On the Wings of Change

Mahinder Lall

L.G. PUBLISHERS DISTRIBUTORS

On the Wings of Change
Mahinder Lall

First Published, 2012

ISBN 978-81-910382-4-8

Published by
LG PUBLISHERS DISTRIBUTORS
49, Gali No. 14, Pratap Nagar
Mayur Vihar Phase I, Delhi 110 091
Tel : 011 2279 5641 email: lgpdist@gmail.com

Printed at
Arpit Printographers, Delhi 110 032
arpitprinto@yahoo.com

Foreword

Mahinder Lall and I became acquainted and grew up together during our years at the Doon School and have remained fast friends ever since.

Even during our early years together, Kali, as he was known to us, was a prolific reader and had developed a remarkable ability to write graphically, with the capacity to bring out vivid details through his careful choice of words, as this volume aptly demonstrates.

The book is an accurate, perceptive and fascinating description of a turbulent period in India's history from the point of view of a critical and eminently rational commentator.

Kali was never one to mince his words and always put forth strong arguments in defence of his ideas, often resulting in heated arguments between the protagonists, one of whom was my wife, Ratna. The fact is that he was always able to back his theories and ideas with strong, rational arguments, however contrary his point of view might have been and we not only enjoyed his sharp wit and immense capacity to imbibe and digest knowledge, but inevitably, wound up giving in gracefully to the force of his logic and contentions.

Kali's acute memory and pragmatic perceptions of the world as it changed around us, provide a remarkable record of events that shaped this nation and everyone who reads this will be so absorbed that they will not be able to put it down.

Gulab Ramchandani

Preface

History is like a spool of yarn. Once it starts to unravel it seems to be endless, with no beginning and no end, ongoing, open-ended. The goal posts have to be set at the start of the narrative. They are purely arbitrary, depending on the period of history under surveillance. This is basically a personal narrative, written with a heavy bias on life experiences, intertwined with historical events that have shaped the author's thinking and attitude. The focus is on the period before and between WW I and WW II and the events that were the precursors to the latter, leading to this dreadful conflagration. So here are a few introductory comments, which will facilitate writing this narrative and will enlighten the reader, who will, perforce, join me on this journey as a companion through a rather turbulent period of history, which was to be the forge in which my fate and character were to be annealed. Since this is a personal exposition, I will be expressing views which may give offence to some people, but offence is not intended, so please be charitable and read what is being said with an open mind. Disagree by all means. That is your inalienable right, so please exercise it. Equally, I claim my inalienable right to declaim what I have learnt and experienced and to share this with those who wish to accompany me on this journey. Let us embark on this voyage in the spirit of camaraderie and discovery, savouring every experience with the freshness of the young who have not become blasé and tainted with the trauma of memory and the blight of careless insouciance. Lastly, I claim a measure of poetic licence, enabling me to meander across the corridors of history to maintain continuity, yet avoid needless excursions into tedious justifications of what has been said.

Preface

[illegible]

Contents

1

Beginnings

The stage is set in North-Western India, in the populous state of what used to be called The United Provinces or UP for short. In post-Independence India it became Uttar Pradesh, or the Northern Province, a misnomer, as it is not the Northern most part of the country by any means. The biggest town in its most western districts is a large, sprawling, dusty city called Saharanpur. There is very little to commend this typical Northern Indian city with its squat, single and two storied buildings with flat roofs, built cheek by jowl in what are called *mohallas*, an Arabic word denoting an inhabited quarter of a city. The *mohallas* are a strange by-product of India. They are segregated 'ghettos', virtually islands inhabited by a particular community, separated from their neighbours by some inexplicable and unwritten rules. This 'ghetto' system not only separated the major religious groups, like the Hindus and Muslims but also between castes among the Hindus, and major factions among the Muslims, like the Shias, Sunnis and Sufis. There was virtually no socializing among the groups outside work. The clarion call from the workplace brought these very disparate groups together, and by and large, they worked harmoniously under the firm leadership provided by old, large Indian families and estates, a foreign ruler like the East India Company, succeeded by 'The British Raj' after the1857 Indian Mutiny (what is now known as the First War of Independence), or commercial enterprises, both Indian and foreign. However, even at work, the different communities ate separately because of strict dietary taboos and customs. For example, the Indian *'hookah'* or water pipe, *narghila,* is smoked by all Indian communities but the hookah is not shared in leisure time. The different communities will gather together and smoke their separate hookahs, gossip and compare notes on the day's happenings and what is in the news. All this is with bonhomie and good nature and in the shared vernacular language. At the end of the day, the employee bids farewell to the employer, wishes him protection of the almighty and disappears into the labyrinth of the *mohalla* and the seclusion of the family. Among the Muslims, the female members are strictly segregated and veiled from the gaze of all adult male members of the family. This is the *zenana* or female quarter. Among the Muslims, it is not unusual to have multiple wives; they are legally allowed four wives under the Shariat, or Muslim Law. This licence does not extend to the other communities where monogamy is strictly enforced. It is evident that India is a highly complex and inbred society among the working and middle classes, who are traditionally the bastion of orthodoxy in societies all over the world. The social norms lose their sting among the better-educated and more broad-minded elements where people are just people, irrespective of race, origin or religion. This is the intelligentsia, the professionals, the champions of industry, the higher echelons of the bureaucracy as distinct from the clerical *'babu'*, the much despised, totally venal underling, who is always up for sale. This dreadful individual was unwittingly created by the British administration when they were formulating the civil and criminal codes for India. Little did they realize that because of poor education and lack of initiative, every chapter and verse would be taken literally, totally ignoring the spirit underlying the printed word and the purpose of the enacted law. This reluctance to interpret the written word was reason enough for the *'babu'* not to make decisions. Inaction was preferred to action, which could be questioned, followed by a possible reprimand from a superior. The *'babu'* also quickly realized the latent power that inaction gave him vis-à-vis the applicant, who was richer and higher up the social ladder, and therefore an object of envy and resentment. The applicant's file could not move to the next echelon in the hierarchy until the

clerical underling had made his notation in the margin, quoting chapter and verse from the turgid legal tomes and case laws that bedevil the ponderous legal system that prevails in the country. Since India became independent in 1947, the whole legal system has virtually collapsed under its own weight and inadequacies. The *'babu'* reigns supreme, in collusion with an even more corrupt and avaricious political system. Both groups are totally devoid of any feeling of patriotism or sense of duty to the country. It is now axiomatic that to become rich without trying, nothing can rival becoming a politician. Politics is not only the refuge of rascals and criminals, but it is also the haven for the scurrilous nouveau riche. So much for this excursion into the political marshland of India. Its time to head back to dusty Saharanpur which owes its importance and place in history to its strategic location on the border of the UP and the old state of the Punjab. The border is barely 14 miles away defined by the venerated River Jumna or Yamuna, which is its sanskritized name.

The Yamuna rises in the Himalayas at Yamunotri whose cluster of snow capped peaks are clearly visible from Saharanpur in winter. The Yamuna comes roaring out of the Garhwal Himalayas and debouches into the Dehra Dun valley at Kalsi, where it is joined by its main tributary, the River Tons. The confluence of the two rivers at Kalsi produces a logjam of pine trees floated down the two rivers, but mainly the Tons, from the extensive logging operations deep in the mountains. This logjam is called Dak Pathar Boom, where the logs are separated, graded and refloated downstream, destined for the sawmills in the 'old' Punjab just north-west of Saharanpur. At this stage, it should be mentioned that the Dehra Dun Valley, just to the north, is separated from the alluvial rich, Indo-Gangetic Plain of Saharanpur and beyond by a low range of hills called the Siwaliks that rise upto 1,000 meters. The Siwaliks pre-date the Himalayas. The heavily forested valleys and slopes of these hills are the home of the Bengal tiger, panther, the elephant, jackals, the Sloth Bear which is the smallest of the bear family in India, and a host of deer. The Siwaliks run parallel to the Himalayas for hundreds of miles and their dense forests provide conservation national parks for wild life, like the Corbett National Park named after Jim Corbett, the world famous big-game hunter of man-eating tigers and panthers in the Garhwal and Kumaon Himalayas. In his later years, Jim Corbett became an ardent conservationist. At this stage it would be very remiss of me not to say a few words about the Terai, this incredible belt of dense elephant grass, intersected by swamps, clumps of forest and slow-flowing streams that debouch into the plains from the southern slopes of the Himalayas. The terai is virtually impenetrable except on the back of an elephant. The elephant grass grows to a height of nearly 15 feet and has a dense and deep root system. The terai is unhealthy and highly malarial.

The Yamuna used to be a big, powerful river, but so much water has been taken out for irrigation of the Western UP districts that what is left is a pathetic sluggish stream that swings eastward and flows to Delhi and Agra. It eventually has a confluence with the Ganga, the erstwhile Ganges, at the city of Allahabad. According to mythology, the once mighty Saraswati River now flows underground and joins the other two surface rivers to create a highly venerated tri-junction called the Triveni at Allahabad.

In recent times, there has been a lot of speculation about the disappearance of the once mighty Saraswati River, which flowed from the Garhwal Himalayas as the River Yamuna, but instead of swinging east to eventually join the Ganga, it flowed south-west to join the Sutlej River which has its origin near the sacred Mansarovar Lake at the foot of Mount Kailash in Tibet. The Sutlej then cuts through the Himalayas and flows into the Punjab. According to mythology, the combined Sutlej and Yamuna rivers become the Saraswati which receives a lot of tributaries like the River Ghaggar and flows into the present state of Haryana and then into Western Rajasthan where it receives the River Hakra and then onto Gujarat where it empties into the Arabian Sea. The delta of the Saraswati is the shallow swamp of the Rann of Kutch.

While the Saraswati River was flowing, it was a mighty stream which was many miles wide, and along its banks flourished the ancient Indian civilization of Harappa that paralleled the civilization of Mohenjodaro on the banks of the River Indus or the 'River Sindu' of antiquity. These twin civilizations reigned supreme between 3,000 BC and 1,900 BC. Both are cloaked in mystery, as is their eventual disappearance. What we do know is that they were highly developed agrarian societies with vast granaries, having a highly developed system of weights and measures, public sewage systems, irrigation channels and baths. The cities were built in a highly ordered fashion with wide, paved streets set in squares and with commodious dwellings. There is no evidence of looting, plunder or massacre. Western historians and philologists have invented the 'Aryan Invasion Theory', which presages an invasion of India by a Central Asian Indo-European people, reputedly called 'Aryans', who decimated the city of Mohenjodaro, inhabited by an autochthonous people who were driven out. There is no evidence to support this highly evocative theory which is strongly disputed by Indian researchers. For whatever reason, the citizens of Mohenjodaro just left a perfectly liveable city intact and disappeared into history. The demise of Harrapa on the other hand is attributed to the gradual degradation of the Saraswati River and its eventual disappearance underground, leaving in its wake a parched, dessicated landscape which is the Thar or Great Indian Desert. Archealogical research has unearthed evidence of thriving habitations in places like Dholivira, Lothal, Kalibagan, Banawali, Kunal in India and Rehman Dheri, Kot Digi, Amri, Balakot and Mehrgarh in Pakistan. Extensive excavations are still going on, even underwater, in the Rann of Kutch, where there is evidence of land subsidence and remnants of an ancient city drowned due to some cataclysmic event. So did the Saraswati perish due to tectonic factors, climatic changes causing a retreat of the Ice Age, or a change in the course of the Sutlej/Yamuna water flow causing the Sutlej to flow south-west through Bhawalpur to join the Indus and the Yamuna to head east and flow into the Ganga? With the loss of the headwaters of the two main rivers, the fate of the Saraswati was sealed as was the demise of the Harappa civilization. The Yamuna is notoriously fickle and there is plenty of evidence available in Saharanpur District to testify to changes in the river's course. There is 'the Budhi Jumna', that is, the'old Jumna', with a deep lake drained by a small stream. Further south, near the village of Sarsawa, is another deep lake, again drained by the remnants of the Yamuna. Only further extensive research will divulge the mystery of the 'disappeared civilizations of India.'

The British presence in India dates back to the early 1600s with the arrival of the British East India Company as a trading organization in competition with the Dutch and more with the French. The East India Company (EIC) was destined to play a very major role in India's economic and political life in the years to come and merits detailed treatment, which I will endeavour to provide.

However, for the moment I am going to skip over nearly 150 years and land the reader back in Saharanpur which we left in the previous paragraph. As the EIC extended its power over Northern India, it developed an extensive network of roads over thousands of miles to move goods and troops across the country. Whilst this was an enormous engineering feat, a lot of the spadework had already been done by the Mughal Emperors of India, who built what was known as The Grand Trunk Road (GTR) from Lahore in the Punjab to Calcutta in Bengal. The GTR ran through Saharanpur and on to Delhi, as the Mughals realized the strategic location of the city. The EIC was quick to follow suit, but Saharanpur really came into its own with the development of the Indian railway system. The automotive industry was still in its infancy and totally inadequate to meet the needs of the EIC, which followed England's example, and developed the railways as the principal mover of men and materials.

The first railway locomotive was built in the engineering college in Roorkee, a city about 40 miles north-east of Saharanpur. The EIC followed the English system of semi-independent railway lines like the LNER (London and North Eastern Railways) and, LMS (London, Midland & Scottish Railways). The logical location in Northern India was Saharanpur because of its strategic location and this city became the main marshalling yard for two of India's major railway lines.

The North-Western Railway (NWR) covered the Punjab, the North-Western Frontier Province (NWFP), all the way to Peshawar and the troublesome frontier tribesmen on the border with Afghanistan, and then to Delhi. Militarily it was the most important railway line in India. The second railway line was the East India Railway (EIR) that fed the United Provinces and went all the way down to Calcutta. The EIR was the economic artery of the Company. Saharanpur became the hub of the entire railway system in Northern India and sported a huge railway colony and consequently one of the biggest centres of the so-called Anglo-Indian communities in the country. The origin and fate of this community merits special treatment which I will cover separately. Saharanpur was a vital centre of the East India Company and became the home of many of its officials and bureaucrats. The British, unlike the other foreign invaders and rulers, had no intention to integrate and get absorbed in the vast Indian fabric. For the British, India was a stepping stone to wealth and fortune and then a return to Britain. The British, with rare exceptions, never really understood India and Indians. Yet, they wrote prolifically on Indian manners and customs, coloured with their brand of sardonic humour and sometimes paternalistic arrogance. The British in India present a multi-faceted mosaic which is difficult to translate to the outsider in an intelligible form. It is best to present this montage in a piece-meal manner so that injustices are avoided. But let's get back to Saharanpur. Let it be clearly understood that the British lived an opulent lifestyle that they had never known back home. In Saharanpur, with its lack of amenities, the British created an oasis, a home-away-from-home, like the huge municipal garden which was a veritable botanical wonderland to be enjoyed by all the citizens of Saharanpur. Then there was the beautiful Saharanpur Club, built to celebrate the Silver Jubilee of Queen Victoria, with spacious lawn-tennis courts, billiard tables, card rooms for bridge and rummy, reading rooms and a library with copies of the Illustrated *London News, Punch, The Tatler*, and of course, the inevitable bar to slake the thirst after tennis. All very gentlemanly and civilized. Saharanpur had several other claims to fame, such as the magnificent Remount Depot, where horses called 'Walers' were bred for the Indian Cavalry Regiments. The local Indian horses were a small, wiry breed which were used extensively for pulling the traditional two wheeled vehicles called 'tongas', but were too small and puny for the British and Indian cavalry regiments and horse-drawn artillery. The first attempt to cultivate suitable breeds of horses dates back to 1793 when the EIC established stud farms in the three Presidencies, namely Madras, Bombay and Bengal. These were a dismal failure due to a lack of veterinary science and the first two were soon closed down. The Bengal stud would have followed suite but the EIC managed to employ a veterinarian fresh out of the recently created College for Veterinary Science in England. This was William Moorcrof, who arrived in India around 1808, and after considerable experimentation found that neither the English nor the famed Arabian breeds were suitable for Indian conditions. At this stage it should be mentioned that even prior to the arrival of the EIC there existed a brisk trade in horses, with Afghans selling Turkoman horses to Indian chieftains, but the supply was erratic and unsatisfactory for the cavalry. Moorcroft went into Central Asia on two occasions but evidently perished never returning to India. The Remount Depot in Saharanpur came into being in 1875 and fortuitously the Remount Depot found that Australian- bred horses from New South Wales were ideal for use in India. A considerable trade sprang up and 'Walers' became the mounts for the Indian Cavalry and were used as studs for propagating the breed in Saharanpur. One shipment from Botany Bay ran aground off Frazer Island in Queensland and sank. The horses swam ashore and are the present day 'brumbies' that roam wild on the island. The Remount Depot also bred mules, donkeys and camels for the Royal Indian Army Service Corp (RIASC), which had the very onerous duty of supplying the fighting units with arms, equipment, forage and victuals in out-of-the-way frontier areas.

Before we leave Saharanpur, I must mention that the British Tobacco Company's subsidiary, W.D. & H.O.Wills, had built a very substantial cigarette-manufacturing facility in Saharanpur and was the biggest employer in the city. The executive staff was entirely British, and ran a very 'posh' and exclusively British

Club called the 'Peninsula Club', which had the most up-to-date facilities for its members. The business is still thriving, but most of the British staff has been replaced by Indians. In addition, the Indian Tobacco Company (ITCO), the Indian subsidiary of British Tobacco, has diversified its activities and is also a major entrepreneur in the hotel and hospitality industry in India.

The whole of UP and Bihar have a very substantial Muslim population with major centres of education like the Aligarh Muslim University in the city of that name. It was here that the first stirrings for a separate Muslim country were voiced by the founder, Sir Syed Ahmad Khan in 1887. Here lies the birth of what was going to lead to the Partition of India in 1947, and the creation of Pakistan. The UP is also the home of seminaries like the Dar-ul-Uloom in the small town of Deoband, barely 100 miles north-east of Saharanpur, and its sister-school, Mazahir-ul-Uloomin Saharanpur proper. The Deoband seminary was founded in 1867 and is a major centre for Islamic studies and Arabic, and is a puritanical exponent of the fanatical Wahhabi sect in Saudi Arabia. The Deoband version of Islam is the fountainhead of Pakistan's *jihadi* fundmentalism and international terrorism. Pakistan was born and bred in the cities of UP and Bihar yet there has been next to no migration to Pakistan from these areas. Stranger still is the contempt that the indigenous Punjabi and Pathan population of Pakistan has for the miniscule migrant population, who are contemptuously referred to as Mohajirs, that is, refugees.

The Deoband seminary has assumed the mantle of being the authority on all matters relating to Islamic jurisprudence in both India and Pakistan and issues *fatwas* or Islamic diktats that are often in conflict with the national, civil and criminal legal codes.

Now it is time to leave Saharanpur and head north to the lovely Doon Valley, ensconced between the Siwalik range to the south and the massive buttress of the Mussoorie Himalayas to the north.On the western boundary is the valley of the Yumuna and on the east is the valley of the mighty Ganga as it debouches into the plains at Rishikesh, a holy city for the Hindus with its myriad ashrams and temples. A magnificent river wonderland with its roaring rapids and deep, emerald-green, sombre pools. Further south, along the river, is the ancient city of Haridwar, literally 'the doorway to God', and one of the holiest cities for the Hindus. Every twelve years, the city experiences a deluge of humanity as millions of devout Hindus vie to bathe in the river to celebrate the Kumbh Mela, probably the greatest religious gathering in the world. The Kumbh Mela is also vigorously celebrated in the city of Allahabad where the Ganga and the Yamuna have a confluence with the mysterious and mythical Saraswati River that flows underground to emerge at the trijunction. But it is time to return to the heart of the Doon Valley and the city of Dehra Dun. In days gone by, Dehra Dun was a small town with delightful, leafy roads, lined with beautiful bungalows set in spacious gardens and stands of lovely trees. Dehra Dun is at an elevation of about 2500 feet, which makes it considerably cooler than Saharanpur which swelters in summer. The winter temperature plummets close to freezing and it has even had flurries of snow which does not settle. Snow blankets the hills of Mussoorie to the north, which tower to 5,000 feet, and present a lovely panorama. Unfortunately, Dehra Dun has not escaped the Indian penchant to turn every thing lovely into grottos of grubby and untidy, characterless dwellings, which spring up like mushrooms, and bazaars with tiny, mean shops, squawking their wares on blaring loud speakers. Dehra Dun's steady decline commenced with the flood of Hindu and Sikh refugees pouring in from the charnel house of Pakistan in 1947. No open space was spared other than the military cantonment areas of the services. The sheer pressure of population has destroyed the pristine beauty of the town. The city has now become the capital of the newly created State of Uttarakhand that covers the entire hill regions of Garhwal and Kumaon, north of Dehra Dun, right to the Nepal border in the east and the State of Himachal to the west...

Uttarakhand is the latest addition to India's numerous states. It was splintered off from Uttar Pradesh, which wanted to introduce affirmative action granting special rights and reservations for the so-called 'backward classes'. This would have needlessly handicapped the hill areas, where more than 70 per cent of the population consists of high caste Brahmins and the warrior Kshatriya Rajputs. This situation was untenable and a split became inevitable.

Dehra Dun was the logical choice as the provincial capital by virtue of its well-developed infrastructure and proximity to Saharanpur, Mussoorie and Delhi. However, the creation of another state meant the duplication of all the offices and paraphernalia of government. Dehra Dun is a boomtown, bursting at the seams, with soaring land prices. True to form, it is dirtier and grubbier than ever before and promises to get worse.

However there are many redeeming features in Dehra Dun. Probably its world famous 'Dehra Dun *basmati* rice' has catapulted it into fame and fortune, and justifiably so. Its delicious and aromatic long-grain rice is greatly in demand, to such an extent that the local product is almost totally exported to the rich Gulf States. However the' Basmati' name is so well entrenched all over the world that variants grown in Pakistan are marketed everywhere. It is also rumoured that Tamerlane, Timur the Lame, invaded the Yamuna Valley after devastating the city of Delhi in 1399. True to form, he built pyramids with the skulls of his defeated foes and left Delhi a city of fear and tears. It appears that this'Tartar Scourge' acquired a taste for Basmati rice, which he combined with choice pieces of mutton, and the dish called 'biryani' was born. It is one of the favourite dishes consumed in both India and Pakistan. It is best not to dwell on its disreputable origins!!

India was being periodically attacked and plundered by marauding tribesmen from Afghanistan and beyond, who had a sword in one hand and the Quran in the other. The Indian Rajputs, 'the Sons of Kings', put up a valiant defence but they never succeeded in staunching the flood. There are many reasons for their repeated failure but the main factor was that they never presented a consolidated confederacy, plus, they fought with honour and chivalry against an enemy who had the mentality of a street fighter, with no holds barred. The Muslim invaders had plenty of 'elan', driven by the lust for loot, rape and plunder, and the blessings of a religion, which glorified the slaughter of the hated infidel and idolater. Individually, the Rajputs were incomparable for their valour but they lacked 'elan'. There was no uniting force among them and the Indians had not developed a sense of nationhood as understood by the Europeans like the British, French, Dutch and the Portuguese. The Rajputs fought and died as individuals. Even the leader was often a petty prince, and there was no shortage of these squabbling, pathetic individuals, who were forever at each others throats for trifling gains of territory and plunder. Internecine fighting tore out the heart of the country, leaving it wide open to foreign marauders. Strangely enough, the Indians never developed the concept of the professional soldier, paid and equipped by the ruler's treasury. The soldiers were basically 'privateers', who brought their own horses and equipment to fight for the princeling of the moment. They lived off the loot and plunder. Once the ruler was killed or wounded, the 'privateer' cut and ran. Robert Clive, of the East India Company (EIC), discovered this very early in his career. He found that a handful of trained European troops could rout large Indian armies. This became very evident with his easy victories at the Battles of Arcot and Plassey. The marauding Middle-Eastern barbarians had also spotted the Indian Achilles Heel and targeted the ruler, who rode conspicuously, on top of an elephant. The Indian forces were further encumbered with the baggage, which accompanied the ruler and was a severe impediment in combating the fast moving horsemen from the frontier. The valiant Rajputs were never able to consolidate and defend the country. The coup-de-grace came at the Battle of Chitor in 1303, when Rajput men and women fought to the death on the battlements of the city. Those who could not fight, the aged and children, committed suicide rather than fall into the hands of the barbarians. The Rajputs had had enough and they fled into the safety of the Himalayas and established the kingdom of Nepal in a small town called Gorkha. The migration spread over several centuries but probably Nepal emerged as a kingdom when a chieftain called Drabya Shah captured Gorkha in the 16th century. It is not the intention to write a history of

Nepal, so a breviary is necessary to outline the key features. The country around Gorkha is inhabited by two mongoloid races, the Magars who cultivated rice and maize in the lower reaches and the doughty Gurungs, who raised goats and cattle in the more alpine reaches called 'Lekhs' in the shadow of the mighty Annapurna range. To the east, in the Kathmandu Valley, there was another semi-mongoloid race called the Newars, who were a highly skilled, artistic people who built the city and its beautiful temples. The Malla Kings from India ruled Nepal for nearly 400 years and spread their empire to the border of Sikkim in the east and to the Kangra valley on the border of the Sikh Kingdom of the Punjab. The Gorkhas even penetrated into Tibet and went up to the town of Shigatse, raising the ire of the Chinese who claimed suzerainty over Tibet. The Gorkhas were irrepressible and it was inevitable that they would come into conflict with the EIC who were rapidly moving up the Indo-Gangetic Valley. The Nawab of Oudh had ceded his territories to the EIC in 1801. The Rohillas, west of Oudh, were eventually defeated and the EIC now controlled land right up to the Garhwal and Kumaon mountains, which were under Nepal. The EIC was busy cultivating Indigo for dyeing cotton and opium for export to China, which were highly lucrative trades for the Company. Raiding parties of Gorkhas descended into the plains to extract money from the landed gentry called '*zamindars*', who had already paid their taxes to the EIC. The situation became untenable, with both sides flushed with the arrogance of success. An ultimatum was given to the Gorkhas to withdraw. They refused, and war was declared in 1814. General Gillespie was ordered to occupy the Doon Valley. In the Punjab, General Ochterlony was to attack the Gorkhas in the Simla hills and Generals Wood and Marley were to head for Kathmandu. The deadly Terai jungles extracted a terrible toll in men and equipment and Wood and Marley withdrew ignominiously. Gillespie fared better but was killed at the Battle of Kalunga in the Doon Valley.

Late a monument was erected at Kalunga in his honour and his brave soldiers. Next door is another monument would be built to honour the Gorkhas.The Marquis of Hastings now decided to take personal command of the war and advanced into the Sirmoor hills to link up with Ochterlony who was facing an experienced Gorkha General, Amarsing Thapa. Some very heavy fighting took place but the Gorkhas lost nearly a quarter of their force of 2,000 men. In the mountains of Kumaon, hundreds of miles to the east, the EIC captured the fort in the town of Almora. The war was going badly for the Gorkhas and Amarsing sued for peace. Ochterlony's terms stripped Simla, Garhwal and Kumaon from Nepal and restored Sikkim to its traditional ruler, the Raja. However, these terms were not acceptable to the Prime Minister, Bhimsen Thapa, sitting in Kathmandu. He recalled that the EIC forces had faced a debacle in the Terai and generals Wood and Marley had been forced to retire. Furthermore in the Punjab, the EIC was getting a battering from the Sikhs under Maharaja Ranjit Singh and the Maratha confederacy had finally decided to challenge the British around Delhi. The stumbling block was the demand to hand over the Terai, the only flat land in Nepal. This obduracy was unacceptable and a force of 18,000 with artillery support was assembled at Dinapur in Bihar, under the command of the redoubtable General Ochterlony, with order to occupy Kathmandu. Ochterlony crossed the Mahabharat Lekh range that separates the Kathmandu Valley from the Terai. Extremely heavy fighting ensued at Makhwanpur Garhi with the Gorkhas suffering massive losses. Bhimsen Thapa's worry was to keep the foreigners out of the valley and he sued for peace. The British conceded to this demand but insisted that a Resident would be installed in Kathmandu, a procedure that had been adopted by the EIC in its dealings with the numerous independent princes of India. Ochterlony was greatly impressed by the magnificent fighting quality and tenacity of his adversary and realized that the Gorkhas would be an invaluable asset to the armies of the EIC. The recruitment of Gorkhas became a clause in the Treaty of Segauli signed in 1816. An enduring friendship and peace ensued and Gorkha recruiting centres were established in Dehra Dun, Almora and Gorakhpur.

Now we have to sidetrack a little to explain the strange attitude of the British to this new addition to the EIC's armed force. The Gorkhas were to be commanded only by British Officers and were to be insulated from the other Indian units. The reason put forward was absurd and ridiculous in the extreme, namely, that the Gorkhas were not prepared to be commanded by Indian Officers! Yet, the Gorkhas claim descent from the legendary Indian Rajput chiefs and Nepalese Princesses are married to some of the top Maharajas in India. The truth is that the famed British 'Thin Red Line' was not only very thin but it was frayed and tattered. The British felt very vulnerable and fragile in this vast land and covered this dread with the famous British swagger, bluff and bluster, coupled with a healthy swig of class snobbery and racism. I shall write extensively on the subject, so for those of you who don't agree, and that is your right, please be patient and await the denouement. So let us stick to this protective cuirass for the moment as it stands. The Gorkha was the classical Indo-Nepalese Schweitzer. He was a 'loose cannon', to borrow an American expression, but once he took the oath of loyalty to His Majesty, the British Emperor, he was totally committed. Initially, three regiments of Gorkhas were raised and recruitment was from erstwhile Nepal by the EIC. They were in fact Garhwalis and Kumaonis and their regimental names show their origins. The 1st King George V's Own, Gorkha Regiment was the Malaun Regiment that takes its name after the fierce battle fought between Amarsing Thapa and Ochterlony in the Kangra Hills, west of Simla. The 2nd King Edward VII's Own Gorkha Rifles is the Sirmoor Rifles which was raised in the Garhwal Hills in1815 at Nahan the capital.The 3rd Queen Alexandra's Own Gorkha Rifles was also raised in 1815 and named the Kumaon Battalion and was raised in Almora with recruits from the Hills of Kumaon. It is not my intention to write the regimental history of the 10 Gorkha Regiments so let this brief interlude suffice to prove that the British contention was utter rubbish, as the three senior regiments were in fact Indian. The truth of the matter is that commanding the Gorkhas gave the British a sense of security in the event of a revolt by the other Indian soldiers who were, after all, the crutch propping up British rule. Prophetic to say the least, as we will see!! But let's proceed with this narrative about the Gorkhas.

Two major changes were in the offing. The first was within Nepal, where the control and administration were ruthlessly usurped from the King by a cabal of local chieftains called Ranas, the Rajput name for 'ruler'. The King and the throne were left intact, but the rulers of Nepal were the Ranas, a situation that closely paralleled the Japanese Shogun who ruled but did not overthrow the Emperor. The Ranas physically and politically isolated Nepal and extracted revenue from the tillers of the soil. They amassed large fortunes, which were invested in India. The Ranas intermarried with the Princes of India but did not disturb the recruitment of Gorkhas.

The second change was in Garhwal where the British reinstated the local Maharaja of Tehri Garhwal. This territory was now bifurcated into the Princely state of Tehri Garhwal, ruled by the Maharaja, and British Garhwal. The two were separated by a major branch of the Ganga called the Bhagirithi.

I have mentioned earlier that 10 regiments of Gorkhas were raised by the British as the old 'Gurkha Brigade', to use the incorrect spelling used by the British. In peacetime a regiment had two battalions of 1,000 men each but the number of battalions was a variable figure in wartime. Each battalion had a complement of 11 or 12 British Kings'-Commissioned Officers, assisted by Gorkha Officers who were Viceroys-Commissioned Officers(VCO's). This followed the typical hierarchal structure used by the British Army. The British Regimental Sergeant Major's equivalent was the Indian or Gorkha Subedar Major, literally the backbone of the battalion. In both armies, these officers were awesome figures that commanded great respect and power among the men and officers alike.

At this juncture, it is vital to clarify that the Gorkha soldier was not a solitary racial entity. In fact, the recruitment was from a broad ethnic group stretching from the Kumaon border in India in the west to the border of the State of Sikkim and Darjeeling in the east. The largest group was the Magars and Gurungs in the west, followed by the Khas or Chettri from around the town of Gorkha. This is the home of the famous

Thapa Clan that provided the brilliant Generals that fought the EIC. From Eastern Nepal come clansmen such as the Rais, Limbus, Lamas, Puns and Khandkas. Gorkha regiments recruited troops by their clan origins even though there was a common language and culture throughout.

The Gorkhas covered themselves with honour in India and in WWI and II. A history of their exploits would fill volumes and is way beyond the scope of this narrative, which is intended to bridge the entry of the Gorkhas into the Indian and British Armies. To do this, I have to make a quantum leap from the mid-1800s to India's Independence in 1947, when the Brigade of Gorkhas, consisting of 10 regiments, was split, with 6 regiments staying with the Indian Army and 4 regiments joining the British Army. The British wanted to retain the Gorkhas as they still separeted vestiges of their tattered Empire, and a Chinese-led Communist insurgency threatening the colonies in Malaya, Sarawak and Brunei required the Gorkha to patrol the border in the New Territories in Hong Kong. The Sultan of Brunei insisted on a permanent contingent of Gorkhas to safeguard his kingdom. The British Army had been whittled down to a meagre 113,500 men and the presence of a few thousand Gorkhas was highly welcomed. The 4 Gorkha regiments selected by the British were the 2nd, 6th, 7th and 10th Gorkha Rifles, with their recruiting centre at Pokhra, overlooked by the massive Annapurna Range and Machapuchre, the Fishes Tail. A truly magnificent setting. On the Indian side, the 6 Gorkhas Rifles are a solid 40,000 contingent totally integrated into the 1.1 million-strong Indian Army. Gorkhas are also recruited to serve in mixed battalions like The Guards Brigade and in the Border Security Forces like the Indo-Tibet Border Police (ITBP) and The Assam Rifles. The recruitment and deployment of Gorkhas is huge as there are no passport or border restrictions between India and Nepal and the two currencies are totally inter-changeable. The British Gorkhas, on the other hand, are a dying breed as they provide mainly a ceremonial service although they saw minor action in the Falklands War. However, there are a few interesting injunctions imposed by the Nepal Government in the 1947 separation. The first and foremost of these was that Gorkhas would not be asked to take up arms against a Hindu enemy. Secondly the salary and pensions in both armies would be on par although the British Gorkhas are now demanding parity with British soldiers. This is merely making them more expensive and less employable. The logical solution is to transfer the British Gorkhas to the Australian Army when they eventually become defunct in Britain. In a paper that I have written on 'The Defence of Australia', I have suggested this but so far no action is forthcoming. Australia has a severe shortage of recruits in its army and the addition of about 5,000 highly trained and brilliant jungle fighters would be invaluable assets, particularly in the Asian hinterland where they would readily blend with the local population. Should my suggestion become a reality at some stage, further recruitment could be negotiated with the Indian and Nepal Governments. Only time will tell!!

We have covered the Gorkhas fairly extensively but Dehra Dun has many more institutions that need to be covered, like The Indian Military Academy (IMA), (India's 'Sandhurst'); the Doon School (DS) (India's Eton) and the magnificent Forest Research Institute (FRI), that must rank with the world's top forest research and forest protection institutions. So let us proceed in a methodical manner. The first in the line of fire is the IMA.

2

The Indian Military Academy

True to form, the British felt that Indians lacked the qualities of leadership and command. Let me quote from Lieutenant General Alexander Cobbe, Sec. Gen. of the Military Department of the India Office:

> As proof, he cited incidents during WW I, when Indian troops, deprived of their British leadership' showed a tendency to deteriorate seriously and quickly...few, if any, Indians apparently having the natural aptitude for leadership possessed by the average Englishman.

As a consequence of the Indian Mutiny of 1857, the blustering confidence of the British was severely shaken. They felt terribly insecure, knowing full well, but never admitting, that British rule was only possible by the tacit consent of the Indians who propped up the Indian Army. Some very crafty leger-de-main and obtuse psychology was vitally necessary to convince the Indians about British superiority and invincibility and the necessity for continuation of British Rule. We have already seen one snippet of this game plan with the Gorkhas having only British officers. This little ploy assured the British of enduring loyalty from one segment of the Indian Army. But this was not enough by any means. The troublesome segments were all from the Bengal Army recruited from the States of Bihar and the UP. These had to be eliminated gradually and replaced by recruits from the Punjab and the NWFP (North-Western Frontier Province) but to do this, the British invented the myth of the so-called 'Martial Classes', created by the genius of none other than

'Bob Bahadur', Lord Roberts of Kandahar, who was Commander-in-Chief from 1885 to 1893. The total reorganization of the Indian Army was in the offing with the creation of 'Class Regiments' which had sole recruitment of the so-called 'reliable' troops like the Sikhs and Dogras and 'Class Company Regiments', in which companies were ethnic but the battalion was mixed. The *'langar'*, or mess, was separated to cater to the religious and social taboos of the troops but all the training and sports facilities were shared. This also ensured that there would be minimal opportunity for collusion to mutiny. All very crafty, but this was only the tip of the iceberg. Long Range Artillery was entirely British. The Indian Artillery was equipped with short-range mountain guns or Howitzers. The argument put forward was that the Indians had never mastered the subtle nuances of gunnery. Utter rubbish of course but an excuse is just an excuse. And lastly, the Indian was mentally and physically incapable of combating his European counterpart in the field. In other words, the Indian soldier was unfit to serve in a European theatre of war. World War I was the turning point when the sheer logistics of man power shortages in the 'killing fields' of Flanders forced the British to pump Indian troops into this charnel house. As was to be expected, the Indians excelled and covered themselves with glory and the myth of European Supremacy were finally laid to rest. The blood letting exhausted the Allies and the Germans. Post WW I found Britain a rather anaemic and tired version of the original boisterous ruler. Changes were in the wind in India also, with a surge in the demand for freedom and independence. The leaders of the Indian National Congress Party were in the vanguard of the Independence Movement but they were an ambivalent group that espoused the Hindu concept of 'ahimsa' or non-violence and therefore deplored the military, which was the flagpole for the Union Jack. Fortunately there were more balanced and pragmatic leaders outside the Congress who were demanding that Indian officers should get the opportunity of promotion into the ranks of the King's Commissioned Officers (KCOs). A tired and dispirited Britain was gradually beginning to accept the idea that was so eloquently voiced by Colonel John Hodgson:

'We cannot hold India save with the Indians'. A far cry from the stiff-upper-lipped imperialists who felt that it was a God-given right for Britain to bring British values and decency into the benighted lives of its subjects, willing or unwilling.

The first major break-through came in 1919 during the tenure of General Henry S. Rawlinson, Commander in-Chief. Some of the epic changes were as under:

1. The admission of Indians into all branches of the Indian Military;
2. A quota of 25 per cent of all new KCOs to be reserved for Indians; and
3. Indian facilities for pre-Sandhurst training, especially for the sons of Indian Officers.
4. In 1922, the government established the Prince of Wales Royal Indian Military College (RIMC), in Dehra Dun, run on the lines of an English Public School. Its purpose was to prepare the students for training in Sandhurst. Initially, ten vacancies per year were made available. The British were adamant that an English public school-type Education was essential for Indian recruitment into the ranks of the KCO and even into the Indian Civil Service (ICS), which was on the drawing-board and was destined to become the best and most prestigious Civil Service in the world. It must be said to the credit of the British in India that when they moved they did not make any compromises with quality, even though this was tinged with their inimitable sense of class distinction and protocol. The RIMC was meant for the sons of KCOs, both Indian and British. The Lawrence Military School at Sanawar, in the Simla Hills, was for sons of British NCOs up to the rank of Warrant Officer, the highest rank in this cadre. Similarly, they set up several KG RIMCs (King George's Royal Indian Military Colleges) for the sons of Indian VCO's, that is, Indian NCOs.

All very neat and tidy but the Rawlinson remit did not cover the creation of an Indian Military Academy equivalent to Sandhurst. As a compromise, the number of vacancies in

Sandhurst was raised to 20 per year but this was inadequate to meet the needs of the army. Eventually, the Indian Military Academy (IMA) was opened in Dehra Dun in the autumn of 1932 with a capacity for 60 cadets from the Indian Army and 20 cadets from the Indian State forces. The course was for 2½ years, somewhat longer than Sandhurst.

Further recruitment into Sandhurst ceased after 1932. The IMA-commissioned officers were called Indian Commissioned Officers (ICOs) as distinct from the Sandhurst group, which still carried the title of KCO and earned higher pay and allowances.

It is now time to leave the fait accompli of the IMA and to turn our attention to the Doon School, my old alma mater, and that of my two brothers.

3

The Doon School

The school took over the premises of the Forest Research Institute, vacated when the FRI moved into new and much more palatial premises next door to the IMA. Coincidentally, adjoining is the RIMC. So, by a bit of fortuitous 'serendipity', two public schools grew up side by side and were destined to be locked in 'friendly combat' on the playing field, on the cricket pitch, the swimming pool and even in the boxing ring. During WW II, we even sat side-by-side doing our Senior Cambridge (SC) examination. I spent the entire war years in the Doon School and the RIMC boys were my constant competitors and a finer bunch of boys would be difficult to find, both Indian and British.

Now it is time to give the reader of this narrative the gist of the birth of an idea and its eventual growth into what was going to become India's 'Eton'. As British hegemony grew, the EIC, and its evangelist arm, realized that effective control of the country could only be accomplished by proper education of the Indian intelligentsia through the medium of the English language. India, which was falling into the lap of the EIC, was an educational wasteland, with very poorly developed indigenous institutions of learning. The Muslims had their 'madrassas', which were religious seminaries that taught the Quran in Arabic by rote learning. The graduates were only fit to say prayers in mosques and function as clerics in religious seminaries. The Hindu situation was hardly any better and centred on religious schools run by 'gurus' or educated holy men. Neither system lent itself for the creation of a modern educational institution. The Christian Church was quick to react to this hiatus and built church-run schools for boys and convent-run schools for girls. In all fairness, it must be said that the education standards were quite acceptable but the centre piece of the system was the conversion of the 'heathen native'. Proper education was a secondary consideration.

The British had another problem on their hands, namely imparting a modicum of education to the scions of the 564 Princely States, which were not directly under British rule but were in individual treaties with the British monarch. The Indian Princes—Hindu, Muslim and Sikh—were autocratic noblemen who did not take kindly to discipline, or indeed, any form of regimentation The 'princelings' were thoroughly spoilt brats with scores of subservient retainers bending over backwards to fulfil every wish of the churlish 'enfant terrible' in their charge.

The first step was the introduction of the English 'governess', who would take over the tedious role of bringing up the brood of spoilt children. This was a group of remarkable English women, from good middle-class families, exuding the self-confidence, without arrogance, that seems to come naturally to being British. They could not be bothered learning those unpronounceable and 'silly' Indian names and proceeded to give 'nice' English names to their charges, like 'Billy', 'Mickey', 'Margaret' and so forth. In turn, the British Government established a series of 'Chiefs' Colleges', whose function and purpose is clouded in mystery. Education and the rigours of learning did not come naturally to these peevish individuals who would rather have a few *'chakars'* of polo, go galloping into the sunset or shoot a brace of partridges. The so-called students arrived with a full retinue of servants to fetch and carry and a stable of horses. Rajkumar College, Rajkot was probably the worst of a bad lot. Other Chiefs' Colleges were Daly College, Indore, Mayo College, Ajmer, Scindia School, Gwalior and Acheason College, Lahore. None of these institutions were suitable for the establishment of a genuine Indian public school.

The intelligentsia in India was quick to realize that there was a serious lacuna in education in the country. They had seen first-hand the quality of the British officials who had been through the public school education in England in stark contrast to those who had not. The upper echelons of Indian society decided that it was time to take full advantage of this excellent system and started sending their sons to highly acclaimed schools like Eton, Harrow, Rugby, Winchester, Charter House, and many others. The boys left India at the age of about nine and after completing their school education, they entered Oxford, Cambridge or the prestigious INNS OF COURT to become barristers, like my father and grandfather, who were 'Called to the Bar' at Middle Temple and Lincoln's Inn respectively. A marvellous education to say the least and one that produced a first class product, but they were 'Brown Englishmen' and totally un-Indian—a sad commentary after the parents had spent a fortune on their education. A classical example of this era was Pandit Jawaharlal Nehru, India's first Prime Minister, who went to Harrow and then Cambridge. One day, he jokingly said to a bemused John Galbraith, the American ambassador, 'that he was the last Englishman to rule India'. A similar fate awaited Satish Ranjan Das, the scion of a wealthy Bengali family, who was sent to England to study at Manchester Grammar School and then went on to study law at the Inns of Court. S.R. Das was an inspired man of vision. He could clearly see the huge advantages offered by the English public school system and was determined to make this the template for an Indian public school, which would eliminate the need for boys to go to England. He was hoping that the reverse would happen and England would come to India, bringing with it a raft of English schoolteachers and the legacy of a brilliant education system refined over centuries. To the uninitiated reader of this narrative, the trials and tribulations experienced by S.R. Das in setting up the infrastructure of the Doon School, India's Eton, is a futile and boring study and needs to be ruthlessly short-circuited. This is precisely what I intend to do. Let it suffice to say that by June, 1927, pledges for sufficient money had been received from a variety of benefactors to enable a committee under the chairmanship of Lord Halifax, a former Viceroy of India and now President of The Board of Education of England, to select a Headmaster for the school. Out of 32 applicants, the committee selected Arthur Edward Foot, a science master at Eton. Foot had studied at Winchester College, Trinity College, Cambridge and Oxford, and had taught at Marylebone Grammar School before joining Eton. He had never been to India but he exuded a sense of self-confidence and sincerity that won over the panel of selectors. He was barely 34 years old when he set sail for India with his new bride. He was a brilliant choice as he had the breadth of vision to synthesize an odd assortment of British public school systems, that he shamelessly plagiarized, and blended these with his own unique concepts on education which he felt that a fledgling school could use to turn out the young men of integrity and leadership that the country needed.

From Harrow he took soccer, or what was called football in those days. Rugby's illustrious Headmaster, Dr Thomas Arnold, was the inspiration for the strong prefect system under which boys controlled the discipline within the school, loosely supervised by the masters. Rugby also gave the system of 'toy rooms' where boys did their 'prep' at the end of the day, under the watchful eye of prefects. The game of rugby was not introduced as Foot felt that it was too rough for the smaller built Indian boys, the ground was too hard and there could be severe injuries from falls. Marlborough set the pattern for a strong emphasis on sports and athleticism. Foot also eliminated the traditional public school 'fag' system, which was demeaning to young boys who had to fetch and carry for senior boys. Caning and all forms of corporal punishment were banned and replaced by a system of 'cards', which deprived the student of certain privileges, or put the student into detention. A 'blue card', or Prefects' card, was a physical endurance nuisance that involved running 'rounds' of the playing field between the end of breakfast and school assembly, and woe betide if you were late. The system worked very well. Reams could be written on the innovative ideas that flowed from the versatile mind of Foot, now that he had a unique opportunity to create a totally novel system of education. The constraints of time and space, however, demand a *vade mecum* that would give the reader a gist of what was happening in this remarkable institution. I have already highlighted the importance given to sports with the delineation of the major sports like cricket, soccer and hockey, played every evening by term times, with the exception of Saturday and Sunday and half-day on Wednesday. The half-day every Wednesday was set aside for a compulsory unit of 'social labour quota', when every student could pick an area that suited him and could entail educating the children of the workers who lived on the premises, teach the families basic hygiene, or cycle down to the village of Tunwalla which the school had adopted, help build the school or dispensary and help the villagers in every way. Foot believed that the sons of India's elite must be taught that privilege could not be taken for granted and demanded recompense by way of helping the weak, needy and poor. In this, he has been singularly successful and Doon School Boys, now given the honorific of DOSCOS, are always in the forefront to help the citizens whenever flood, earthquakes, tsunamis or any misfortune strikes the land. A great achievement set by the personal example of a most remarkable man.

The Doon School is totally non-denominational, in total contrast to the British public schools, which have a strong leavening from the Church. There is no formal institutionalized religious teaching. Instead, Foot introduced a selection of prayers which he had personally handpicked from a huge range of poets and authors, Indian and foreign, which had a powerful message to impart to the laity on moral and ethical values. One prayer was read out by the Headmaster (HM) at Assembly every working day. For Assembly, the entire school trooped in by forms, led by a Prefect or the Form Teacher. Assembly was after breakfast and before the start of school. The HM read out any messages that he wanted the school to hear, followed by a school song, led by the Music Master, and sung lustily by the boys. Talking about Music and the Arts, the Doon School was again quite unique among public schools as a great deal of emphasis was laid on the Humanities, to round off the education of Doscos. The Doon School has a magnificent edifice for The Art School and another one for the Music School. These are run by the Art and Music Masters. They are another chevron for the HM's innovative genius.

Another of Foot's remarkable achievements was the 'Doon School Weekly', a joust into the field of journalism, freedom of speech and thought. The 'Weekly' is written, edited and published every week, except holidays, by the editorial staff made up of boys, and since its inception in 1936, it hasn't missed an issue. It is a forum for the expression of views of all types. The HM was a regular contributor but he never sign off as 'The Headmaster' but used his name only, so there was no pulling of rank. So typical of the man!!

The Doon School is also unique in several other ways. It is totally residential and all the boys, teaching staff, the workers and their families, live on the estate. It is a self-contained entity, but not insulated from the outside world by any means, but which is 'out of bounds' for the students. 'Breaking Bounds' is a serious offence. As a part of this discipline, money is not permitted to be kept by the boys who have to hand in all cash and valuables to the safe-keeping of the Matron, who is now called 'Dame', a much revered personage, who is in every sense a substitute parent to the boys. In place of cash, the boys are allowed limited 'pocket money', which can be encashed for coupons by using a school-issued chequebook.

Considering its antecedents the Doon School is a highly egalitarian society, which draws children from the wealthiest families to students on scholarships and bursaries funded by the school. The school is a 'meritocracy', always striving to be the best in the classroom and on the playing field, but abjuring the encomium of mindless elitism.

There can be no doubt that the grand architect of the Doon School was Arthur Edward Foot, a dyed-in-the-wool Englishman, who was totally imbued with a great sense of responsibility towards educating Indians to eventually take over the leadership of this ancient land and its people. On one occasion, Lord Wavell, the Viceroy of India, and his entourage, attended Assembly in 1945 and when it ended, everybody stood to attention while the boys sang *Jana Gana Mana* lustily. Lord Wavell asked Foot what was the song that made everybody stand to attention. Foot replied 'Your Excellency, that was India's National Anthem'.

Great men achieve great goals but they cannot do this single-handedly. A part of their greatness is the ability to build a team of like-minded individuals who can pull together but who still retain their unique individuality to bring freshness of thought to the centre stage. Into this illustrious group of Masters were people like John Martyn, Jack Gibson (Gibby to the boys) and R.L. Holdsworth (affectionately called 'Holdie'). The contribution of each individual is so enormous that they deserve individual accolades. So lets start with John Martyn, who succeeded Foot as HM in 1948. Foot first met John Martyn when he interviewed him at Harrow, where he was teaching English and History. What impressed him most was Martyn's enormous *joie de vivre* and natural good nature, which were a good foil for Foot's more serious, matter-of-fact and down-to-earth demeanour. They made an excellent pair and worked very well in tandem. John Martyn came to India closely following in the footsteps of Foot and became the Housemaster of Hyderabad House, a responsibility that he carried with great élan till he became the HM in 1948. Martyn brought with him a totally new education system, pioneered by another great educationist, Kurt Hahn, in Germany, the founder of the Outward Bound Movement and England's Gordonstoun School, which became the Alma Mater of Prince Phillip Mountbatten and his son, Prince Charles. Kurt Hahn believed that education should not be a dreary drudgery of forced learning but a vibrant and creative experience in workshops, art and music schools, tempered with a sense of excitement and adventure engendered while climbing mountains or sailing at sea. The Doon School espoused the Outward Bound Movement with alacrity and mountain climbing, with the Himalayas on its doorstep, became a way of life for many Doscos. I shall write in greater detail when I write about Holdie. For the moment let it suffice to say that the Outward Bound Schools have a close network with a regular exchange of teachers and students.

After an illustrious career as the HM, Martyn retired and lived in his beloved Dehra Dun with his wife, Mady. In his retirement, he actively worked with the local Cheshire Home, named after Baron Leonard Cheshire, V.C., the intrepid bomber pilot of WW II. Martyn was awarded the O.B.E. by Britain and the Padma Shri by India for his services to the country. He died in 1984, grieved for and missed by Doscos all over the world—another giant of a man who has left an indelible imprint in India and the Doon School in particular.

The next pillar supporting the Doon School was J.T.M. Gibson, who was the most peripatetic of this group of English masters. He was destined to wear three hats. The first was as the illustrious Housemaster of Kashmir House, followed by a stint in the Navy during WW II, and back again to school where he taught geography in his inimitable and unorthodox manner. He was in the forefront of the school's numerous forays into the Himalayas and introduced white-water rafting on the Yamuna and the Ganga. India, in the meantime, had adopted the concept of a Joint Services Wing (JSW) for the three services. This entailed a competitive examination to select young boys destined for careers in the three services and to educate them for three years as cadets at a senior-school level before sending them to their respective academies. Jack was the first Principal of the JSW. A singular honour!!

Jack Gibson could be called the Grand Architect of India's JSW. No mean achievement. After leaving the JSW, Jack Gibson was appointed as the Principal of Mayo College, Ajmere, one of the most prestigious Chiefs Colleges, established by the British to educate the sons of India's autocratic princes. The task of converting a Chiefs College, populated with pampered, spoilt and privilege-ridden brats, into anything even remotely resembling a public school, was a Herculean endeavour. Jack Gibson succeeded and today Mayo College is one of India's premier public schools. The incredible achievement at Mayo College started a veritable avalanche of change in the other Chiefs Colleges. India was desperately short of good schools and had a burgeoning middle class, which had the wherewithal to pay the fees demanded by good schools. Jack Gibson was awarded the O.B.E. by Britain and the Padma Shri by a grateful India for his enormous service to education. Like John Martyn, Jack Gibson never left India and passed away in Ajmere after retiring from Mayo, greatly respected and missed by the Old

Boys of the Doon School and Mayo College, whose lives he had moulded.

R.L. Holdsworth (Holdie) was the last of the triad that Foot had recruited. He was teaching in Harrow, which he left to become the Headmaster of Islamia College in Peshawar, right in the heart of the turbulent North-Western Frontier Province (NWFP) bordering on Afghanistan. Here he developed a deep respect for the fiercely independent Pathans, to the extent that, in the hot summer months, he used to wear their dress and turban. Holdie brought this idiosyncrasy to the Doon School. He would remove his turban which was respectfully placed on his table before commencing his lecture. Over his Pathan regalia, he sported the obligatory master's gown. Holdie, brought many attributes with him. He had a 'Blue' in cricket from Oxford and soon took over as the coach. Cricket flourished under Holdie's tutelage. This highly talented individual had many strings to his bow. Mountaineering, fishing, knowledge of high-altitude alpine plants and skiing were among his many attributes. Holdie, accompanied by the redoubtable Eric Shipton, had climbed Mt. Kamet (25,263 ft.), the highest Himalayan peak to be climbed at that time. Holdie also had the distinction of smoking his pipe on the summit and skiing down the face of the mountain. On his return journey, Holdie discovered the Bhayunder valley, the incomparable 'Valley of Flowers', a veritable carpet of alpine flowers—an alpine wonderland!!

The Outward Bound Movement took on another dimension with numerous expeditions and high-altitude treks by boys led by Martyn, Gibson and of course, Holdie, climbing the peaks of the Himalayas and orienteering in the marvellous 'Bagyals' or high-alpine pastures of Garhwal. The Doon School pioneered mountaineering in India, but its zenith came when Nandu Jayal, a protégé of Holdie and a Major in the Indian Army, was given the singular honour of being the first foreigner to become a Swiss Alpine Guide. The Government of India made him the Principal of The Himalayan Mountaineering Institute in Darjeeling in 1954. Tenzing Norgay, who climbed to the summit of Mt. Everest with Sir Edmund Hillary on 29 May 1953, was the Chief Instructor under Nandu. Tragically, Nandu lost his life on an expedition to climb Cho Oyu four years later and is buried in the snow on the mountain. The grand tradition of mountaineering was continued by another master at the Doon School, Gurdial Singh (Guru to his friends), who led numerous expeditions in the Garhwal Himalayas. Guru has an encyclopaedic knowledge of high-alpine flowers, which he always shared with his climbing companions. Holdie retired in 1963 and returned to England, where he passed away.

This narrative is assuming the proportions of a saga on the Doon School, which was never intended. Yet, how does one write about the birth of an incredible institution, totally novel in India, and the remarkable people from far away England who made it happen, without a strong leavening of poetic and historical licence? Let me hasten to add that Doon School is by no means the swaddling child of British India. There is a vast team of Indian HMs, masters and Old Boys who have given years of their lives to bring the school to its present pre-eminence as India's Eton. I could write volumes about my Alma Mater and what it has done for me but this borders on a nostalgic journey down 'memory lane'—a delightful experience for the writer but probably a crashing bore for the reader. So I will desist. However, a serious problem remains. I would dearly love to give well—earned accolades to so many, stalwarts who have done so much for the school, but this would turn into a voluminous magnum opus of 'great men that I have known'. I have no alternative but to indulge in a bit of craft and cunning to get out of this dilemma and that is not to isolate the individual but to collectively give them my personal heartfelt thanks and the thanks of all my colleagues and associates for their enormous contribution, in so many spheres, that has made the Doon School the template for all public schools in India. So much for nostalgia!

In the chapters that I have written and the experiences that I have shared with my fellow travellers, I hope that I have been able to convey the remarkable qualities of leadership and character that the English masters at Doon School manifested and inculcated in the students under their care. They were a very special breed and definitely did not typify the 'run-of-the-mill' Britisher who arrived in India under 'The Raj'. It is also not fair or desirable to 'tar' all Britishers with the same brush. They came in all shapes and sizes and it behooves us to identify the obvious categories like the British Army officers, the true commercial 'Moghuls', laconically labelled as the '*Box Wallahs*'; the travelling salesman; the civil servants of he East India Company (EIC), and above all, the individual adventurers and soldiers of fortune who sallied forth to the 'ends of the earth' in search of the fabled 'pot-of-gold'. I am going to take the liberty of setting the ball rolling by giving pride of place to the very last group, that little band of unconventional Britishers who formed the avant-garde of the EIC.

4

Unconventional Britishers

The most prominent in this group was the indomitable James Skinner, son of an adventuring Scot and a Rajput Princess. James Skinner gathered around himself a levy of excellent horsemen and marksmen from around Delhi, unlike the EIC, whose recruiting ground lay hundreds of miles to the east.

'Skinner's Horse', as the troops were called, wore a yellow tunic that earned them the title of 'the yellow boys'. Skinner's Horse started its career in the service of Scindia, the Maratha Chief, harassing the EIC, west of Delhi. This became necessary as, by 1792, a person of mixed blood, like James Skinner, could not get a commission in the British Army or a fitting rank to command troops like the Skinner's Horse. In 1803, the Maratha Confederacy opened hostilities against the British and all European soldiers were dismissed from their service. This left James Skinner in an awful predicament as Skinner's Horse became, like the Japanese Samurai 'Ronin', or Sumarai warriors without loyalty and leadership. Fortunately, the C-in-C, Lord Lake was a man of extraordinary vision and courage, who despite the narrow-minded and racist policies, which were a part and parcel of the baggage inherited by the EIC from London, took on the 'yellow boys' as an irregular cavalry unit. Over the years, James Skinner was referred to as 'Sikander of Hansi' by his men—Sikander being the Indian name for' Alexander the Great'—and Hansi referred to the huge Skinner Estate in the small township of that name not far from Delhi. In 1815, the younger brother, Robert Skinner, became second in command and James Skinner was made Companion of the Bath and elevated to the rank of Brigadier. James Skinner built the lovely St James Cathedral at Kashmiri Gate in Delhi. The Skinner family also had extensive estates in Dehra Dun, which were taken over by the Doon School as it expanded. The Skinner family is very well respected by Indians, but the descendants of James Skinner were given short shrift by the British because of their mixed ancestry—a deplorable attitude considering the service that the Skinner family had given to the British. But racial prejudice is mindless, blind and stupid. Enough said!

I now have to leave the Skinner family and move onto another intrepid adventurer, Sir David Ochterlony, the son of a rich American landowner in the newly settled colony of America, who was impoverished in the re–settlement of the country. The destitute young man had heard that, after the loss of the American colony, the focus of the British had shifted to India and the British East India Company (EIC) was desperate for young men of mettle and adventure to man the ramparts. David Ochterlony entered the service of the EIC in Calcutta with no credentials to his name. By sheer grit and determination, he moved up the ladder. His big opening came when he saved Delhi from the marauding Marathas in 1804, but he achieved his even bigger name as a military commander in the 1814–16 war against Nepal. It was Ochterlony who laid down the terms of surrender and this has been covered in detail earlier in this narrative. The recruitment of Gorkhas into the army of the EIC is also thanks to the foresight and vision of General David Ochterlony. This was a very exceptional individual with many attributes, unlike the relatively dull and staid British servants of the Company in Calcutta. Ochterlony was fluent in several Indian languages and totally at home in the customs and traditions, which he espoused as his own. In his home he lived like an Indian, wearing Indian garb and reputedly, married 13 Indian wives. He had 'gone native'—a deplorable situation in the eyes of the bigoted racists, with their archaic George III values, who blindly followed the rarified and stultified ethos that prevailed in London. But his blood had not been sullied with 'native' blood, unlike Skinner. Plus, the EIC needed him as an intermediary when dealing with the Indians, whom the

British secretly despised and never understood. Ochterlony's health had taken a battering after 54 years in India and there was pressure on him to go back to England, but he politely refused. He had nothing to 'go back to'. India was his home and country. He loved the land and its people and that is where he ended his days—an incredible individual on whose shoulders the EIC grew and prospered.

After the defeat of Bonnie Prince Charlie at The Battle of Culloden in 1746, many Scottish Lairds faced ruin and destitution and were at the mercy of the ruthless English Monarch. The ancestral house of Moniach, the home of the Frazer family, now fell on troubled times and forced members of the family to leave and seek employment elsewhere. The eldest son, William Frazer, arrived in Delhi in 1815. He was a 'freebooter' and lived by his wits. He fell in love with India, married six or seven wives and fathered numerous children. He was a scholar of Sanskrit and Persian, and over the years, became a good friend of James Skinner. These two 'renegade' Britishers and a Mughal nobleman, Ahmad Baksh Khan, set up a lucrative business, importing stallions from Afghanistan and Central Asia. These beautiful animals were stabled on the Skinner estate in Hansi and became the mounts for his famous cavalry regiment. William Frazer's vast knowledge of Delhi and India were invaluable assets for the EIC and he became an advisor to the Resident, Sir Charles Metcalf and later to his nephew, Sir Thomas Metcalf. The peak of his career came in 1833 when he was appointed Resident. He was shot and died on 22 March 1835. The assassin was a disgruntled employee.

There were numerous other Britishers, like Colonel Gardner, who came to India settled in the country, married Indian wives, and formed the 2nd Royal Lancers. I have handpicked four to give the reader a glimpse of the mettle of these intrepid adventurers who are an integral part of Indian history.

The British Army and its brilliant commanders were the shield and the Indian Army was the sword—arm which brought a semblance of peace and order into a turbulent, tattered and disparate collection of warlords who were forever at each others throats. The EIC literally walked into a maelstrom of feuding princelingswho had no concept of nationhood, or respected any centralized authority. As we will see, India was the nursery in which some of Britain's greatest military commanders were reared and nourished. Immortal names like Lord Herbert Kitchener of Khartoum; Lord Frederick Sleigh Roberts of Kandahar; Marquis Richard Wellesley, the elder brother of Arthur Wellesley, who later became the Duke of Wellington. Both brothers distinguished themselves on Indian battlefields. Marquis Charles Cornwallis, who introduced the Cornwallis Code, and was the Governor-General of India in 1804; General Sir Samuel, J. Browne, V.C., lost his left arm in 1858, making him design the famous 'Sam Browne' belt, worn by officers of many Countries as a part of their standard uniform. These are but a few of the immortal names in British military history that catapulted the country to the forefront of fame and fortune and created the fabled reign of Pax Britannica, not only in India but in the Empire.

5

The Indian Army

It is very difficult to pinpoint the genesis of The Indian Army as a separate entity. Indian soldiers were recruited by the British as *sepoys*, a corruption of the Persian word *'sephai'*, for soldier or watchman, and who fought alongside British soldiers in the prolonged wars with the French. In fact the sepoy army outnumbered the British by as much as two to one. Both the British and French realized the excellent fighting qualities of the sepoy when he was properly trained and disciplined, in total contrast to the 'rag tag' soldiery of the levies that joined the Indian princes in their incessant squabbles. The very first step was a proper salaried force paid by the EIC. The next quantum leap was the introduction of the *silladari* system under which the horse and equipment was supplied by the EIC and paid off by the trooper by regular deductions from his salary. In the event of death or retirement, the next incumbent took on the burden of repayment. The *silladari* system ensured uniformity in dress and training. However, in all fairness, credit must be given to the French Generals like Dumas and Dupleix, who were the first to recognize the excellent inherent fighting qualities of the Indian, when properly led and disciplined, and recruited them into their army.

Robert Clive arrived in Madras as a clerk, working for the EIC, but he soon transferred to the army. There was fierce rivalry between the French and the British in the Deccan area with the dwindling power of the Mughal emperor in Delhi and the rampaging forays of the Marathas. Dupleix and the Nawab of Carnatica jointly attacked and captured Madras in 1744. They then turned their attention to Fort David but were repulsed by the British under the command of Major Stringer Lawrence, a remarkable man who gave Robert Clive the permission to attack the fort at Arcot, even though Clive was an unknown and untried entity at the time. Clive took Arcot in 1751 and resisted the siege that followed for 53 days. Clive's reputation as a military commander was now legendary. It should be mentioned that most of the fighting was done by sepoys under his command. The scene now shifts to Bengal where the local bully boy, Nawab Siraj-ud-Daulah, became alarmed at the growing power and wealth of the EIC. He attacked and took Calcutta. The local British residents were ill treated and humiliated. This was the so-called 'Black Hole of Calcutta' that scarred the psyche of the British and left a seething resentment, which would surface as a furious hatred and vindictiveness against Indians in the Mutiny of 1857. But let us get back to the fall of Calcutta to Siraj-ud-Daulah. When news of this debacle reached Madras, Clive was dispatched with a small force to relieve the city. His army was mostly composed of sepoys who displayed considerable panache, precision and steadfastness under fire and a flare for attacking the enemy head on with the bayonet. Facing Clive was a massive force of 50,000 foot soldiers, 10,000 cavalry and 56 pieces of artillery, consisting mainly of heavy guns. Clive was heavily out numbered but the enemy was plagued with deceit and intrigue and was easily routed. Siraj-ud-Daulah fled and was replaced by his uncle, Mir Jafir who was proclaimed as the Nawab by Clive. This grateful upstart paid Clive £234,000 as a personal gift. An enormous sum of money, plus £3,000,000, plus jewels and coinage for the Directors of the EIC. Clive now attacked and captured the French Fort at Chandernagore near Calcutta and the Dutch enclave at Chinsura. The entire Ganges delta was now under the control of the EIC. The Battle of Plassey once again proved that a small force of well trained soldiers—either European, sepoys or mixed—could rout massive indigenous formations. Plassey was not militarily a great victory but it established British hegemony in a huge area of India, plus it laid the base for the establishment of an incipient Indian Army. The Nawab's army was disbanded and the EIC was given the right to raise taxes.

After Clive's victories at Arcot and Plassey, he returned to England as an extremely wealthy man. Some reckon that he was the richest man in England and earned the derisive title of 'Nabob', a corruption of the Indian title of 'Nawab' or ruler. The EIC servants, loaded with their ill-gotten loot from India, were an object of envy and derision and created a feeble attempt by the Directors of the EIC to put an end to this pillaging. The impeachment of Warren Hastings was the consequence and his trial lasted seven years at the end of which he was exonerated. Unlike Clive, who was an unmitigated, self-serving scoundrel, Warren Hastings was a good and genuine administrator. In their misguided wisdom, the Directors of the EIC sent out to India a mischievous intriguer, Phillip Francis, as a Councillor. Francis and Hastings clashed immediately. Francis was a typical bureaucrat whilst Hastings was a wise and sensible administrator. Matters came to a head and a duel resulted in which Francis was wounded. A malicious and conniving Francis concocted a forged charge of bribery and corruption against Hastings, which led to his Impeachment. A sad case of miscarriage of justice. It should be mentioned that Warren Hastings and Sir William Jones jointly founded The Asiatic Society dedicated to the study of oriental languages, history and culture.

The EIC was not out of the woods by any means. In the Deccan, the Hindu State of Mysore was overrun by Hyder Ali, a renegade Punjabi adventurer who was succeeded by his son, Tippu Sultan, a tyrannical and erratic ruler forever playing a sort of political roulette with the British and the French. He defeated the EIC in a battle in 1782 took over a 1,000 prisoners whom he put into dungeons and ill-treated them. He over-stepped the mark when he invaded the State of Travancore, which was under the protection of the EIC. By this time Richard Wellesley had become the Governor-General, who sent an ultimatum for withdrawal, which was ignored. Major General David Baird, who had spent time in the dungeons of Tippu Sultan, was ordered to attack Tippu Sultan in his capital of Seringapatam in

1789. Tippu Sultan put up a valiant fight but was killed in the encounter. This finally put a cap on the efforts of the French, under Dupleix, to gain ascendancy over the British.

The Wellesley brothers, Richard and his younger brother, Arthur, who was destined to become the Duke of Wellington, did not take kindly to India, Indians or, for that matter, the British civilians in Madras and Calcutta. Arthur Wellesley described the latter as 'vulgar, ignorant, rude, familiar and stupid' and India as 'a miserable country to live in'. He commiserated with the returning 'Nabobs', and their ill-gotten loot, as just recompense for living in that God forsaken country. In spite of this derogatory attitude, both brothers did signal service on the battlefield against the Maratha Confederacy and gained considerable territory for the EIC, causing consternation in London.

The EIC was now poised for changes in direction and it was necessary to do a quick stock-take of its territory and financial position.

The EIC had overreached itself with the fresh conquests of the Wellesley brothers that virtually covered the entire Deccan Plàteau, and the defeat of Dupleix removed the threat of any fresh incursion by the French. The aftermath of The Battle of Plassey was that the EIC had open access to the whole of Northern India right up to Delhi, and the annexation of Oudh in 1803 brought the EIC to the borders of Nepal. This period of history has been covered in detail in the war against Nepal. Arthur Wellesley defeated Scindia of Gwalior, the biggest Maratha chief, at the bloody battle of Assaye in 1803 which earned him the sobriquet of 'The Sepoy General.' Effectively, the EIC now controlled the whole of India, barring the Princely States, Punjab and Sind. The Treaty of Poona in 1817 put an end to Maratha power but unleashed the marauding bandits called Pindarris, who will be dealt with separately in this narrative. So far the EIC has been engrossed in increasing its territory and administration. It has not meddled in social reforms, education or Evangelism. All this was about to change with the arrival of three 'griffins' or 'grifs', the term used in Calcutta for fresh arrivals from England.

6

The Reformers

Before we dwell on the handiwork of the reformers, it is desirable to understand the landscape that had to be altered and reshaped. The recipients were the inhabitants of India, the Muslims who were the erstwhile rulers and the Hindus who were the overwhelming population of subjugated people who had suffered under the Muslim yoke for nearly 800 years. The arrival of the British was like a life raft for the Muslims who had lost their Mughal Empire through decadence and lasciviousness and were under assault from the Hindu Marathas, who were ascendant everywhere. Let us deal with the Muslim first of all. Evangelism was an almost impossibility as apostasy is punishable by death under Islamic Sharia law and preaching the Bible is forbidden. The Muslim did not readily take to western-styled education in English and tended to stick to their *madrassa* seminary system. This attitude bred isolation, conservatism and backwardness, which would boomerang back on the community when it had to compete against the Hindus who are now in the spotlight.

Over the centuries, Hinduism was degraded from the Empyrean Heights of its ancient philosophical discourses in the *Rig Veda* and the *Upanishads* and its pre-eminence in science and mathematics, to a tawdry, decadent, ritual-ridden, corrupt society that lived off its wits. The subjugation of over 90 per cent of the population by barely 9 per cent of Muslims for nearly 800 years was not only demeaning but it destroyed the last vestige of pride and self-reliance. We now have to see the Hindus as the EIC encountered them. To do this we have to cast aside the sham, bluff and hum-bug of the cast Hindus who snivelled before the British overtly, but despised them as 'untouchables'—'Chandals', behind their back. The British openly despised the Hindus, which the Hindus paid back in kind, but in a sneaking surreptitious manner. Let me hasten to add that these comments do not apply to the healthy relationship that was developing between the British and Indian fighting-men, but to the civilians of both communities that were hell-bent on exploiting each other. Over the centuries Hinduism had degenerated into a sick and ugly society in which expediency and venality had over ridden decency and morality. Although Hindus have always boasted about the honourable place of women in their society, in contrast to the debased status of women in Islam, the truth presents a very different picture. Female infanticide was rife and child-marriages were arranged by families to compact beneficial financial or political alliances. Widow re-marriage was forbidden and the life of a widow was a living hell. Her blood family's attitude was that she no longer belonged to them as she had been given to her husband's family thus she was their responsibility. To her in-laws she was a nuisance and a financial burden so the disgusting practice of *sati* or *suttee* was born, that is, the widow should be immolated on her husband's funeral pyre, not necessarily of her own choice. Once again, I have to digress to distinguish between this disgraceful behaviour and the custom of *'jauhar'*, or the ceremony of 'the saffron robe', practiced by that noble race of Rajputs who place honour and chivalry above everything in life.

At the Battle of Chitor, this tiny principality, in 1567, refused to surrender to the mighty forces of the Mughal Emperor, Akbar the Great, who laid siege to the fort. The defenders were a mere 8,000 Rajput men and women, led by their chiefs, Jaimal and Patta, who were going to fight to the death. Every able-bodied woman picked up her spear and went onto the ramparts to fight alongside the Rajput warriors. The sick, old and children committed suicide rather than fall into the hands of the barbarians. This was all done after the ceremony of *jauhar* when the women broke their bangles and proclaimed their widowhood, thereby freeing the men of any responsibility. A saffron cloak was put over the shoulders of the men. Not a single man or woman survived that day. Chitor was a city of the dead. The mighty Akbar, the descendant of Chenghiz Khan, was so impressed by such valour that he decided that Rajput blood must run in his family and he married a Rajput princess. Such was the valour and chivalry of the Rajput, these doughty warriors, from whom the valiant Gorkhas claim their descent. I have covered this earlier in the narrative. However, what a comparison between the honour and nobility of *jauhar* and the despicable degradation of *sati*! How the mighty have fallen. Hinduism had debased itself and the ritualistic murder of widows by '*sati*' could no longer be tolerated. It was banned by Lord William Bentinck (WB) when he became the Governor-General in 1928.

There were howls of protest from the Hindus but he was undeterred in his determination to 'improve the Indian race morally and materially by westernization'. The seven-year reign of Bentinck was very eventful, but then he was not a person who would turn a blind eye to obvious iniquities around him like the practice of 'Thugee', or human sacrifice in the name of the bloodthirsty Hindu Goddess, Bhiwani, Kali or Durga, the consort of the God Shiva. The Thugs roamed around the countryside in gangs, which would ingratiate themselves with caravans and then would garrotte their victims while they slept, with a specially prepared handkerchief, called a *roomal*. The Thugs would loot, that is, pillage the caravan, and bury their victims in shallow graves after offering them as sacrifices to Bhiwani, their Goddess. The words, 'thug' and' loot' have entered into the English language from the nefarious exploits of these criminals. Lord Bentinck appointed a special Commissioner, Sir William Sleeman, to eradicate the Thugee cult. In six years, Sleeman executed over 3,000 Thugs, which put an end to this menace. Sleeman was also responsible for eliminating two other criminal problems which were ravaging the Indian countryside. The Treaty of Poona, in 1817, put an end to Maratha insurgency but this left the Maratha forces unemployed and without proper leadership. The Maratha irregulars now took to banditry and were called Pindarris. They were a mixed group of freebooters with no fixed territory, race or religion. They were progressively eliminated by Marquis Francis Hastings—no relation of Warren Hastings—in what came to be known as the Pindarri Wars.

After the death of the Mughal Emperor, Aurangzeb, in 1707, the dynasty went into a sharp decline, and with decadence, lawlessness increased. Dacoits, or armed bandits, roamed the countryside, looting and pillaging at random.

The suppression of dacoity became a priority for Sleeman and with his usual ruthless efficiency, dacoity was greatly reduced.

The EIC Directors, like their counterparts in the British Government, were obsessed with what can be best described as Russo-phobia, exacerbated by the gradual expansion of Russia into the Middle-East towards Persia and Afghanistan. The British were the dominant power after the defeat of France, but Russia, under Czar Nicholas II, was seen as a continuation of Russian hegemony under Catherine the Great, with Russia looking for a warm-weather port. Russo-phobia gave birth to what came to be known as 'The Great Game', with the Russians surreptitiously probing into the tribal Khanates, east of the Caspian Sea, and extending their influence towards Persia and Afghanistan, and the British in India, percolating into the same area with their spies and informants. I shall deal with this subject in more depth once the EIC extends its domain to the Afghan border. For the moment we have to return to the reform-agenda of Lord William Bentinck (WB) who abolished the flogging of Indian sepoys, as this meant a loss of *izzat*, loosely translated into English as a' loss of face', but in fact the repercussions were much deeper. Flogging was so demeaning to them that it virtually destroyed the individual as a man. Incidentally, flogging continued in the British Army for many years after it was banned in the Indian Army.

In 1824, the EIC invaded and conquered Burma in order to safeguard its eastern border and then moved into the Assam Valley, which was ruled by the Burmese Asom Kings. The invasion of Burma had further repercussions as this was accomplished by using Indian troops who mutinied at

Barrackpore and Vellore. The Indians resented being sent overseas.

1827 saw the arrival of a 20-year-old Charles Trevelyan in Delhi, fresh out of the EIC's Haileybury College, created by the Company in 1806, to train its employees prior to posting in India. Charles Trevelyan was the son of the Arch Deacon of Taunton. He was a bit of a prig, imbued with strong evangelical ideas and an over-zealous sense of morality. One of his teachers at Haileybury was Reverend Thomas Malthus who needs no introduction. At this juncture, a slight digression is necessary in order to understand what follows:

In India, there was a long-standing custom called *nazar*, which dictated that underlings of all types down the pecking order, gave a token gift (tribute)to the 'lord' or senior, of money, called *nazar*, literally a vision, glance or favour. Incidentally, at one time *nazar* was paid in gold 'mohars' or English Sovreigns. To refuse *nazar* was an unforgivable insult. It was unthinkable and the epitome of bad manners. The British understood this custom and Lord Cornwallis had decreed that all gifts and *nazar* must be deposited in the treasury. Sir Edward Colebrooke was the senior magistrate in Delhi. At the age of sixty-five he had neglected to do this. When this came to the attention of Trevelyan, he was infuriated and reported the matter to Calcutta. The old man was sent back to England in disgrace. Such was the fulminating anger of the 21-year-old Trevelyan. A well-educated and intelligent man he set about learning Indian languages, but he was appalled by Hinduism and its pantheon of deities. For a while, he was the tutor of the son of the Raja of Bhurtpore.

The last of the triad of reformers was Thomas Babington Macaulay, who arrived in Calcutta with his sister Hannah. He was a Member of the Governors' Council and developed an Indian Penal Code for the EIC. Unlike Trevelyan who was a bit of an intellectual, Macaulay could not be bothered with this sort of palaver. Allow me to quote from what Macaulay had to say about oriental languages:

> 'I have never found anyone distinguished by their proficiencies in the Eastern tongues who would deny that a single shelf of a

European library was worth the whole native literature of India and Arabia.'

So much for the culture and history of the land that was going to be his home for many years. Dismissed by a stroke of the pen, Macaulay was a strange, mixed-up man who knew what he has to do because of his English upbringing, but he was laced with a Christian evangelism which breeds intolerance of other religions and beliefs. Watch what he has to say, as Lord Macaulay, to the British Parliament on 2 February,1835:

> 'I have traversed across the length and breadth of India and I have not seen one person who is a beggar, who is a thief, such wealth I have seen in this country, such high moral values, people of such calibre, that I do not think we would ever conquer this country, unless we break the very backbone of this nation, which is her spiritual and cultural heritage, and therefore I propose that we replace her old and ancient education system, her culture, for if the Indians think that all that is esteem, their native culture, and they will become what we want them, a truly dominated nation.'

Unbelievable but true! Macaulay was determined to destroy every vestige of Indian education and culture and on the ruins he was going to erect a so-called modern and western education system based on the English language and create an educated class of Indian in blood and colour but English in taste, opinions, morals and intellect.

Macaulay was obsessed with the virtues of the English language and this laid the foundation of 'western-styled education' in India, with the evangelist church opening up a plethora of schools for men and convents for women. Little did Macaulay realize that in the years to come, with this legacy, India would become the whetstone on which the English language would be honed and would create a renaissance which would make it the 'lingua franca' of the world. India today is probably the most prolific source of English literature and writing in the world.

Before we leave Macaulay and his legacy of the English language to India, it is worth mentioning as an *obiter dictum*, that Trevelyan married Hannah, Macaulay's sister. Macaulay continues to be a thorn in the side of India's so-called Hindu

Nationalists, who persist in blaming him for the destruction of a non-existant Hindu education system. I have written about this lacuna in India's education system which gave rise to the 'diaspora' of Indian boys being sent to English Public Schools and the eventual genesis of the Doon School. Thank God for Macaulay!

There were two terrible blights in the life of the young Britisher fresh out of England—the so-called 'Griffin'. The first and foremost was the dreadful shortage of English women. The fresh arrival was an unwed bachelor with a 'roaring libido' and no English consorts in sight. The tiny female population in Metropolitan Calcutta, were the wives of senior EIC administrators who had earned the derisive sobriquet of 'the *Burra Memsahib*'. A veritable 'pain in the neck', full of her own importance and riddled with archaic victorian 'starchy' values. I shall write at length about this dreadful phenomenon, but, for the moment, let us revert to the terrible plight of the poor 'Griffin'. So there was no joy to be had in this quarter. The Indian population was in a sort of 'quarantine'. The Muslim women were cloistered in their *zanana* or female quarter, out of sight of all males. Among the Hindus, the British were *Chandals*, the lowest category of the 'untouchable', the carrion-removers. The British detested the Indian and vice versa, a novel experience for the swaggering EIC bully boys, who, after all, were 'British' and the Indians were only 'natives', after all - a term of derision and blatant racism. What was left were the Hindu outcasts, these poor defenceless victims of a dreadful and pernicious caste system that was pitiless in its victimization of a people whose only crime was that were born 'out of cast'. Obviously a just punishment for crimes committed in past lives. Utter garbage of course. The untouchables were segregated and lived in ghettos. This was the only community that welcomed the sexual advances of the equally untouchable Britisher, who created the so-called '*Bibi Ghar*' or the house of 'women'. This was all very well in the '*Mouffasil*', the district or countryside, out of sight of the prying eyes of the puritanical Administration. The Bibi Ghar was an institution that survived until the arrival of the so-called 'Fishing Fleet', the influx of single British women desperate to find a husband in the swarm of eligible bachelors in the army and civilian services in India. The 'Fishing Fleet' started to arrive even before the opening of the Suez Canal. Once the EIC had annexed Sind, the Indus River became available for steam ships to ply from the Arabian Sea to the Punjab which had fallen to the EIC after the death of Maharaja Ranjit Singh, the 'Lion of the Punjab'. The travellers to India would disembark at Port Said, travel overland to Suez, board steam ships that would ply the Red Sea, picking up coal and fresh water at Aden and then proceed to what would eventually become the Port of Karachi. Then came the journey by steam ships up the Indus River to the Punjab. A tedious journey but infinitely better than six months on an 'Indiaman', buffeted by high seas as it went around the Cape of Good Hope.

But lets get back to the *bibi ghar* that was the saving grace for the desperate young Britisher. Inevitably the *bibi ghar* became the nursery for the progeny of these alliances and the so-called 'Anglo-Indian' came into being. This name is a misnomer and should rightly apply to the British living in India but the British would not have a bar of this nonsense. A Britisher was a Britisher no matter where he lived. Everybody else was a 'bloody foreigner', poor devil!. Typically, the Hindu could only sneer and call the poor Eurasian a 'chee chee', that is, dirty or unclean. The British were equally unkind and referred to them as 'black and white' or 'chutney Marys'. Disgraceful behaviour considering that the British had fathered their off spring. But at least the British felt that they had a responsibility towards the Anglo-Indian, even though this was strongly flavoured with a sense of exploiting the Anglo-Indians' with his distorted sense of being 'British' by proxy. Here was another totally reliable 'ally' in an otherwise hostile India. The Indian Railways and The Post and Telegraph Services became a reservoir for the Anglo-Indian in the lower echelons. Stationmasters, guards, ticketmasters and engine drivers were almost exclusively manned by Anglo-Indians, who lived in Railway Colonies. Another area was in the field of nursing and teaching in convents, which the caste Hindus disdained. Of course, the Anglo-Indians were Christians and the church used the community to evangelize. Kindergarten teachers were almost exclusively Anglo-Indian women with a sprinkling of British women who either set up exclusive preparatory schools or became governesses to the children of Indian princes Church schools were often referred to as Anglo-Indian Schools and they provided a sound education, laced with compulsory Bible classes for all students, irrespective of their own religion.

India is a land of inexplicable and often ridiculous contradictions. Here is a classic example. Children from mixed marriages, where the father was Indian and the mother was either British or some other European, were regarded as Indian. There was no stigma or slur and these children became top generals and headed giant corporations. They were regarded as Indians and no questions asked. A very different story to the Anglo-Indian I have described in detail. A part of their misery was of their own making, as they totally disowned their Indian ancestry, understandably, and put on airs and fancies of being 'British'. All very silly and laughable. When India became independent the poor Anglo-Indian was left high and dry. Tens of thousands immigrated to England but the climate was too cold and British acceptance of the Anglo-Indian as 'one of them' came with severe reservations. Many Anglo-Indians then migrated to Australia, mainly Western Australia, where they introduced the Aussie to the intricacies of hockey. Australia today is one of the top hockey playing countries in the world, thanks to the immigrant Anglo-Indian.

Fortunately India has grown up and matured since independence and today the Anglo- Indian is happy and proud to be an Indian. He is totally in the main stream of Indian life and not before time. Having covered the main blight of the young male Britisher in India, the lack of available young British women, before the arrival of the 'Fishing Fleet', brings us to the second serious affliction that marred life in the country, and that was the dreadful summer heat. In Northern India the arrival of April heralded the start of searing heat' without respite' for the next three to four months. The British had picked up some very useful tips from the Indians, who, over centuries had become experts in 'evaporative cooling' of their homes. This is such a vast topic that a separate section needs to be devoted to it to do it justice. For the moment let it suffice that the poor Britisher suffered badly in India's merciless summer heat. The defeat of the Gorkhas and the Treaty of Segauli, gave the EIC access to the Himalayas, stretching from the Punjab to the western border of Nepal. The EIC made Simla, at a height if 7,000 feet, its summer capital in1827. a most welcome escape from Delhi's enervating climate. A chain of so-called 'hill stations' followed suit, like my hometown of Mussoorie, perched 5,000 feet above Dehra Dun. My family did an annual 'safari',a migration, every year when we left our winter home in Saharanpur in April, and moved to Mussoorie, 64 miles away, which was our summer residence. As the cold blast of winter brought hail and snow, the reverse migration would start in November. An incredible feat for my mother who had to organize and supervise this enormous movement of servants and household paraphernalia twice a year. But we were extremely fortunate for we had the best of both worlds. The bracing climate of Mussoorie was like a draught of wine and a breath of fresh air. From our home we had an uninterrupted view of 800 miles of snow capped Himalayan peaks. A truly magnificent panorama that was non-pareil anywhere. Winter in Saharanpur had its own charm, sitting by a roaring fire as the temperature was close to freezing. Although my family did not have to put up with the ghastly summer months of Saharanpur, a lot of our friends were not so fortunate. When I write about living in this environment, I am not talking from personal experience but knowledge acquired from friends and associates who could not escape into the hills. But, more of that anon.

The building of The Suez Canal was the brain child of a French engineer, Ferdinand de Lessepe, who surveyed the land and set about forming The Suez Canal Company. The shareholders were the French, the British and the Khadive of Egypt. Work was started in 1859 to widen and deepen the rudimentary waterway between Port Said on the Mediterranean and the Port of Suez on the Red Sea.The work was completed in 1869 and cost £17,800,000. The Prime Minister, Benjamin

Disraeli, quickly realized that the Canal was the principal artery connecting Britain with its 'jewel in the crown', which was India, but did not have a controlling interest in the affairs of the Company, a highly unsatisfactory situation that had to be remedied immediately. But Britain was 'broke'! Disraeli went to see Baron Rothschild and asked for a loan of £1,000,000 to buy out the shares of the highly unpopular Khadive. Baron Rothschild asked Disraeli what security was he offering? Disraeli replied, 'the word of the Prime Minister of England'. Without another word, Baron Rothschild wrote out the cheque. This happened in 1875 and in1876 Disraeli pronounced Queen Victoria, as Empress of India.

The journey through the Suez Canal now took a mere 15 hours and Britain's iron grip on India was total. In 1857 the Indian Mutiny nearly cost Britain its Indian Empire and it very quickly realized it was an absurdity to allow a commercial enterprise, with its Directors sitting in London, to rule over such a huge and extremely valuable piece of real estate. The British took over the reigns of government in 1858.

With the advent of the Suez Canal, the tentacles of British Imperialism stretched far and wide into Asia and Australasia. It all started with the birth of the European Thalassocracies of Britain, France, Holland, Spain and Portugal, and even earlier with the Greek Argonauts and the German Hanseatic League. The driving force was 'lebensraum', the ever-increasing pressure of population, driving races and nations to look for greener pastures. The development of the caravelle and the galleon enabled the ancient mariners to venture further afield', financed by traders and the City States always on the lookout for goods to buy and sell. The travels of Marco Polo along the Silk Road to Xanadu whetted the desire to buy the marvellous silks of China and the delightful spices of India. The early 1600s saw the birth of the East India Companies of Britain, France and Holland. Sir Thomas Roe was given a letter by King James I to be personally delivered to the Mughal Emperor, Jehangir, requesting permission to open up trade between the two countries. Sir Thomas Roe landed in Surat on the west coast in1615 and then proceeded to Delhi The Permission was eventually granted and a 'factory' was opened in Madras in1639. However, the Dutch and the Portuguese had already started trade with the latter, buying calico and indigo. With the arrival of the French, the rivalry was between the two major powers and this has been covered in detail in this narrative. With the course of time Dutch commercial influence virtually disappeared in India but moved down the coast to Ceylon. The 'Bergers' in Ceylon, or Sri Lanka, are the descendants of mixed marriages between the Dutch and the local women. The Portuguese in India receded into their enclaves of Goa, south of Bombay, and the tiny settlements of Daman and Diu. These colonies were eventually absorbed into independent India.

The Charter of the British East India Company allowed the Company to use British troops to protect their forts, but they were remunerated by the Company. The Company also owned its own naval vessels and managed its harbours and jetties. Trade was the 'name of the game', not conquest or territorial acquisition. The EIC literally blundered into the conquest of Indian Territory. The country was just ready for conquest. India was not a nation but a loosely held confederation of about 20 different nationalities, owing no fealty to any central authority but a fidelity of convenience to the local warlords. We have already travelled over this ground and we need to move on. The commercial 'shenanigans' of the EIC will be given its own corner of history. For the moment, we are now entering troubled waters that lead into the dreadful events, which were the precursor to the Indian Mutiny of 1857, which almost ended British rule in India.

I do not intend to give a blow-by-blow account of what the mutineers did to British women and other civilians of the EIC, or the terrible reprisals that the British perpetrated on not only the mutineers, but the hapless citizens of India who were caught in the crossfire. Once madness is in the air all sense of morality and decency disappears and an animalistic blood-lust takes over. Revenge, cruelty and viciousness cloud rationality. However, the crisis of 1857 is such a landmark in the history of British rule in India that I cannot gloss over the event and dismiss it as though it never happened. What are truly cogent are the precursors that eventually caused the Mutiny and on these I will concentrate.

There is an old saying that there is no such thing as a bad soldier, only bad officers. The EIC had entrenched itself and won huge areas in wars against the French and sundry Indian warlords, largely on the back of the Indian sepoy. Unfortunately, the fabled bond of camaraderie between the British officers and the Indian soldiers was still in the melting pot and was being forged on the battle field. What existed in 'Civvy Street' was a disdain for everything Indian and a contemptuous arrogance by the British. The Indian felt demeaned and insulted. This was compounded by the reform agendas of Lord William Bentineck abolishing *Suttee* and *Thugee*, traditional but entrenched practices. To the orthodox Hindus this was a frontal assault on their religion. These dreadful practices had to go but orthodoxy was not going to give in without a fight. The arrival of Trevelyan and Macaulay now compounded the problem with a deliberate drive to destroy Indian culture and superimpose an education system based on the English language.

At the same time, there was a surge in evangelism by opening education to the Church which eagerly responded by starting schools for men and convents for women. None of this was going to endear the British to the Indian. But worse was to come. We are now going to witness rapacious greed on the part of the EIC. Lord Dalhousie introduced what came to be known as 'The Doctrine of Lapse'. Under this iniquitous Act the EIC reserved the right to annex any state or territory where there was not a rightful male heir or if the EIC felt that the ruler was not fit to rule. Large areas were forcibly annexed, like the States of Satara and Nagpur and, of course, the huge Muslim State of Oudh, which was one of the principal causes of the revolt Rani Lakshmi Bai, of the State of Jhansi, was widowed when she was just 18 and was childless. Jhansi was duly annexed by Dalhousie in spite of the Rani pleading her case for clemency. Dalhousie callously and contemptuously dismissed her from his presence. The Rani of Jhansi became a heroine and led strong forces of her men against the British during the Mutiny. She became a legend in India and during WW II a contingent of

Indian women fought against the British-Indian IV Army in Burma, as a part of the Indian National Army. They were called the Rani of Jhansi Regiment. Captain Lakshmi, who commanded the unit, was tried for treason by the British, along with the other Indian National Army officers (INA). This trial created such an uproar in India that the trial was dropped. For the Indians the INA internees were patriots, fighting for independence from Britain. Such was the long reach of the Mutiny, which was called India's First War of Independence by Indian patriots.

A bit far-fetched considering that the Presidential Armies of Bombay and Madras were not involved and in the Bengal Army only two battalions revolted. Furthermore, Britain would never have turned the tide against the mutineers had it not been for the solid support of the loyal sections of the sepoys like the Sikhs and their Princely States, and other soldiers from the Punjab, The incredible 'tour de force' by The Guides Cavalry, who left their head quarters in the frontier town of Hoti Mardan on 13 May 1857, under Captain Daly, and arrived in Delhi on the 9 June after having ridden 580 miles. They were in constant action with the 2nd Gorkhas and the 60th Rifles (King's Royal Rifle Corp). Such was the close association of the 2nd Gorkhas and the 60th Rifles that the latter insisted that the 2nd Gorkhas would henceforth be The 2nd Gorkha Rifles. This, incidentally, set the pattern for all Gorkha regiments to become Rifle regiments and would carry their weapons at trail arms. The 2nd Gorkhas were in fact Garhwalis, from the hills north and east of Mussoorie, and this close link gave the Garhwal Regiment, later to be named the 18th Royal Garhwal Rifles, the right to wear the Gorkha *khukri*. The Regimental Headquarters are at Lansdown in eastern Garhwal.

The seething resentment was also fuelled by the deployment of sepoys in the EIC ventures overseas, like the war in Burma, which resulted in the Mutiny in Barrackpore and Vellore.

Bad management and attitude on the part of the British is typified by the patronising and racist attitude in the following pronouncement by Lord Elgin, which speaks for itself: 'all orientals are children, amused and gratified by external trappings, ceremonies and titles and ready to put up with loss of real dignity if only they are permitted to enjoy the semblance of it.'

The powder-keg was primed and ready to explode once the fuse was lit and this was by a strange happenstance. The Army had been issued with the latest Lee Enfield rifles which needed the shot to be bitten off before it was fed into the breech. The shot was covered in a grease of unknown composition and a rumour was started that the grease was fat from a pig or cow or both. Religious defilement of both Hindus and Muslims was the excuse to mutiny.

The coup-de-grace came in 1842, when Dr Brydon staggered into the cantonment at Jallalabad as the sole survivor of Britain's ill-fated expedition into Afghanistan to unseat the ruler, Dost Mahommed, and replace him with their puppet, Shah Shuja. About 4,500 troops and 12,000 camp followers perished at the hands of the merciless Afghans. The myth about 'white invincibility' was shattered forever. If the Afghans could oust the British so could the Indians!

The EIC won the Mutiny by the skin of its teeth. The British were 'cut to the quick' that the Indian 'niggers' had the gumption to take them on and had clobbered them. How dare an inferior and degraded race like the Indian have the gall to challenge the might of the British, who were merely fulfilling their right to rule, given to them by a Divine Providence. Retribution was swift and severe. Unfortunately, at the receiving end was the senile and hapless last survivor of the Mughal dynasty, Bahadur Shah Zafar, who met the furious onslaught cowering in his ancestor's tomb, the mausoleum of the Emperor Humayun. His two sons were shot and Bahadur Shah Zafar was exiled to Rangoon, where he died a broken man, in November 1862. Bahadur Shah was an accomplished poet who wrote his pathos-filled verses under the nom de plume of 'Zafar'. The needless viciousness of the British and total disdain of any sense of decency and respect for the descendant of a great dynasty speaks ill of the British. There was no call to demean the poor man in his perilous dotage—shades of 'King Lear'?

One is sorely tempted to indulge in casting blame on the

British, but this does little to the cause of impartial historicity, and this, after all, is the sole purpose of this narrative. However, I have to make the observation that the City of Delhi was razed to the ground and its citizens were brutalized, irrespective of whether they were involved in the uprising or not, has to be said to the credit of the British Government that it realized that the days of the EIC were well and truly over and that it was no longer fit to rule over India. It acted swiftly, ending the Charter on 1 November 1858.

We are now entering a dreadful phase in the history of both Britain and India, but particularly Britain, as it was the paramount power controlling the destiny of millions around the world. I have already written about the inexorable pressure of population growth and the imperative for 'Lebensraum' and the constant search for greener pastures. But it was the destiny of the Reverend Thomas Robert Malthus, at Haileybury College, to propound his essay on 'The Principles of Population' which stated in succinct terms that population growth tended to outgrow the' means of subsistence'. Malthus further stated that growth of population must be arrested, either by self-restraint or birth control measures. The ghastly repercussions of this treatise became a reality when the 'potato-blight' hit Ireland, between 1846 and 1850. In County Mayo alone 30 per cent of the population perished and over 1 million migrated to America, Australia and Britain itself. The population of Ireland had tripled from 2.6 million to 8.5 million between the middle of the eighteenth century to 1845. What was termed 'potatophagia', the over-dependence on one foodstuff, only compounded the problem. Trevelyan, a student of Malthus at Haileybury, believed that it was the 'way of Providence to teach an indolent and un-self-reliant people a lesson'. A rather callous attitude, but fairly typical of the man. The tragedy of Ireland was ameliorated by the safety valve of emigration to the colonies and England, and the Repeal of The Corn Laws in February 1846, by the Prime Minister, Sir Robert Peel, which allowed American corn to be imported by Britain to feed the starving Irish. Let us leave Ireland and switch to our focus on India, a land traditionally ravaged by the vagaries of nature. India has always been at the mercy of an unpredictable south-west monsoon, the annual downpour from the Arabian Sea, or the north-eastern monsoon from the Bay of Bengal. Deluge and floods, interspersed with withering droughts, flowed in an unpredictable cycle. In spite of being made a concerted effort to master this cyclic tragedy, ascribing it to fate or destiny. The Indian languages are replete with words that describe this Human condition. Famine has decimated all parts of India, In 1860, two million people died of starvation in the Punjab. In i866, 800,000 died in Orissa, that is nearly 27 per cent of the population. In 1868, 25 per cent of the population of the city of Ajmere starved to death. During the Governorship of Lord Lytton, between 1877-8, 7 million Indians starved to death. It's an endless saga of misery and death. All that the Indian could do was to stoically 'grin and bear it' for centuries. A ghastly indictment of the Indian's laid-back attitude to nature's vicissitudes. Fortunately, the English, with first-hand experience of the Irish calamity, were moved to try and remedy this recurring disaster. India is blessed with vast tracts of highly fertile arable land, intersected by massive rivers flowing down from the Himalayas, which inundate the Indo-Gangetic valley and spread a carpet of loam on the land. The Northern Indian has thrived on nature's fecundity but has neither understood its ecology or conserved its abundance. India under the EIC and the Princely States was an agricultural economy, whose prosperity rested on the shoulders of the 'ryot' or peasant farmer who was mercilessly exploited by rapacious landlords called *talukdars* or *zamindars*, who looted and pillaged at random. As usual revenue collection was a haphazard, parlous and erratic affair that hinged on the local landlords' whims and fancies. The EIC was faced with a 'double whammy, apropos its tax reforms and the revitalization of Indian agriculture, the lifeblood of the economy. First and foremost was the horrendous task to introduce justice and fairness in collecting taxes and revenue from the 'ryot' and away from the rapacious hands of the *talukdars*. The EIC achieved this by the induction of the Indian Civil Service (ICS) and its hand-picked band of 'collectors' who were forever roaming the countryside on horseback, living in tents, with a Westley Richards rifle by his side and dispensing rough and ready, but common sense, justice, as 'honorary magistrates'. The ICS was originally called the Covenanted Civil Service as its members entered into a covenant with the EIC and, after 1858, with the Secretary of State in Council. In fact as early as 1853, entrance was opened to all British subjects by a competitive examination. The ICS was destined to become the crème de la crème of all Civil Services in the world with its hand picked officers, seasoned in the rough and ready milieu of the Indian countryside. After the departure of the British in 1947, the ICS was replaced by the Indian Administrative Service (IAS), with its training school in my home town of Mussoorie. It has to be said, to the credit of the EIC, that the induction of the brilliant ICS paved the way for modern India to become a contender for world power status. It is now time to move onto another remarkable achievement of the EIC, the induction of the Indian Irrigation Service.

Having sorted out the nightmare of revenue collection, the next task facing the EIC was the control of floods and irrigation to counter-act drought that ravaged the country. The motivation was not entirely humanitarian, although this prima facie was the principal engine for action. Irrigation greatly improved crop yields and, therefore, revenue for the EIC. Irrigation also brought arid and semi-desert land under the plough. In fact irrigation of the Punjab turned a semi-desert land into the granary of India. And lastly, the switchover from the Oudh and Bihar recruiting area of The Bengal Army to the so-called 'martial classes' of the Punjab opened up the Sikh, Punjabi Mussalman (PM) and Gujjar peasant-yeoman as recruits for the Army. The Punjab was destined to become the 'sword arm' of the Indian Army and, ipso facto, the mace, wielded by Britain, to protect her Empire.

Work started on the Great Ganges Canal and the East and West Yamuna Canals with their headworks in the Dehra Dun Valley. These massive canals took care of the irrigation needs of the United Provinces. Irrigation engineers, recruited into the newly created Indian Irrigation Service, were responsible for the maintenance of the main canals and subsidiary feeder canals that spread out into the countryside and regulated the discharge of water into the system at the weir. A very specialized and responsible job. The engineers were very well paid and lived in spacious canal bungalows with their families and a complete entourage of junior officials and staff to cater to their needs. As the canal system was very extensive, the engineer and his immediate staff were always on the move, living in a chain of well-constructed canal bungalows built on the canal embankments. The canal bungalows could be used by officials from other departments, like The Public Works Department, (PWD) and the public for a nominal fee when vacant. The Irrigation Service was also responsible for the collection of water-usage fees from the farmers and to ensure that the individual farmer got his fair share of water when water was released into his fields. Theft of water was a common offence and often led to family feuds and murder.

We now have to move westward into the Punjab, whose very name defines the character of the country—the land of the 'Five Rivers'. Moving westward, these rivers are the Beas, the Sutlej, that originated in Tibet near the sacred Mansarovar Lake, the Chenab, the Ravi and lastly the Jhelum, that originates in the Kashmir Valley. In addition to the five Punjab rivers, we have to add the Indus that arises in Tibet, near Lake Mansarovar, enters Ladakh in Kashmir, takes a sharp bend to the south-west, to flow into the western-most end of the Punjab .The Indus collects the total flow of the Punjabi rivers before it debouches into the Arabian Sea near the Port of Karachi. The collective area of the Punjab and Sind is huge and, until the EIC established its massive network of weirs and canals, the countryside was semi-arid in the Punjab and a part of the Great Indian Desert, or Thar, in Sind. In one' fell swoop', the EIC and later the British Government, changed the entire countryside and created what must still be the biggest irrigation system in the world and brought prosperity to millions of destitute farmers. As an obiter dictum it can be said that unwittingly it planted the seed for the Partition of India and the creation of Pakistan, the hot bed of Islamic terrorism that is going to haunt Britain for years to come. An undeserved slap in the face!!

Talking about Partition introduces another conundrum and

that is the inequitable division of the waters of the Indus Valley System between India and Pakistan. A treaty was hastily signed by India's incompetent Prime Minister, Jawaharlal Nehru, in 1950, which gave India the tiny river Beas and the massive Sutlej. The Indus and the other three Punjab rivers were bestowed to Pakistan. There was no logic, rhyme .or reason behind this division. It was not based on population or the area under cultivation. For example, the Indus was handed over to Pakistan, lock, stock and barrel, thereby denying Ladakh and the valleys of Dras and Kargil, of any water from the Indus. I foresee big problems looming ahead over this vital issue. Water for hydroelectricity, agriculture and day to day living are key factors. Dissension has already started by India building a hydroelectric power station at Baglihar on the Chenab River. No water is being diverted or used, so Pakistan is not affected by the scheme, but because the Chenab has been designated to Pakistan under the Indus Valley System (IVS), Pakistan is demanding its pound of flesh. How does India compensate Pakistan for having extracted electricity out of the river? Has the Chenab been 'de-energised' in some way? But this is only the start of this riparian nightmare. Another serious problem is brewing in north-eastern India, in the Assam Valley. China is planning to divert the waters of the Brahmaputra River, the Tsangpo, in Tibet, to the dry north-eastern part of China, fed by the Yellow River. This will seriously affect the water flowing into the Assam Valley through the Dihang River, which is the Brahmaputra.

In closing this chapter, a huge accolade has to be given to the EIC and its successor, the British Government in India, for leaving behind this incredible legacy of the ICS and The Irrigation Service.

7

The Great Game

Now its time to back-track to Lord Auckland, who succeeded Lord William Bentinck. Lord Auckland subscribed strongly to Britain's Russo-phobia, which precipitated the disastrous misadventure into Afghanistan, to depose the ruler, Dost Mahommed, and replace him with the despised Shah Shuja. The trouble started when Persian forces, assisted by the Russian, occupied the city of Herat in Western Afghanistan. The British responded by moving into Kandahar in southern Afghanistan and Kabul. But treachery was in the air. Burnes, the British Resident was murdered and Akbar Khan, the son of Dost Mahommad, stabbed and killed the British envoy, MacNghten, whose mutilated body was paraded through the bazaars of Kabul. Instead of retaliating, it was decided to return to India in the Afghan winter in deep snow. What eventuated was an absolute debacle and a solitary survivor, Dr Brydon, staggered into Jallalabad as a stern reminder that the Afghans do not tolerate intrusion by foreigners. For the British it was a clarion-call to seal her frontiers and precipitated the annexation of Sind, which saddles the Indus and abuts on the Afghan frontier. The conqueror of Sind was the redoubtable General Sir Charles Napier, who said it was a 'very advantageous, useful human piece of rascality'. The area was ruled by hereditary tribal chiefs called *Amirs* who were fierce, decadent and ruthless. The climate was like purgatory. All told, a posting to Sind was highly unpopular among the sepoys. In addition, there were constant raids by the wild tribesmen from Balochistan. The problem became so bad that the EIC decided to raise a special cavalry unit called the Scinde Irregular Horse under the command of Lieut. John Jacob of the Bombay Artillery. This unit joined the force under Sir Charles Napier and subjugated the Amirs at the decisive Battle of Meanee in 1846. So effective was John Jacob that another corp was raised and placed under his command.

After the death of Maharaja Ranjit Singh in 1839, there was internecine fighting among his descendants. Intrigue and deceit were rampant, with no clear leadership. There was a strong feeling that they could take on the EIC which had suffered a humiliating withdrawal from Afghanistan in 1842 and was deeply involved in subduing the Amirs in Sind. The Sikh army or 'Khalsa', the army of the Pure, were about 75,000. Two Sikh Wars were fought, in 1845–46 and 1848–49. All told, seven pitched battles were fought by Sir Hugh Gough, later Lord Gough, a doughty warrior who nearly lost the decisive Battle of Chillianwallah in the Second Sikh War. If the Sikhs had been united and had attacked him they would have won the battle, but of course they did not and Gough's exhausted troops had time to recover and turned the tide. The Punjab was annexed and Sir Henry Lawence became the Governor. The EIC now governed the whole of India, an incredible achievement for a trading company that had no formal mandate to conquer. An off-shoot of the Sikh Wars was the sale of Kashmir to a Dogra Hindu General in the Sikh Army for £750,000.

We have covered the trials and tribulations of the EIC in establishing British rule in India at considerable length. None of this would have been possible without the enormous contribution of the Indian soldier, who was literally the backbone of British power, not only in India but through out the Empire. It would be an exercise in stupidity to try and quantify the relative importance of officers and men in the Indian Army. The two worked together like a well-oiled machine and are indivisible. It is now time to put this incredible military formation under scrutiny.

Our *Sahib*! The title of *Sahib* is of Arabic origin and denotes a leader, or master. It is a title of respect which has been used in India for centuries and is no longer a foreign word. The corollary is *Pukka Sahib*, combining the Indian word, *pukka*, meaning correct and proper, signifying a well and truly tried leader. Both words have entered into the English language. In the Indian Army the title of *Sahib* applies to both British and Indian Officers. It would be highly impertinent to address a *Havildar* (Sergeant) or *Subedar* (Sergeant- Major) without the suffix of '*Sahib*'. Such are the niceties of protocol and etiquette accorded to rank. The penultimate honour is when the 'other ranks' refer to their Officers as *Hamara Sahib—Our Sahib*. This is an honour that has to be earned through courage, fortitude and leadership in battle. It does not automatically go with rank. It signifies that the men accept you as one of them and the Indian soldier will follow his *Sahib* into the jaws of death without a murmur. What more can an officer demand of his men!!

The EIC fielded a mixed bag of administrators and generals, ranging from the best that Britain could produce to pathetic incompetents, who should never have left their shores—puffed-up little men whose only claim to fame was a sneering contempt of anything and everything Indian and a misplaced hauteur of being 'British'. Luckily, these 'unfortunates' tended to congregate in the musty offices of the Calcutta '*Box Wallahs*' and have earned a pride of place of their own in this narrative.

The battlefield quickly sorts out the sheep from the goats. The true mettle of a man shows up when his survival depends on his compatriots' verve and fortitude. The battlefield has no place for the faint-hearted to duck for cover. The British soldier, and particularly the British officer, quickly realized that the Indian sepoy, fighting by his side, was a man of courage and honour, provided he was well-trained, respected and well led. In the Indian Army there were no snide racial jibes. It goes to the credit of the British that they realized very early in the piece that the Indian soldier could not be bluffed into accepting a second rate officer as their '*sahib*'. As a result the pride of place at Sandhurst was given to officers destined for India. In addition there was a tradition in Sandhurst that good officer material was not just being physically robust and smart on the parade ground but involved the intangible qualities of a strong sense of justice and fair play and to take hardship as a fact of life. These qualities were ingrained into Public School boys in

England and were greatly coveted in Sandhurst, which was regarded by the Public School boy as a mere extension of his school days. The crucial but imperative ability to obey and to command are contradictory values that are instilled in a Public School boy from early childhood. This odd-ball quality is what The Duke of Wellington was referring to when he said that '...the Battle of Waterloo was won on the playing-fields of Eton.'

In 1815, the British nearly lost the battle but for the rigid discipline of 'The British Square', manned by the dogged Welsh 'Taffy', and the rallying-cry of the Coldstream Guards: 'Up Guards' and at 'em!'.

The British held fast until the late arrival of the Prussian General Blucher which finished Napoleon.

There is another aspect to recruiting Public School boys in Sandhurst and that was the fact that the boys came from the top aristocratic families of England and had private means. Life in the Army in India was expensive, especially in the elite cavalry regiments. The British officers were paid a handsome 'overseas allowance' to augment their normal pay, but this was never enough to meet the expenses of mess-bills, a multitude of uniforms, at least four horses for polo and at least two *sai*s or grooms, and the list of expenses kept mounting. It was taken for granted that the young officers would be in debt to the regimental *banya* or Hindu money-lender, who never cavilled and embarrassed the *sahib* for money. When debts became unwieldy, the *banya* would approach the commandant who would delicately broach the subject with the young man, knowing full-well that a degree of 'financial embarrassment' was only natural for a young cavalry officer in the Indian Army. He would not have it otherwise! The cavalry officer lived life 'on the gallop', verging on the edge of recklessness, what with polo, tent-pegging, which entailed plucking out a tent-peg with his lance, or hunting wild boar on horse back. All highly dangerous activities acquired from Indian horsemen, who were equally 'mad' and 'devil-may-care'. They made a good pair in the field!!.

The British are a strange race and some of their actions are incomprehensible, even reprehensible. For instance the British and Indians have fought valiantly, side by side, on many battle fields. The British officers and men earned the coveted Victoria Cross, instituted in 1856 'For Valour' beyond the Call of Duty, but this honour was denied to Indians and no reason given. The highest decoration given to Indians was the IDSM (Indian Distinguished Service Medal) and that, too, for rescuing or saving a British life in the field. The first Victoria Cross (VC) to be awarded to an Indian was to Sepoy Khudadad Khan, of the 129th Baluchis, on 30/31 October at Ypres. Once the ice was broken the Indians won dozens of V.C.s in both WW I & WW II. It is a matter of pride that the first Indian V.C. in WW II was awarded to Lieut. Prem Bhagat of the Bombay Sappers. Prem was born and bred in Mussoorie and was the son of old family friends.

One is sorely tempted to list the names of those British Officers who qualified for the honoured title of' *'Hamara Sahib'* but the chances of errors by omission or commission are daunting. It is best not to venture into this minefield for fear of giving offence when only giving honour is intended. However, let it be said that the list of *'Hamara Sahibs'* is huge. The Indian Army, was and is, one of the most proficient and professional armies in the world, forged in the fire of some of the world's bloodiest battlefields; keeping the peace between implacable enemies in modern times; fighting floods and famine and bringing hope and succour to the desperate needy wherever and whenever the clarion call for help is sounded. An amazing body of men, both officers and other ranks, British and Indian. Let me quote Field Marshal Lord Roberts of Kandahar V.C., G.C.B., G.C.S.I, G.C.I.E., in his autobiography, *forty-one Years in India*:

'To the Country to which I am so proud of belonging.
To the Army to which I am so deeply indebted,
And to my wife,
Without whose loving help
'My forty-one years in India'
could not be the happy retrospect it is,
I dedicate this book.'

Lord Roberts won his V.C. in 1858 for saving the life of an

Indian trooper at the hands of some Indian mutineers.

Lord Roberts, 'Bob Bahadur', that is, 'Bob the Brave' to his men, was born in Cawnpore (Kanpur), the U.P. in India. He was the son of another distinguished English General, Sir Abraham Roberts, who retired from service with the EIC when he was in his sixties, an incredibly long service on active duty in those days. Lord Roberts was sent back to England as an infant, had his schooling at Eton and was commissioned through Sandhurst. The Roberts family has roots in India spread over two generations. No one can be a better exemplar of *'Hamara Sahib'* than 'Bob *Bahadur'*.

I have to leave the Indian Army temporarily and switch the focus onto another segment of the British presence in India, namely the British trader, who, after all, was the raison d'etre for the creation of the British East India Company (EIC) in 1612. The territorial acquisitions were purely adventitious. India fell to the EIC like an over-ripe fruit. America had not yet cast off its colonial shackles and the Industrial Revolution was still on the drawing board. Trade for the British meant the slave trade and the transportation of nearly 28 million African slaves to work in the plantations owned by British settlers in America and the Caribbean. The other big attraction was the spice trade in Asia. The EIC started trade in Surat, north of Bombay, and eventually moved its factory to Madras. I have covered the change of focus to Calcutta, which was destined to become the financial and trading hub of the EIC. The Portuguese had a saying that 'whichever country controlled the Moluccas, held Europe by the throat' .The British were late-comers to the spice trade, which was dominated by the Portuguese, but the Dutch, in particular, were surreptitiously colonising the East Indies and exploring Van Diemen's Land which was also-called 'Terra Incognita'—the unknown land, or Terra Hollandia, later to be called Terra Australis.

So how was the Calcutta *'Box Wallah'* (BW) surviving in those lean years? He started off as a 'merchant' representing a variety of small manufacturers in Britain. The EIC imported large quantities of Stilton cheese and claret which was normal fare for the services and the BW, plus a strong beer was brewed locally and bottled. Chile Salt Peter was imported and used for cooling water and drinks. In later years, huge blocks of ice were shipped from America across the Pacific. For the British, ice was not a luxury but an absolute necessity in India's torrid climate. The *Ab dar* or drinks waiter was a highly valued and prized member of any BW establishment, family or club. He was discretely secreted around the corner, within hailing distance, and responded to the call of '*Koi Hai*'—is any one there? By a response of extreme politeness—'*ji Hazoor-Hukum*?'—'yes Sir, your wish or order'. All very civilized and proper!! Excluding the services, the EIC cadres earned the somewhat jocular sobriquet of '*Koi Hai*s' (KH), an expression that I will use frequently when writing or referring to this group of '*Box Wallahs*', in Calcutta or the Moufassil, that is, up country.

The big break-through for the 'KH' came with the discovery of coal in the District of Dhanbad in Bengal. The EIC became the first colliery owners and large fortunes were going to be made in the coal trade in Calcutta. With the arrival of steam powered railway locomotives and steam boats on the river system of the Ganges, the financial future of the KHs was secured.

The arrival of steam opened up the districts up-stream on the Ganges as river traffic was far more comfortable and faster than the tedious journeys by the pot-holed, almost non-existent roads. Once the country was opened up along the Ganges, the next 'El Dorado' was the massive cultivation of indigo by the EIC in Bihar. The indigo plant was native to India and belonged to the genus of Indigofera Tinctoria and had been cultivated for centuries and greatly valued for the brilliant blue dye that was extracted from it. Indigo was also known to the British as *wode,* extracted from a local plant in England called *Isatis Tinctoria,* but the cost was prohibitive. The EIC had 1,750,000 acres planted with indigo in 1897 and over £17,000,000 of indigo dye was exported by the company. Unfortunately, this cornucopia came to an untimely death when the German chemical monolith, IG FARBEN's subsidiary, Hoechst, produced synthetic indigo in 1883.

The loss of such a lucrative market was a severe blow to the finances of the EIC, but the company had another string in its bow and that was the cultivation of opium in India and sale to the Chinese. China was being ruled by the powerful Quing Dynasty that was arrogant and so totally self-confident that China did not need any trade from the 'foreigners'. All ports were gradually shut down and only Guangzhou (Canton) was left open. The European traders had to buy Chinese merchandise like silks, tea and porcelain with payment in silver and gold. There was next to nothing that the Chinese wanted from the Europeans This one-sided trade was totally unacceptable. The British were smuggling 5,000 barrels of opium every year through crime syndicates and the trade was increasing by leaps and bounds. The Emperor designated a senior commissioner, Lin Zexu, to procede to Guangzhou and put an end to this illicit trade. Lin Zexu seized 20,000 chests of British opium in 1839. This triggered off what became known as the First Opium War between Britain and China. British warships sailed into Chinese rivers, destroyed and captured ports and harbours, including Shanghai. A deeply humiliated China was forced to sign the 1842 Treaty of Nanjing, opening up 10 more ports for the British. Now the French and the Americans demanded and secured similar concessions from a cowed Chinese Emperor. Under the treaty, Britain occupied the island of Hong Kong, which got officially ceded to them in 1842.

China was now entering a very crucial page in its history, with the Europeans and Americans squeezing totally unfair concessions from her. As if this was not enough, a massive famine engulfed the country in 1849–50, causing the Taiping Rebellion, which resulted in a disastrous civil war and the death of 20 million Chinese. The rebellion was crushed with the help of foreign troops. In the meantime the British were busily cultivating opium in India and selling it through a British company called Jardine Mathieson (JM), based in Hong Kong. By 1900, nearly 40 million Chinese were smoking opium including 15 million addicts. Jardine Mathieson was amassing a gigantic fortune out of this vile trade but the British plutocrats sitting in London and Calcutta were totally mindless of the terrible havoc that they were wreaking in China. Jardine

Mathieson became known as a 'Taipan' in Hong Kong, a term designating a handful of extremely wealthy business enterprises that virtually ran the colony.

Ruthlessness was the name of the game and money was the engine that drove the British aristocracy to such incredible depths of depravity. Human values only mattered when it affected this tiny cabal of the landed gentry. They were equally ruthless and pitiless with their own countrymen, who were mercilessly exploited in their 'press gangs' who 'shanghai'd' unwary merchant-seamen and drunks in taverns. This legacy of ruthlessness was going to be handed down to the manufacturing tycoons who were waiting in the wings for the industrial revolution to begin. If you happen to be born on the 'wrong side of the railway line', you did not count as a human being.

But let's get back to the Opium Trade and what was going to be termed the 'Second Opium War', of 1856–60. Chinese forces boarded a British ship, the 'Arrow,' on the suspicion that it was indulging in piracy, and took the crew into custody. British, French and American forces defeated the Chinese and extracted further concessions, which enabled these countries to penetrate deep into China. Britain acquired Kowloon, a part of the mainland adjacent to Hong Kong. A defeated China now had to sign the Treaty of Tianjin.

The Europeans and the Americans started a major evangelical drive now that they had access to areas deep inside the country. This ever increasing foreign intrusion bred intense resentment and a secret society called 'The Harmonious Fists', better known as 'The Boxers', began to take the law into their own hands and started burning foreign missions and killing foreigners and Christian Chinese. In Peking, foreign envoys were besieged for nearly two months. The siege was lifted when troops from Britain, France, America and Japan invaded China and defeated the Boxers and occupied Peking. The Indian Army dispatched Skinner's Horse and the 6th Duke of Connaught's Own Lancers to spearhead the assault on Peking and were the first troops to enter the city. It is worth mentioning that Skinner's Horse and an American cavalry unit made a joint mounted attack against a Tartar cavalry force and defeated them. This was the first time that Indian and American troops had fought together. The 6th D.C.O. Lancers were the first to relieve the American Legation and, as a token of esteem, were presented with the 'Stars and Stripes' flag that had flown over the Legation during the siege. This flag now decorates the wall of the Officers Mess. Several Indian infantry units followed to complete the total rout of the Chinese. There is a strange irony in this chronicle as it was Indian-grown opium that started this disgraceful episode at the hands of the British rulers and then Indian soldiers were used to give China its coup-de-grace and establish 'Pax Britannica' and British hegemony over a cowed nation. China was going to redeem its honour by thrashing the Indian Army in the border war of 1962.

China was happy to sell processed tea to the foreigners but the actual shrub was closely protected and it was strictly guarded. Jardine Mathieson succeeded in extracting a few shrubs which were secretly shipped to their subsidiary in India called Jardine Henderson, one of the many KH companies of the EIC. The tea shrub was identified as *Camellia Sinensis* and was planted in an area called The Dooars in northern Bengal, where it flourished. This humble beginning was to become a giant tea industry in the years to come. The KH's were just waiting in the wings to start a gigantic investment in the propagation of the tea shrub into the Assam valley, the Hills of Darjeeling, the Nilgiri Hills in South India and Ceylon. India and Ceylon were destined to become the major centres of production of tea in the world. At this stage it should be clarified that Camelia Sinensis continued to be cultivated in Darjeeling but was superseded by the Indian genus, Camellia Thea, later named Camellia Kissi, which was introduced in all the other tea gardens as it was more robust and gave bigger yields.

The tea companies, with their HQ's centred in Calcutta, fell into several categories. First and foremost were the tea planters who had cleared vast tracts and planted beautifully manicured tea estates all along the Brahmaputra river in Assam and its tributaries. It took the dour and doughty Scots to battle with forest, rain and pestilence, to carve out these magnificent tea plantations with their cover of shade trees. Needless to say, most of the planters were Scots with a heavy admixture of Indian public school boys from institutions like the Doon School. My younger brother was one of this of 'huntin', 'shootin' and 'fishin' fraternity, who took to this isolated life in India's' boon-docks'. The company provided spacious bungalows and gardens to the managerial staff, which was some compensation for this life of isolation in out-of-the-way places. Social life centred around clubs scattered around plantations which held 'club nights' by rotation and provided amenities like golf, squash and tennis, billiards, cards, dancing to tinny gramophone records and, of course, the ubiquitous bar was the centre of club life. Some of the tea plantations, especially on the North Bank of the Brahmaputra, were so isolated that their only contact with the outside world was by privately owned derelict airlines, flying WW II Dakotas, which did a weekly 'milk run' from Calcutta. My brother's tea garden called Baradighi, was on the border of NEFA (North-Eastern Frontier Agency) which is a part of the wild and heavily forested state called Arunachal Pradesh. It was customary to stop plucking tea by 4 pm in the outer garden as there was danger of attack by wild animals wandering in from the adjoining forest.

I have taken the liberty of writing at length on life in a tea plantation to give the reader an insight into the ardous task of growing the 'cup that cheers'. I will finish this segment by saying that plucking tea is a fine and tedious process. The picker plucks 'two leaves and a bud' from the bush. It is very labour-intensive and the Assam and Dooar plantations employ indigenous tribal Munda and Oryia labour. Nepalese labour is employed in the Darjeeling hills. The Ceylon tea gardens employ Tamil Indians, Ceylon citizens from north-eastern Ceylon, as the local Singhalese consider this work demeaning.

The plucked crop is now moved to the plantations factory where the bulk is roasted, carefully, and rolled to produce the familiar packaged tea. Unroasted or 'green tea' is exported to Tibet where it is consumed as a gruel with ground barley. This is the national dish called '*tsampa*'. Green tea is also the national drink in Afghanistan and Pakistan's NWFP called *kawa,* which is drunk out of shallow saucers. Tea is called *chai*, the original Chinese word for the brew. Chai is continuously brewed in tea urns called *samovars* throughout Russia and Central Asia. The ubiquitous Samovar sits in every 'Caravan Serai' and hostelry and is the centrepiece of the establishment.

The processed tea now enters the bulk warehouse of the 'Tea Company', awaiting grading and classification by teams of expert 'Tea Tasters'. The tea taster is an expert who works full-time for companies which hire his services to the giant tea companies in Calcutta like Jardine Henderson, James Findlay, Williamson Magor, Mcleod, J. Warren, and many others who will supply tea to London-based and India-based marketing companies like Brooke Bonds, Liptons, Rickett and Coleman, and others. On the recommendation of the tea taster, tea is bought and blended and either exported in bulk or supplied to the local marketing company for packaging. The international tea trade is controlled in London.

The KH controlled the commercial life of Calcutta for decades with their domination of the coal trade, tea, and lastly the jute industry, which manufactured burlap for sacking. Close behind the KH were Indian entrepreneurs who were much more hard-working, abstemious and aggressive. The KH were too full of their own importance and the British arrogance that the 'sun would never set on the British Empire'. The soft life of the KH, with legions of domestic carers; the bumptious pretentions of the *burra memsahibs* and the priggish snobbery of the exclusive Bengal Club, were all militating towards the eventual collapse of this obsolete edifice. The Bengal Club was only one of a stream of supercilious exclusive British Clubs that dotted the Indian landscape, each outdoing the others in their silliness. Classical examples are the Royal Bombay Yacht Club, exclusively for 'whites' if you please, even after Indian Independence. The Bombay Gymkhana Club was laughable with its archaic membership rules and regulations. Of course Indians were strictly *'verboten'*. But even the British were strictly regimented. British membership was only open to officers of the three services, the ICS and senior police officers, employed by the government in Delhi but excluded other police officers, no matter how senior, if they were in the state cadre. All other bureaucrats were excluded, as were all *'Box Wallahs,'* irrespective of whether they were multi millionaire owners or CEOs. The KH were very 'infra dig', which must have gone down well with the Bengal Club fraternity, and the *'burra memsahibs'* in particular.This snootiness would have really stuck in their craw. But there is a humourous sequel to this absurdity. The President of The Bombay Gymkhana asked the Viceroy, Lord Willingdon, to preside over one of the Club's grand functions. A perspicacious Lord Willingdon noted the total absence of Indians and asked the President to present some senior Indians, only to be told that Indians were strictly prohibited entry into the hallowed precincts. After the function, Lord Willingdon arranged a meeting with Bombay's leading citizens and asked them to open a separate club under his aegis, and the prestigious Willingdon Club was born. The British are such an incredible nation!! Incidentally, Mr Foot, the Headmaster of Doon School, refused to become a member of the Dehra Dun Club because it denied membership to Indians. What really put the cat among the pigeons was Mrs Foot's decision to wear a sari on formal occasions.

I have written at length on the life style of the KH in Calcutta and the Moufassil but further elaboration is necessary. Oddly enough there was relatively little socializing between the British civilian and the Indian intelligentsia. For the British, India was a transit point where you made your fortune, sent the children to England for education, and hoped to join them 'backhome' with enough money to retire comfortably on a small farm. With few exceptions they did not put down roots. I have already written about those who buried their bones in India. The British lived on the fringes of Indian cities, in what were called The Civil Lines, with spacious bungalows and lovely gardens. The word bungalow is a corruption of the Indian word *'bangla'* for a compact home surrounded by a verandah, taken from the Indian word *biranda,* which sheltered the house from the direct rays of the sun and rain. Even In the Civil Lines, the *'burra memsahib'*s presence was everywhere. She made sure that her home was a replica of 'dear ole Blighty', with afternoon tea served with cucumber and watercress sandwiches on beautifully manicured lawns. The junior wives were au fait with the strict protocol exercised by our 'Grande Dame'. They had earlier made their obeisance by dropping their 'calling cards' in the receptacle held by 'Sambo', at the entrance hall. 'Sambo' typified the racist kitsch of the Georgian and Victorian eras, with its golliwogs and Negroid cartoon characters in comics. 'Sambo' stood about four feet tall, was made of wood and was painted in the gaudy colours associated with the Negro servant. The 'calling cards' were carefully scrutinized and appropriate invitations were sent to the junior wives to join the 'regal presence' for tea and croquet, whist or Mah Jongg All very British and civilized. The husband more often than not, was in the revered ICS, the Police, or the forest service and was usually on 'tour' in his district with his camp followers in tow. In the ICS he was labelled a 'Collector' in charge of a district, or a Commissioner who covered five to six districts—a very senior bureaucrat with direct access to the Governor. While on tour the British official was entertained and feted by the local Indian gentry, both Muslim and Hindu, often with a bout of '*nautch* girls'—professional singers and their accompanist musicians, who whirled and pirouetted before the audience with gay abandon. The British visitor was totally fascinated by the nut-brown, lissome, full-breasted Indian female, who was such a total contrast to the pale, wasp-waisted female sitting at home. The '*nautch* girl' was in great demand and several made fortunes, like Begum Sumroe, a beautiful girl from Kashmir, who had several wealthy European suitors who left her sizeable estates around the city of Meerut. In her day, Begum Sumroe 'held court' and became a power to be reckoned with. At this stage, a distinction must be drawn between the rather tawdry *nautch* performance that has been described above and the highly refined and sophisticated *Mujra*, which was very much a part of the culture and refinement of Northern India. The singers and dancers were not '*nautch*' girls but these ladies were courtesans of great refinement and were extremely well-versed in the arts, poetry and music of the land They were like the Geishas of Japan. The sophisticated intelligentsia, both Hindu and Muslim, relished what is known as a '*Mahfil*'— a gathering of intellectuals who would gravitate together to listen to music and recitation of poetry, discuss philosophy and listen attentively to the ladies of the *mujra* as they sang and entertained the *mahfil*. The Begums of the *mujra* were treated with great respect and courtesy. The *mahfil* and the *mujra* were an integral part of the cultural life of Northern India. To this group we must add the *mushaira*, which is a gathering of poets and the lovers of poetry, who listen with rapt attention to the recitation of poetry, both old and new, with spontaneous exclamations of appreciation from the audience. Rather like the Spanish *Ole* in flamenco performances.

Now it is time to return to the Civil Lines and that 'dragon', the *burra memsahib*, who had no intention of suffocating in the infernal summer heat of India and would be heading to the hills once April arrived, minus her husband, who had to languish in the plains doing his job. To make life more bareable, all the windows and doors of the bungalow were swathed in wet matting called *tattis*, made from an aromatic rush called *Khas*. Cross-ventilation caused evaporation and cooling of the inside of the house. The *Khas* was kept wet by an employee called the *bhisti*, literally the 'provider of paradise', who carted water in a goatskin bag called a *mushk*.

The British acquired a taste for gin and tonic Water, which was one easy and palatable way of ingesting quinine as an antidote to malaria.

The services lived in a separate section of the city called the 'cantonment', which was totally independent of the civil administration, except for the common amenities like water, electricity and sewage. The management and maintenance of buildings, roads, health facilities et cetra, were under military control. British and Indian forces were billeted separately, with their independent messes for troops and NCOs Commissioned Officers, both British and Indian, lived and dined in common regimental messes.

There was some fraternizing between the 'Westernized' Indian (a hateful term that signifies nothing other than aping the British) and the senior echelon of the British Civil Services who lived in the Civil Lines. They met at the club for tennis, a round of billiards, a game of bridge or rummy and the inevitable bar room. In the cantonment the senior army messes were totally integrated. Over the years, a working bonhomie and mutual respect had developed, especially among the civil services where British and Indian officials had to work and pull their weight together. But what about the orthodox Hindus and Muslim urban communities? It is time to address this issue in some depth, starting with the Hindus who constitute the overwhelming population.

The orthodox Hindus constitute over 80 per cent of India's population. The backbone of the Hindu community is the Hindu Joint Family or The Hindu United Family (HUF). There is no primogeniture as all male members are co-parceners in the family estate, but the society is totally patriarchal, with the father being the head of the entire family. He is called the *Karta* and his word is law for all members of the family. On his demise, the eldest son becomes the *Karta* and so on. The same pecking order applies to a family business and in all matters that affect the family. The death-knell of the system came at the hand of the Income Tax authorities as the entire income of the family was accessed as a single corporate entity. The level of taxation became unbearable because of its sheer size and forced a dissolution of the HUF. In many ways, this was regrettable as the entire family lived in a huge mansion called a *Haveli*. Each family had a separate section of the mansion for privacy, but the family ate together and performed all religious ceremonies and rituals together. This created an incredible family bondage and unity and some of India's giant commercial enterprises had their genesis as HUFs. The entire indigenous banking system called *hawala* is based on word of mouth transactions and a total unspoken trust. In the *hawala* system there are no defaults and enormous sums of money are remitted all over the world by businesses, politicians and crime syndicates. The working of the *hawala* system is cloaked in secrecy. *Omerta*, or the code of silence applies to the Mafia as much as it does to the code of the *hawala*. Only the Orthodox Hasidim Jews have a comparable system that runs through the diamond trade. The *hawala* and the HUF go hand in hand. Many HUFs have wound up but the *hawala* system is alive and flourishing in spite of government efforts to close it down. It is so much a part of Indian life that it procreates itself.

It is time to return to the *haveli*, the ancient centrepiece of Hindu urban life. The epitome of Haveli life is to be seen in the township of Shekhawati, not far from Jaipur, which has about 5,000 *haveli*s that are open to the tourist during the Shekhawati Festival at the end of autumn. The crème-de-la-crème is the Morarka Haveli built in 1900 AD, by the extremely wealthy patron of the arts, Mr Jairamdas Morarka. The culture of the *haveli*s began in 1750 AD and continued into 1900 AD. The *haveli*s were the ancestral homes of the wealthy Marwari business class who thrived on the brisk trade that existed between Rajasthan and Europe, but which declined with the arrival of the EIC when the fulcrum moved to Bombay, but mainly to Calcutta.

The *haveli*s were left in the care of a resident caretaker. The family meets every year to celebrate the festival of Diwali with a religious *pooja* to propitiate the family deity. The external walls of the *haveli*s are lavishly decorated with exquisite frescoes depicting mythological and genre scenes of Rajasthani life. The ground plan of the *haveli* is a rather sparse quadrangle called an *angan* from which rise several floors which provide the living quarters of the family members. The *angan* is the work centre with a *rasoi* or kitchen with charcoal fired braziers on which the *purohit* or Brahman cook prepares his vegetarian meals. Food is eaten fresh from the stove, so the family sits on the floor as the food is served by the kitchen staff.

From the *angan*, steps lead down into a large basement area. This is the *teh khana* which the British called the 'Go Down'. The *teh khana* was cool and moist and was occassionaly used as a refuge from the blistering heat outside. It was the ideal place to store provisions for the family and 'Go Down' became colloquialized to *godam* in Hindi meaning a warehouse. The Indians were literally troglodytes and in royal residences the *teh khana* could be a veritable catacomb, an intricate maze of subterranean passages that often led to the riverbank and was an escape route for the royal family.

But let us surface to the *angan*, which not only served as a dining area but also housed the cool water for drinking which was held in porous earthen vessels called a *surahi*. Water percolated through the porous earthenware walls and on evaporation, cooled the contents. Indians did not have access to ice until the British constructed ice factories, using ammonia as the refrigerant. The Indians were experts in evaporative cooling and we have already seen the use of *khas* to cool houses and offices. What came to be known as the 'coolgardie safe' in Australia was also borrowed from India. It was a safe for storing perishables and stood on bowls of water to stop insects from climbing up the legs. The wire mesh frame was swathed in wet matting which cooled the contents by evaporation. In India it was called a *doli* and was an imperative in every house. In Australia the principle of the *surahi* was used in sheepskin bags, which could be carried on horseback. The sheepskin bags were porous and evaporation kept the contents cool.

I have already mentioned that many of India's giant business enterprises started as HUFs. The classic example is the giant Birla Group of companies, which for many years, was headed by the redoubtable Mr G.D. Birla, who ran the empire with an iron hand and pioneered the group to its position of eminence in business. The biggest problem with the HUF system is that it tends to stifle enterprise and initiative in the younger members of the family and eventually leads to a break-up of the cohesive strength of the family corporate entity. But there is no doubt that, in the early stages of India's entry into the world of global commerce, the Marwari HUFs from Shekhawati played a cardinal role and the fragmented remnants will continue to be major players in the years to come. Business and commerce is in their blood. They are what are called *raes*, the wealthy citizens who do not have to do manual labour.

Attention should be drawn to a strange anomaly in the life of the Hindu *raes* and that is the total absence of gardens and orchards in their surroundings. This is in total contrast to their Muslim counterparts who love their *bagh*s and *bagecha*s, Turkish names for gardens and orchards, usually on the outskirts of the towns or villages, where the Muslim gentry spent a few days and nights savouring the *shab-nam* (dew) and particularly the *bad-e-Sabah* (the cool early morning breeze) in summer. This strange Hindu anomaly astounded the Emperor Babur, who hated India and Indians, and made Kabul his capital. Like all desert dwellers, there is an insatiable love of water and greenery. Babur could not understand how the Hindus of India had never developed a sense of gardens and landscaping. Could the Muslims love for parks, gardens and orchards be a case of atavism harking back to their ancestral origins in harsher and arid climes?

The Orthodox Muslim constitute about 13.4 per cent of the population, amounting to 147 million, making the Muslims the second biggest religious community. We have already touched on differences between the Orthodox Hindus and Muslims. Muslims the world over are not a homogeneous entity and are split into factions that are deeply divided and antagonistic to each other. The three main groups are the Sunnis, Shias and Sufis, The different groups live in clearly defined *mohalla*s and even pray in separate mosques. It is not my intention to make this a dissertation on Islam so I have to be content to write about this community in general terms that are applicable to all sects.

By and large, the Muslim community is economically poorer than the Hindus, Sikhs, Jains and Christians, largely because they have much larger families due to polygamy. Education is at a premium, particularly among their womenfolk who are sheltered and confined to the home. Although government schools are available to all communities, the Muslims have a predilection for their 'madrassas', which are essentially religious seminaries. The standard of education is much lower than in the state-run schools and the graduate from the *madrassa* starts life with a distinct disadvantage. Madrassa education is centred on rote learning of the Quran in Arabic and the Hadith, which are the sayings and pronouncements of the Prophet, Mohammed–scarcely an education for a professional or commercial career. The Muslim suffers from two other severe handicaps. The first is the lack of education of his womenfolk. If 'the hand that rocks the cradle rules the world', then an uneducated Muslim mother has little to impart to her offspring. The second handicap is the blight of consanguineous marriages.

This unfortunate malaise flies against all the rules of natural selection and ensures that congenital weaknesses are perpetuated down the family tree. A veritable disaster waiting to happen. This is in stark contrast to the Hindus, where marriages, even within the same *gotra* or sub-caste, are prohibited to protect the lineage.

The Muslim has to also contend with some challenging demands that his religion imposes on him. Here are a few glaring examples. Islam prohibits usury, or *RIBA* in Arabic. This makes a mockery of modern banking and finance. Devious methods have evolved to get around this archaic and prohibitive law, but all this is just a tedious waste of time. Incidentally, there is a similar prohibition in Christianity, which threw a life raft to the 'usurious Jew'. In orthodox Islam, even insurance is prohibited as this questions Allah's implacable righteousness and totally just handouts to the true believer. Allah is never wrong or unjust and insurance questions this edict. A further imposition is the fundamental concept of *zakat* which makes it imperative for a Muslim to contribute 2.5 per cent of his income to charity. A great deal of time and effort is expended in shifting and moving assets around in order to this impost without openly defying the edict. This absurd game of financial musical chairs is terribly wasteful and time consuming.

Life for the *momin* or 'True Believer' is an endless round of fulfilling religious rituals and obligations from the time he wakes up in the morning till he goes to sleep. Even ablutions, defecation and procreation are carefully ritualized. Nothing is left to chance or choice. The *ummah* or Muslim brotherhood, the laity, is completely dominated by the *ulemah* or clergy, who decree what is right or wrong. The *ulemah* are the judge, jury and prosecutors and issue *fatwa*s or diktats on all matters, religious, civil or criminal. The power of the *ulemah* is prodigious, especially in the hand of radical, fundamentalist groups like The Dar-ul-Uloom based in Deoband, barely 100 miles north-east of Saharanpur, and its close affiliate, Mazahir-ul-Uloom in Saharanpur-proper. Both organizations are puritanical, ultra orthodox and suffused with the *wahhabi* fanatical credo from Saudi Arabia. The Deoband version of Islam is the basic philosophy found in Pakistan and is the root cause of the country's fundamentalism that has inspired the Taliban and the jihadi terrorism that is growing in Britain.

A Muslim's life is dominated by his religion. Questioning the edicts of the faith is blasphemy and is punishable by death. In many ways, Islam is a simplistic faith. The World is bifurcated into Dar-ul-Islam or the land governed and ruled by the true believers (the Muslims) and Dar-ul-Harb, the land of war, occupied and ruled by the infidels or disbelievers in Allah and His Prophet Mahommed. Islam imposes a strict injunction on every Muslim to convert the infidel to Islam or to behead those who refuse. The entire world must become Muslim and the Muslim law or Sharia must prevail universally. The Muslim cannot live in peace with other religions, as witnessed by the situation in Palestine, Lebanon, Chechynea, Kosovo or Kashmir.

Intolerance is ingrained in the Muslim ethos and this implacable bigotry percolates the entire religion, with intense internecine warfare erupting throughout the Muslim world between Shias and Sunnis and total discrimination against any deviant sect like the Sufis, Ismailis, Ahmedyas, Qaidianis and so many other variant sects.

There are two other Islamic characteristics that must be highlighted. The first is 'revanchism'. Any territory that was ever under Islam must revert back to the Muslims. It is because of this patent absurdity that the Muslims are re-claiming Andalusia in Spain. No justification for the loss is an acceptable excuse. Under this implausible dictum, India should come under Muslim rule, which was extinguished by the arrival of the British. This is the inspiration behind the Student Islamic Movement of India (SIMI), which is a banned terrorist organization. The second, and even more virulent advent, is the treatment of the female gender under Islam. Many argue that a female has no dignity, respect or rights. She is a sex object, available at all times for male licentiousness and abuse. Mutilation of her genitals to destroy her libido is quite common in Islam.

All said and done, it is extremely difficult to bring an orthodox Muslim into the mainstream of modern Indian life.

This community has caged itself into the narrow confines of Islamic orthodoxy, which is self-destructive and inimical to growth and development. The only hope lies with the slender segment of educated Muslims who have shed the shackles of orthodoxy, and have entered the burgeoning world of India's corporate 'wunderland', like Azam Premji's Wipro and Cipla Laboratories. Azam Premji is probably the richest individual in India and Wipro is the third largest IT company in the country. Its eminence is largely due to the fact that it is totally non-denominational in character and corporate leadership is dictated by merit only.

When British hegemony displaced Muslim dominance in India, a miniscule 9 per cent of Muslims ruled over 90 per cent of timorous Hindus, who were forever bickering and squabbling over petty issues. They could never get their act together to throw off the Muslim yoke that had held them in a state of servitude for over 800 years. The Muslims were anything but benign rulers. They despised the idolatrous infidel underdog and inflicted the utmost savagery and brutality on the menfolk whom they butchered mercilessly, raped their women and sold them and their children in the slave markets of Central Asia. The Hindu temples were looted and razed to the ground and mosques were erected over the ruins as a final act of contempt and disdain.

The arrival of the British put an end to this brutishness. For the Muslims, the British were a life-raft that saved them from an impending backlash at the hands of a resurgent Maratha Hindu Confederacy. The Moghul Empire was in tatters, eaten from within by degeneracy and lasciviousness. In turn, the British felt vulnerable and insecure in this vast and strange land, inhabited by people who not only looked different but had totally different values and customs. The inevitable British 'snootiness' and bluff were a good cuirass but they did not get rid of the 'colly-wobbles' in the tummy. The British desperately needed friends in high places. The Hindus were quite hopeless with their absurd beliefs and customs that defied common sense and reason. The Muslims were pathetic in their faded degeneracy and decay, but at least they had a semblance of

Judeo-Christian values. The Muslim was the logical choice out of a bad lot, and the Realpolitik of *Divide Et Impera*— 'divide and rule' was born. The British were past masters at this game, and under the guise of being even-handed, they pampered the Muslim. For example, the Muslims were barely 9 per cent of the population, but the British gave them a third of the job-vacancies in the Civil Services and considerably more in the army. The Muslims were given separate electorates under the guise of protecting a minority from getting swamped by a politically active Hindu majority, which was already clamouring for independence. By contrast, the Muslim was happy to live under the British umbrella. The Indian Muslim was one of the pillars of British dominance in the country, which explains why there were very few Muslim political agitators imprisoned. If one looks at the Pakistan leadership and hierarchy, it is almost totally devoid of politicians who suffered any privation to earn the country's independence. Pakistan literally 'piggy-backed' to freedom on the sacrifices made by the Indian political movement. This partly explains the paucity of any genuine political leadership in Pakistan and its periodic slide into military dictatorship. The second crucial factor is that democracy is an alien concept in Islam the world over. Leadership is supposed to rest with the *caliph,* who presides supreme over the whole faith in all matters.

The Indian Muslim was one of the staunchest pillars of 'The Raj' and he had to be suitably rewarded and pampered. He was also a pliable tool in the hands of a ruthless British ruler, who was constantly creating religious clashes between Hindus and Muslims to prevent any national cohesion. Religious riots were carefully engineered by the police and civil authorities. India was constantly in a state of turmoil and civil unrest. This suited the British admirably who kept the pot boiling.

It must be remembered that Britain never ruled over the whole of India, as over a third of the country was ruled by a galaxy of 560 Princely States of varying sizes and importance. The incredible part is that all the states were in personal treaty with the British Monarch. Some of the states were miniscule, reminiscent of the principalities of Europe. Others like

Hyderabad, Mysore and Kashmir were comparable in size to France, with their own currencies, postage stamps and armies. With great stagecraft and diplomacy, the British kept a fatherly eye on the rulers by appointing a British Resident who lived in pomp and splendour in the capital of the state and exerted an advisory role on the prince. In the case of a frontier state like Kashmir, there was even an independent Resident in the remote area of Gilgit, bordering on Afghanistan and Tibet. This was a very lonely and isolated posting. It was customary for this solitary Britisher to dress every evening for dinner—a ritual to stop the individual from 'going to seed'. The British also kept the princes in harness by establishing the Princes' Colleges, on which I have written extensively. The Officer Corps of the State Forces was trained at the IMA in Dehra Dun, alongside the regular cadets of the Indian Army. And last, and by no means least, was the British recognition that that the Indian princes were totally captivated by the pomp and ceremony that surrounded the British monarchy with its flamboyant pageantry and protocol. The British responded by assigning artillery gun salutes to the most prominent rulers and decorating them with British decorations like the KCSI and KCIE, which were worn with great pride over the left breast on ceremonial occasions. The rulers were given the title of His Highness The Maharaja, Raja, or Nawab or in the case of the Nizam of Hyderabad, His Exalted Highness. The British had the princes eating out of their hand. The finishing touch was provided by the Grand Durbar of 1911, held in Delhi to honour King George V and Queen Mary. The Grand Durbar was Britain's flourish and seal of approval to confirm its destiny to rule the Empire and India in particular, its 'Jewel in the Crown'. All the princes and citizens of importance in the land, including my grandfather, were invited to be presented to their Majesties. This is probably the appropriate time to write about a small but significant incident that illustrates how royalty recognizes the vows and oaths of other royals. The greatly revered and senior-most Rajput prince, the Maharana of Udaipur, wrote to the Viceroy of India, apologizing for his inability to attend the Durbar in Delhi as his ancestors had taken an oath never to enter Delhi except as conquerors. As a part of this vow the royal family slept on a bed of straw with a sword at hand. Instead of taking umbrage, the Royal Train stopped outside the city so that His Highness could present himself to their Majesties. A marvellous gesture of one Royal recognizing the vows of another. As a matter of fact, the Keys of the City of Delhi were ceremoniously handed over to the ruling Maharana by India's Prime Minister, Jawaharlal Nehru, as a symbolic gesture of surrendering the city.

The British Raj was well and truly entrenched in India with British manufactured goods garnishing the table and homes, clothing the people with cotton cloth manufactured in Manchester from Indian cotton, an enormous railway system built on rolling stock made in Glasgow and Birmingham and a substantial army, both British and Indian, equipped by Britain. The Indian Army consumed 35 per cent of the revenue of the government and was the main pillar holding up the British Empire, built on the solid foundation of extremely cordial relations between the British and Indian Officers and their men. What is missing is the relationship between the Hindu and Muslim intelligentsia who have to work together in the Civil Services and industry. Fortunately, the more extreme Muslims elements stay within their own confined ghettos and there is little interaction with the Hindus. Most of the orthodox Muslims are petty traders and self-employed artisans. Over the centuries, India had become a haven for a Muslim eclectic sect called 'Sufis', which had originated in Persia. The founder of the Sufi faith was Jallal-ud-din Rumi who lived in the thirteenth century (1207–3 AD). The 'Whirling Dervishes' in the Middle East belong to this sect, who whip themselves into a trance as they dance. Music and dancing are frowned upon by the Sunnis. In contrast, the Sufis are great proponents of the arts, and the *quwalli* in Indian music, is a major expression of their love and adoration of God. Sufi shrines, like the *dargah* of Khwaja Moin-ud-din Chisti in Ajmere, which is 700 years old, venerated by both Hindus and Muslims. There is a great rapport between the Sufis and Hindus. At this stage, it must be mentioned that in spite of the Sunni objections to the arts, classical Indian music, which is based on Hindu culture, has some of its greatest exponents from the Muslim community. Tragically, orthodoxy and Islamic fundamentalism have almost wiped out music and the arts in Pakistan and has created a desolate landscape 'where no birds sing'.

There is a saying in India that, as soon as an Indian opens his mouth he lays bare his entire culture, family background and education. The whole concept is embodied in the word *tehzeeb*, which is not easily translated into English, rather like another word, *izzat*, which signifies honour, respect, loss of face,' noblesse oblige' and so much more. One has to grow up in the cultural milieu of India in order to wear these linguistic refinements comfortably and naturally. Indian languages present other hurdles as there are three grades of address—when speaking to someone superior or of equal status, when the language is formal and respectful and prefaced by the word *Aap*, equivalent to the German *Sie*. Next we have the 'familiar' with the preface of *too* or the German *Du*. And lastly we have the preface of *Tum*, when addressing someone junior or subordinate. So in this jungle of lexicology, father is *Aap*, mother and God are the familiar, *Too*. God is an intimate and personal entity, not an alien or superior being by any means, as in the Abrahamic faiths of Judaism, Christianity and Islam.

At this stage, I will illustrate the importance of correct speech in India by a personal anecdote, so please bear with me.

I come from an old and very well respected family of prominent Barristers in Saharanpur, that dusty and rather musty orthodox city in what was the UP of yesteryears. The family ran a large establishment with a retinue of over 30 employees, a mixed bag of Muslims and Hindus who worked very harmoniously together, thanks to my mother, who had that rare talent of getting things done without fuss and bother. The 'major domo' of this substantial entourage was my grandfather's Court Clerk, Munshi Ibrahim, a venerable Muslim gentleman of the old school, who was the epitome of Northern Indian culture and politeness. The title of *munshi* identified him as a man of letters and learning. One day, in my childhood and ignorance, I addressed him as *tum* (that is, as an inferior). After all he was our 'employee'! My father overheard this and was livid. He took me into his study, gave me a clip over the ear and called me a *jungli jahil* translated to read an 'illiterate savage' to put it mildly. He told me in no uncertain manner that I must never address *munshiji* as an inferior and demanded that I apologise to him for this dreadful gaffe, which I did in his presence. The dear old soul put his arm around me and said that he had not taken this faux pas personally and apologised on my behalf to my furious father, saying that I was 'only a child'. My father retorted, 'and an uncivilized one at that'. Such are the subtleties of language in old cultures. Incidentally, *munshiji* served the family for over 70 years and even in the dreadful days of Partition, when murder and killing were destroying the equanimity of Saharanpur, he refused my father's instructions not to travel to the estate to manage the affairs of the family in such troublesome times. Such is true loyalty!! Here was a conservative Muslim, working for a Hindu family that he regarded as his own, and nary a word of dissent.

The family 'butler' and *Ab-dar* was Nazir Khan, next to Munshi Ibrahim in the order of seniority. Another Muslim, who had served the family for over 40 years, and so the pecking order went. These people were never regarded as servants but as members of the family. I will share another precious incident with you.

I had made a promise to my father that my first alcoholic drink would be shared with him. I was studying at Delhi University and during the holidays, I went home to Mussoorie. One evening, I said to my father that I would like a drink of Scotch. My father was delighted and called Nazir to bring out the bottle of Black Label that he had ferreted away for the occasion. Nazir put on his butler's regalia and with great ceremony brought the bottle on a lovely silver salver and asked my father for permission to share the event, saying 'Sir, my son is becoming a man today'.

This was an India that the British civilian never knew and could never hope to understand. The British officer in the Indian Army was a part of this Indian family and brotherhood and needed no induction.

Imperial Britain

It is impossible to conquer and rule nations and people without ruthlessness, sefishness and a total contempt for those who are destined to be ruled. Above all else the ruler must be obsessed with a sense of divine destiny to conquer. This ruthlessness is the Hall Mark of all conquerors through the ages. The other imperative is the pressure of population and the compulsion to look for greener pastures and riches. And last and by no means least, Evangelism, the burning desire to bring civilization and decency to the savage.

Britain was no exception to these draconian rules. To be more explicit, it was the English aristocracy and the landed-rich who mercilessly exploited the poor crofters in Scotland, after the defeat of William Wallace, and scattered the destitute Scots to fend for themselves overseas. In Ireland there was the added dimension of a Catholic peasantry, brutalised and thoroughly exploited by Protestant English landlords. And even in England—'that England that was wont to conquer others, Hath made a shameful conquest of itself'.

The poor had to doff their cap and touch their forelock as a sign of submission before the rich landowners. This, then, is the English aristocracy that created the East India Company and implanted all its Archaic, Georgian, then-Victorian norms in the Board Rooms of the EIC and created the vile opium trade in China. It must be made emphatically clear that Britain was out to rule and exploit the Indian milch cow. It did not have the slightest intention of befriending the Indian. At the same time it must be said, to the credit of the British, that they were not unmindful of the terrible injustices and the crass and revolting practices of the Hindus, like *Suttee* Thugee, and female infanticide, which they eliminated. Elsewhere, the British had become the biggest slave-traders and over 28 million African slaves were transported to America and the Caribbean. There is no record of how many African slaves perished in transit, but it must have been in millions. Once again, it was a Britisher, William Wilberforce, who abolished the slave trade in 1834 in Britain and Abraham Lincoln, of British descent, who issued the Emancipation Proclamation in

1863 which virtually ended slavery in the Southern States of America.

The British are a strange and contradictory race. Terrible racists and oppressive exploiters on the one hand and reformers and idealists on the other. It was this dreadful legacy of ruthlessness and greed that the English aristocracy bequeathed to the Business Class that was riding high on the crest of the Industrial Revolution. We are now going to witness the birth of Britain's notorious 'sweat shops' and the pathetic 'mud-larks'—the street urchins who crawled through the murk and filth of the streets of industrial England. First it was Charles Dickens who was appalled by the squalour and misery of Britain's working-class, to be followed by Karl Marx's *Das Kapital*, which would become the manifesto of the Communists, with its strident denouncement of capitalism. Britain was the birthplace of Communism; yet strangely enough it never found roots in Britain, although it had the ideal milieu for a massive revolt by the dreadfully oppressed and exploited proletariat. It eventually found roots in distant Russia, which had barely witnessed the Industrial Revolution. The English landed rich, the so-called 'nobles', were only concerned with preserving their privileges and rights, the hallowed sanctity of their estates and rivers, their grouse fields, trout and salmon runs, and their fox-hunts—all preserved by a team of gamekeepers to keep the hungry poachers off their estates. Poaching was a heinous offence, comparable to stealing a loaf of bread, and could finish one up with transportation-for-life to the penal colony of Australia. Nothing must ruffle His Lordship's equanimity or present a hurdle to the expansion of trade and commerce, which could disrupt profit. As British settlers started to penetrate into Indian Territory in America, the Red Indians were a nuisance and the British decided to eliminate the entire population and establish *terra nullius*, an empty land. In pursuit of this strategy was born the disgraceful practice of 'scalping' and the payment of a bounty for every Indian scalp produced by the settlers. When this ploy did not eliminate the Indian, it was decided to starve the Indians to death by the massacre of the buffalo on the prairies. Millions of buffalo were shot by the likes of 'Buffalo

Bill' and his cohorts and left to rot. In the end, the Indians were corralled into 'reservations'. Australia was going to witness the same ruthlessness, particularly in Tasmania, where the last aborigine died only a few years ago.

With the opening of the Suez Canal, the long reach of the British aristocracy and capitalism penetrated into the very heart of Asia and Africa. Burma had already been subjugated in 1824 and was being thoroughly exploited by the steamships plying up and down the Irrawaddy River carrying teak, mahogany and minerals. When Malaya came under British control, huge rubber plantations needed Indian labour to tap the latex. Tamil labour was indentured to work in these plantations and today Indians constitute about 8 per cent of the population of Malaysia. In Fiji, Indian labour was needed to farm sugar cane and to work in the gold mines. Indians make up nearly 50 per cent of Fiji's population and run most of the commercial enterprises on the islands. In East and South Africa, indentured Indian labour built the roads and railways.

Born to Rule

Conquerors come in all shapes and sizes. Most were megalomaniacs who had no clear-cut philosophy to justify what they were doing other than the sheer joy of conquest, loot and plunder. This was the raison d'être for conquerors like Chenghiz Khan and his marauding Mongol hordes that swarmed out of the steppes of Central Asia, and devastated Eastern Europe. The same could be said for Attila the Hun and Tamerlane, who revelled in the sheer blood-lust of killing, rape and plunder. At least Tamerlane became a patron of the arts in his later years and left a legacy of refined architecture in his beautiful city of Samarkand. Alexander the Great is an enigma and there is no clear-cut motivation for moving his army out of Macedonia other than the fact that Macedonia was regarded as a 'backward back water' by the Athenians. Scarcely a reason for world conquest. It was Alexander's descendant, Ptolemy, who left a legacy of art, culture and refinement. Alexander was little more than a militarist and a remarkable leader of men.

Now we are going to witness the strange spectacle of a tiny

island, off the coast of continental Europe, which would have the temerity to aspire to fame, fortune and world domination. This was 'Merrie England', 'this Royal Throne of Kings, this Sceptered Isle.'

This was a Nation that had a tryst with destiny.

As Professor J.R. Seeley of Cambridge University put it: 'Britain had a civilising destiny.'

To be 'great', one must feel great, think great and this must suffuse through to the very bones. 'Greatness' cannot stomach doubt, uncertainty, and the endless prattle of righteousness. 'Greatness' demands belief and confidence and not a skerrick of uncertainty must muddy the water of positive action.

There were the aristocratic empire-builders in England who ran the EIC, the plutocrats who ran the infamous 'sweat shops', the dreadful coal mines. The colliers, cutters and Indiamen, were totally oblivious of those who worked for them, or the subjugated American Indians whose land they were expropriating. Profit at any cost was their goal. The greater ideals of Empire were still burgeoning in their breast as was the zeal of Evangelism. These would find expression as the Empire unfolded.

It is almost impossible to pinpoint when British imperialism began. Obviously the birth of the Thalassocracies of Britain, France, Spain, Portugal, Holland and the Hanseatic League, opened the vistas of trade with distant lands, triggered by the exploits of Marco Polo along the Silk Road to China. Trade was the spur for maritime exploration and the promise of untold riches with each argosy. With trade came the adventitious opportunity of actual conquest and pillage. The scene was all set for ruthless oppression and exploitation.

Trade and growing wealth fed the insatiable appetite for more of the same. Avarice fueled the furnace.

The Empire Builders

It is difficult to ascribe this honour to any one particular individual or individuals. As I have said earlier, with the gradual demise of the Mughal Empire, India became a mess of squabbling princes, a decaying fabric that made for easy pickings by the EIC which was the only stabilizing institution after the demise of the French. If honours have to be meted out among the galaxy of Empire Builders of the EIC, pride of place must go to Governor-General Richard Wellesley, the elder brother of the Duke of Wellington, who greatly expanded the domain of the EIC with his victorious armies, manned by the Scots, Irish and Welsh, particularly the Scottish soldier-scholars like Sir Thomas Munroe, Sir John Malcolm and Mountstuart Elphingstone. And, of course, we cannot omit the names of Sir Charles Trevelyan and his brother-in-law, Thomas Babbington Macaulay, who laid the foundation of modern education based on the English language in India. But the vision of a glorious and triumphant Britain was the brainchild of Prime Minister, Benjamin Disraeli, who opened the Suez Canal and proclaimed Queen Victoria, Empress of India in 1876. This was a masterstroke of diplomacy as it broke the spell of inertia for a grieving widow, Queen Victoria, and gave life to a triumphant monarch. This was the start of Britain's most profound and glorious epoch of imperial destiny.

The baton was now passed on to another peer of the realm, Lord George Nathaniel Curzon, who was totally convinced that he was born to rule. Curzon was imbued with the implacable conviction that 'Britain was the greatest force for good the world had ever seen', and that he was going to be instrumental in perpetuating this saga. Curzon was a man in a hurry to fulfil his destiny of greatness. At the age of 32, he became an Under-Secretary in the India Office. Never backward in coming forward, he nominated himself for the august office of Viceroy and audacity paid off. Unbelievable but true, he got the appointment and high-tailed for Calcutta with his rich American bride by his side. In London, Queen Victoria was celebrating her Diamond Jubilee with a pomp and pageantry that the world had never witnessed before. The public was ecstatic, swept away with the euphoria of being British. The brilliant composer, Edward Elgar, composed his immortal Imperial March—'Pomp and Circumstace'—in honour of the Empress. Britain's hour of Glory had arrived and the world lay at her feet. An incredible achievement for a miniscule Nation. Henceforth Britain would bear the honorific title of 'Great' Britain. Then the inevitable happened. Britain had barely reached her zenith of greatness when Queen Victoria died in January 1901, throwing the entire Empire into mourning. The death of the Empress shattered Curzon, the epitome of the grand pillar of The Raj and all it stood for. He decided that her memory must be enshrined in stone and mortar .The magnificent Victoria Memorial in Calcutta was the brainchild of Curzon, built in a superb garden setting. Work was started in 1904 when India was in the grip of a dreadful famine. According to the historian Burton Stein, 6.5 million Indians starved to death between 1899 and 1900. Others put the figure as high as 10 million.

In 1901, 250,000 people died of the bubonic plague around Bombay. Another three million were going to perish from cholera by 1905. In the midst of all this suffering and misery, Curzon remained undaunted in his Vice-Regal agenda. These were mere contretemps in an India where death and starvation were endemic. The Government of Bengal was paralysed by riots, strikes, boycotts and the strident call for Independence. Bengal was seething with unrest and political intrigue. It was time to truncate the state in 1905 and to separate the state into East Bengal, with its preponderance of Muslims, with the capital at Dacca, and West Bengal, with Calcutta as the capital. Orissa and Bihar became separate states. This draconian step by Curzon presaged the creation of Pakistan in 1947. Curzon's next dramatic step was to move the Capital from Calcutta to the old traditional capital of Delhi. Calcutta still remained the commercial hub of the EIC. Curzon now created a new state, the North-Western Frontier Province (NWFP), separating the Punjab from the turbulent and almost ungovernable tribal Pathans who straddled the frontier with Afghanistan. Curzon was clearly a man with a mission. He was an absolute autocrat who brooked no nonsense or opposition. He had travelled extensively and had a deep and abiding sense of history and was appalled by the neglect of India's ancient architectural monuments. He was the inspiration in repairing and restoring the country's rich cultural past.

The Clash of the Titans

Britain was the incubator of men of steel and purpose. A burgeoning Empire had no place for wimps and snivellers. The times demanded men of action and a benign providence heard this call and delivered the men to do the job, men like Governor-General Richard Wellesley, The Duke of Wellington, Lord Roberts, Lord Curzon and Lord Horatio Herbert Kitchener. The last two were destined to clash. The stage was just not big enough to accommodate the aristocratic Curzon and the autocratic Kitchener. Both men were very similar yet very dissimilar. They were both 'loners' who made their own rules as they went. They refused to suffer fools and sycophants and they had a clear vision of what they had to achieve. So here we have Curzon, securely established in Delhi as the Viceroy, while Kitchener was busy carving his name as a military commander in Africa. He retrieved Khartoum for Britain by defeating the Mahdis who had killed General Gordon in 1885. On 2 September 1898, at the Battle of Omurduman, near Khartoum, he defeated the forces of the Khalifa decisively and finally broke the power of the Mahdis. Sudan once again came under Egyptian rule. Next came the Boer Wars, in which he served as Chief-of-Staff to General Roberts. Although the Boer War was inconclusive, victory was in fact won by the Boers, who were able to establish the Federated State of South Africa while guaranteeing protection to British possessions. Kitchener returned to England to a hero's welcome. He was offered several senior positions in The War Office, which he turned down but accepted the position of Commander-in-Chief in India. His appointment was well received by Curzon who could not have foreseen the clash of personalities that was in the making. Kitchener's remit was to update the Indian Army, which had grown into a huge lumbering organization in dire need of a major overhaul, consuming 35 per cent of the government's revenue and saddled with the archaic bureaucracy of the EIC. To start with, there were still the three Presidential armies of Madras, Bombay and Bengal, each with its own Commander-in-Chief, reporting directly to the Army Member on the Viceroy's Council, who out ranked the C-in-C. The Viceroy could override any decision taken by the Council and Curzon, in his usual peremptory, sarcastic manner, was quick to criticize any suggestion put forward by the military, for which he had utter contempt, and regarded them as subservient to civilian authority. Kitchener, on the other hand, disliked politicians as self-serving and conniving rascals. Not a conducive atmosphere by any means and something would have to give. Curzon was confident that, as the Viceroy, he not only out-ranked Kitchener, buthad made such major changes for the better that when the matter was being arbitrated in London he was bound to win. What he had forgotten was that Kitchener was Britain's darling and hero. Curzon was recalled, ending a remarkable reign. While all this skirmishing was going on in the political arena in Delhi, Kitchener rolled up his sleeves and started reorganizing the Indian Army. His first, and most important, step was to amalgamate the three Presidential armies under his command as C-in-C. The next step was to put order in the classification of regiments and battalions, naming and numbering them. The eventual goal was to prepare the army for frontier-duty along the Afghan border, in order to prevent insurrection among the tribal Pathans and to provide a deterrent to any moves by the Russian Bear towards India. Russophobia was still alive and well. The two vulnerable points along the frontier were Quetta, in Balochistan, leading into southern Afghanistan and Kandahar and Peshawar, sitting at the head of the Khyber Pass leading to Kabul. The Indian Army was composed of nine Divisions, out of which Northern Command got five, based in Peshawar, whereas Southern Command got four Divisions, with HQ's in Quetta. Kitchener also established a Staff College for senior officers in Quetta, run on the lines of the Staff College in Camberley. Each Division consisted of one Brigade of British troops and two Brigades of Indians. The Indian Army had a total strength of 150,000 including cavalry and artillery. There was no air support yet, and very little mechanized transport. The mule was still the indispensable carrier of arms, ammunition and provender for men and beasts to the remotest pickets. Kitchener had insisted that the legacy of the Mutiny had to be scrapped and both British and Indian forces must have identical equipment. The Lee Enfield rifle and bayonet was still the mainstay of the infantry, interspersed with units of machine gunners, with water-cooled Vickers heavy machine guns. The cavalry were experts with the lance and sabre and were divided into light cavalry, equipped with the sabre, and lancers, wielding the fearsome lance.

But let us return to the endless skirmishing that was going on between Curzon and Kitchener. The main bone of contention was that Curzon believed that as the King's and Parliament's representative in Delhi, final authority was vested in him and he could over-ride decisions taken by his council, even on military matters, as the Army and the C-in-C were subordinate to civilian authority. This raised Kitchener's hackle, who demanded independent command and authority to act and not have to go cap in hand to his subordinate, the Army Member in the council, for permission to implement his orders. One side or the other had to win. Kitchener had placed India on a war footing apropos the Afghan frontier and this tedious bureaucratic wrangling came between swift action as dictated by military necessity and Curzon's courtly demands. As we know, Curzon lost and was recalled to London.

The Gathering Storm

Kitchener had modernized the Indian Army. He had trimmed off all the fat and a lean and trim, highly motivated body of men was straining at the bit for action. The African campaigns had endeared him to the British public and government. His work in India had been completed in record time and he was called back to England. Lord Kitchener was succeeded by General Sir O'Moore Creagh.

The twentieth century can be rightfully called the 'European Century' as the major players on the political stage were, Great Britain, that dominated the globe with over 350 million subjects, with France, a close second but slipping behind after the defeat of Napoleon at Waterloo. Then came the 'Johnny-come-lately's': Germany and Italy, who had gained national unification in the late 1800's, under Bismark and Garibaldi respectively. Both countries had missed out on the massive land grab in Asia and

Africa and were determined to rectify this unfortunate mishap as soon as possible. The Austro-Hungarian Empire of The Habsburg dynasty was teetering and the 'hounds of war' were snapping at its heels. The serf kingdom of Czarist Russia was desperately trying to hold back the Turks and was only too happy to side with the French and the British when hostilities commenced in 1914. Europe was a mess of floundering nations, snarling and gnashing their teeth. One would imagine that, in this insecure milieu' Britain would be sitting high in the saddle with its massive Empire supplying raw materials to its ravenous mills at highly subsidized prices and its exports protected by Imperial Preference duties to keep out the products of other countries from its Empire. India was by far the biggest export market for Britain. Over 10 per cent of Britain's exports came to India. But life was not meant to be easy and there was seething unrest in Ireland, where the Sinn Fein party was demanding independence for the country,and a nascent independence movement was gathering momentum in India under the demand for 'Swaraj', or freedom, under the ferocious onslaught by the patriot, Bal Gangadhar Tilak, who exclaimed 'Swaraj is my birth right and I will have it'. Tilak was paving the way for the arrival of Mohandas Karamchand Gandhi, who was destined to become the doyen of the Indian Independence Movement. Back home, the Suffragette Movement was gathering strength, with women demanding voting rights. This privilege would eventually be granted in 1928, but in the meantime more radical women like Annie Besant were hammering at the door, demanding social reform. Strongly influenced by a Ukrainian émigré, Helena Petrovna Blavatsky, she joined the Theosophical Society, an eclectic philosophical movement started by her. Theosophy brought them to Adiyar, a suburb of Madras, which became the centre for the movement. But Annie Besant was not content with just being a leading light in the Theosophical Society. Her socialist background revolted at the sight of the colonial subjugation of India by Britain and she joined the Indian National Congress.

M.K. Gandhi was born in India but was brought up and educated in South Africa and became a lawyer in England. On returning to South Africa he was outraged by Afrikaaner and British racism and discrimination that made it almost impossible for him to practise law. The fountainhead of this abominable racism was Britain, which had to be assailed where it would hurt it most, and that was in India which was reeling under colonialism. This inspired him to move back to India and join the movement demanding 'Swaraj'. But more of that anon.

It is time to go back to Mother England, which was beset with industrial unrest and the birth of a ferocious Labour Movement and the anaemic 'pink' Fabian Socialism. Across the Channel, Germany was flexing its newfound industrial muscle, spurred on by Kaiser Wilhelm, who jealously resented the stupendous rise of his relatives, the English Royal Family, to such pre-eminence in World affairs. Europe was a powder keg, primed and ready to explode. The assassination of Francis Ferdinand, the heir to the Hapsburg Throne, on 28 June 1914 at Sarajevo, led to a declaration of war on Serbia by Austria. Russia responded by siding with Serbia and declaring war on Austria. Germany declared war on Russia on 1 August and on France on 8 August. German troops poured into Belgium on 4 August, in accordance with what was known as the Schlieffen Plan, carefully developed by the Prussian High Command well before hostilities triggered World War I (WWI). The Invasion of France brought Britain into the fray, and the British Expeditionary Force crossed the Channel with four divisions, which clashed with the Germans at the First Battle of Ypres. Close behind the British were two divisions of the Indian Army, the 3rd Lahore and the 7 Meerut Divisions, still dressed in khaki and totally ill-equipped for the September cold weather in France. I do not intend to write a blow-by-blow account of the trials and tribulations of the Indian Forces in the terrible days that followed, as this is not an expose on WW I. I shall have to be content with highlighting the dreadful blunders, both military and political that fed the charnel house of the Western Front. The European powers that took the centre-stage were totally inexperienced in massive warfare, with perhaps the exception of the annihilation of Napolean's 'Grande Armee' in Russia in 1812. For the rest, their only experience was confined to 'battles', although the grandiose title of 'war' was frequently used in these conflicts. Thus it is not surprising that the massive break-through by the nearly 2,000,000 Germans in September, 1914, caught the French and British armies left-footed, and the Battle of The Marne commenced, with France throwing into the fray 1,300,000 troops and the British Expeditionary Force of 100,000 trying to staunch the hemorrhage caused by the German onslaught. Had the Germans stuck to the Schlieffen Plan they would have encircled the French Army and captured Paris and the Battle of The Marne would not have taken place. However, General Helmuth von Moltke diverted a large force to the Eastern Front against the Russians and the Schlieffen Plan was aborted. The Battle of The Marne cost both sides nearly 500,000 in dead and wounded. The Allies were too exhausted to follow up the retreating Germans. What followed then was the endless slaughter in the waterlogged trenches of Flanders, with the three combatants slugging it out in a meaningless effort to dislodge the enemy and gain a few miserable meters of 'no man's land'. The war in Flanders had deteriorated to a senseless impasse. Neither side had a clear-cut military plan to extricate the embattled troops out of the quagmire into which they had plunged the hapless soldiers. The sodden trenches, barbed wire, the deafening roar of mortar and artillery fire and the staccato chatter of machine guns kept demanding an endless supply of oblations to the Gods of War. General Erich von Falkenhayn of The German General Staff, deliberately embarked on a campaign of attrition to 'bleed France white' and knock it out of the war. What followed was the pointless Battle of Verdun. For the French the defence of Verdun was a matter of national pride. It had no military significance. France's General Joseph Joffre walked straight into von Falkenhayn's plan. Neither side won this stupid battle, which lasted ten months and cost France 542,000 casualties and Germany 434,000. The catch phrase of the French was *'Ils ne passerant pas'*—'They shall not pass'! The carnage on the Western front was to continue until the Armistice was signed in October 1918, and military history would be written on the massacres on 'The Somme', a military disaster organized by Lord Kitchener. It is now time to move to other theatres of war.

On the Eastern Front the Czarist Russian Armies were, numerically, much bigger than the Germans, and they went on the offensive in East Prussia, poorly trained and badly led. The Germans, on the other hand, were brilliantly led by the redoubtable combination of Field Marshals Paul von Hindenberg and Erich von Ludendorf. The Russians, under General Alexander Samsonov, were badly mauled and forced to retire to the city of Tannenberg on 25 August 1914. Samsonov had not bothered to reconnoitre the enemy's position and did not even bother to code his messages, which were read by Ludendorf, disclosing his plans and positions. The Russians were surrounded and slaughtered as they tried to escape. Over 125,000 Russians were killed or wounded and 500 guns were captured. Samsonov committed suicide, leaving his army leaderless. The only advantage gained by this disastrous campaign was the transfer of German troops, by von Moltke, from the Western Front to the Eastern Front, which aborted the Schlieffen Plan.

On the Eastern Front, a second Russian army, under General Pavel Rennenkampf, managed to escape encirclement by the Germans, but lost another 125,000 men and 150 guns. The rout of Czar Nicholas II's army was a complete national disgrace and demoralization of the entire country was going to precipitate the Bolshevik Revolution in 1917. Russia, also, had not forgotten its humiliating defeat, in 1905, in the Russo-Japanese War. Russia was effectively out of the war, giving the ruthless Ottoman Empire open slather to ravage the countries of the Balkans, especially Serbia, its traditional enemy.

The war in Flanders had ground to a stalemate and was nothing more than a charnel house, which destroyed men and material on both sides. The weary combatants did not have an exit strategy in sight.

The focus now shifted to Turkey. Winston Churchill was the First Lord of the Admiralty and the chief architect of the Dardanelles Campaign. The plan was simple and straightforward. The British and the French fleets would destroy the Turkish defences on the Gallipoli Peninsula by a massive bombardment, opening up the passage for the fleet to sail through the Dardanelles and capture Constantinople With the destruction of the Turkish defences by naval bombardment on the Gallipoli Peninsula, British, Australian and New Zealand (ANZAC) forces would clamber up the cliffs and occupy the ridges overlooking the Dardanelles The British force included the Indian Army's 29th Infantry Brigade, under the command of Sir Ian Hamilton. The Brigade was mostly made up of the 6th Gorkha Rifles, who distinguished themselves by capturing a 300 foot high cliff in the Cape Helles sector. Mariner charts still show this feature under the caption of 'Gurkha Bluff'. The whole plan rested on the element of surprise, and this crucial expedient was sacrificed by a series of tactical blunders that alerted the Turks to their inadequate defences on the Gallipoli Peninsula. They were quick to remedy this weakness, with the result that the Allies were faced by a strong, well-dug-in enemy, sitting on the heights overlooking the beaches where the landings took place. On 25 April 1915, a force of 78,000 ANZACS and British troops made two separate landings, but they were too far apart to be able to support each other. To compound matters, there was no naval support as both navies had suffered losses from submarine attacks and carefully laid minefields, and had pulled out. For nearly a year the Allied troops clung to their precarious foothold on the beaches below, while the Turks rained shell and mortar-fire on their helpless enemy. Gallipoli cost the Allies 252,000 casualties and the Turks 251,000. At least the Turks were fighting to protect their homeland. The Allies got a bloody nose and nothing else, other than a page in history. Gallipoli exemplified the basic tenets of warfare: careful preparedness to execute a battle plan; a political philosophy to be pursued through military means; and, last and by no means least, an exit strategy, should the battle plan fail. Above all else, a careful assessment of the enemy, either potential or factual, and his strengths and weaknesses'.

It is time to do a stock-take of what has been gained and lost. Flanders is still a 'meat-grinder' for the armies on both sides, with a total stalemate. Russia has been eliminated and Turkey has emerged stronger than ever. Neither side has gained any superiority and both sides have suffered prodigious manpower losses. With the collapse of the Gallipoli Campaign, a direct attack on Turkey was not a viable prospect. Britain was faced with the two-fold task of protecting the Suez Canal, its lifeline to India, and the safety of the Persian Gulf, so that oil from Saudi Arabia could be transported through the Straits of Hormuz, even though Mesopotamia was in Turkish hands. The Turkish Khadive in Egypt had been deposed in 1879, with British intervention, and Egypt became a British protectorate in1914. The Suez Canal was safe but Mesopotamia was still a bleeding sore. An Indian Army Expeditionary Force was mustered with 11,000 men, 28 guns and a small flotilla of riverboats to navigate through the treacherous shifting channels of the Shatt -al- Arab, the delta of the combined Tigris and Euphrates rivers. The force was under the command of Major General Charles Townsend. The Indian Army captured Basra on 23 October 1914, and advanced up-stream on the Tigris. The Turks mounted a massive attack from three directions with 18,000 men but were repulsed with heavy losses and fell back on the township of Amara with the Indians in hot pursuit. Over-confidence is as dangerous as under-confidence. The former breeds recklessness and the latter, timidity. After the debacle of Gallipoli the British public and politicians wanted the salve of victory, and put pressure on Townsend to push onto Baghdad. A grave error, as the advance lengthened the tenuous supply-line from Basra by river, as there was no railway to fall back on. The rainy season had started, causing floods on the rivers, and the roads were turning into a quagmire. The troops were tired and weary, ill equipped for the cold weather that followed and were on reduced rations. The Turks, on the other hand, had transferred their Gallipoli veterans into this theatre, to protect Baghdad with a leavening of Germans under the command of General Falkenhayn, who had sworn to 'bleed France white'.

Townsend advanced towards Baghdad and, by 12 November, he got to within 30 miles of the city, defended by 20,000 Turks. In this operation he lost 4,500 men, a third of his force. He had no choice but to retreat to the town of Kut, where he planned to hold out against the pursuing Turks and await relief by the Indian 3rd Lahore and the 7th Meerut Divisions, which had been fighting in Flanders, and had been pulled out for deployment in Mesopotamia. The rainy-season had begun, the rivers were in flood and the roads had become impassable. All attempts to relieve Kut were to no avail, but the gallant Indians and their British compatriots held out for 150 days, suffering terribly with disease and half-rations. Finally, Townsend surrendered on 29 April 1916 when 6,000 Indians and 2,000 British troops were captured. It should be mentioned that four separate relief attempts were beaten off by four determined Turkish divisions under the command of the German General, Count Kolmar von der Goltz. The ineffectual relief efforts cost 21,000 casualties. Egged on by the politicians and the War Office in London, Townsend had thrown caution to the winds, over estimated his resources and the poor lines of supply from Basra, and fell prey to over-confidence .He was replaced by General Sir Stanley Maude. The Indian Army had regrouped and was ready to redress the Seige of Kut-al Amara, which was taken from the Turks in February, followed by Baghdad on 11 March 1917, after some very heavy fighting. The next decision was whether to advance to Mosul or to transfer the emphasis to Palestine, where General Sir Edmund Allenby had met with some spectacular successes. His forces had captured Jerusalem in December 1917, a most welcome Christmas present to Lloyd George, the Prime Minister. In the meantime General Maude died of cholera in November 1917, at Tekrit, half way between Baghdad and Mosul. This town was to come into prominence many years later as the birthplace of the dictator, Saddam Hussein.

The war against the Germans was now pivotal in defeating the Ottoman Empire in Palestine. The Turks had re-grouped under the German general, Liman von Sanders, with 36,000 men and 350 guns facing Allenby with 57,000 Infantry and 12,000 Cavalry, and mounted infantry like the Australian Light Horse, which was going to blaze its way into the annals of military history at Megiddo. The Battle of Megiddo opened with a massive artillery barrage on 19 September 1918, which opened a gap for The Australian Light Horse and the Indian 2nd Royal Lancers (Gardner's Horse) to charge through and rout the

Turkish Eighth Army. The Turkish Seventh Army reeled back towards the Jordan River, with Allenby in hot pursuit. Shock tactics paid off and Allenby advanced 360 miles, destroyed three Turkish armies, took 76,000 prisoners and captured 300 guns. British and Indian losses were 853 dead, 4,482 wounded and 385 missing. The charge by the 2nd Royal Lancers and Australian Light Horse was going to be the last cavalry charge in WW I. Earlier, the regiment had rendered sterling service in Flanders as a part of the 7th Meerut Division. The Mesopotamian Campaign was turning into an Indian Army battleground deploying over 600,000 troops.

8

The Beginning of the End

It is time to do a quick stock take of the war. The war in Mesopotamia was over, with a total defeat of the Ottoman Empire, and the end of the brutal Caliphate dynasty that had ravaged the Balkans for nearly 600 years.

Although this narrative is intended to cover the combined British and Indian involvement in WW I, history demands that, for the sake of thoroughness, two battles need to be summarized, even though they did not involve Indians. The first is the massive naval Battle of Jutland, May 1916–1 June 1916, which was fought between the German High-Seas Fleet, under Admiral Reinhard Scheer, and the British Grand Fleet, under Admiral Sir John Jellicoe.This was the first time that Germany's freshly built Armada was going to take on the might of the undisputed British Naval supremacy on the high seas.The British Fleet had numerical superiority and it's massive dreadnoughts, with their 14" guns, had no equivalent in the German fleet. But Britain had a major problem. The propulsive power of 'black powder' was inadequate for the heavy guns of the dreadnoughts, which severely limited their range. These guns needed the propulsive power of 'cordite', which was in very short supply due to the scarcity of the acetone needed in the manufacture of the propellant. At this stage I have to digress:

Anti-Semitism had been the bane of the Jews for centuries, who suffered cruel indignities at the hands of Catholics and the Eastern Orthodox Church, particularly in Russia. The Jews had had enough, and Zionism was the only foreseeable alternative. It appealed to the Jewish intelligentsia like the brilliant chemist,

Chaim Weizmann, who had migrated to Manchester to lecture at the University. Weizmann was approached by Earl Arthur Balfour, the Foreign Secretary, requesting him to produce 20,000 tons of acetone for Britain. In return, a grateful Britain would push the Zionist cause now that Russia and the Ottoman Empires had virtually collapsed. Wonders will never cease!!

Weizmann manufactured the 20,000 tons of acetone and the Balfour Declaration was issued in the form of a letter to Lord Rothschild, dated 2 November 1917, which stated that 'His Majesty's Government looks with favour upon the establishment in Palestine of a national homeland for the Jewish people.'

It is worth mentioning that the Turks surrendered Jerusalem to the British in December 1917. Earlier, Balfour had offered Weizmann beautiful farmland in Uganda or Rhodesia, as an alternative to Palestine, which was still in Turkish hands. The offer was refused. The Zionists wanted the stony, semi-desert and blighted land of 'Eretz Israel' for their home. Such is the power of faith and belief in an idea. Israel was born on the back of 20,000 tons of acetone and the British fleet won the Battle of Jutland, thanks to Weizmann, and sent the Germans seeking safety in Wilhelmshaven. The German Navy would have to confine its warfare with its submarines, sinking Allied merchant ships in the Atlantic Ocean.

It is a strange quirk of fate that it was Benjamin Disreali who opened the Suez Canal for Britain, with money borrowed from Lord Rothschild; two Jews who were responsible for perpetuating British hegemony and, in return, Britain was responsible for the birth of Israel.

So far, two major players have not featured in WWI, namely Italy and Austria. This brings us to the dreadful Battle of Caporetto, 24 October to 12 November 1917, which was the culmination of extensive fighting between the Italians and the Austrians in the Alps above Trieste. Like Flanders, the two armies had exhausted themselves into a 'no win' situation. The stalemate was broken on the 24 October by a massive barrage from 3,000 guns, plus mortars from the German 14th Army' under General Otto von Bulow, and two Austrian armies. The

Italians reeled under this onslaught and had to retreat from Caporetto, losing almost 70 miles of territory; almost 40,000 killed or wounded; 275,000 prisoners and 2,500 guns. Caporetto was a disaster that virtually eliminated Italy from the war. In this campaign, a young German officer, Erwin Rommel, distinguished himself and was awarded Germany's highest military award, the 'Pour la Merite'.

The German Reichswehr was still well entrenched in Flanders and the Allies had hardly made an impression on the front line, in spite of all the fighting and bloodletting. On the Eastern Front the Russians had been soundly defeated and had become totally ineffectual. After the decisive Battle of Caporetto the Italians had become a spent force. In Mesopotamia and Palestine, the Indian and British forces had some spectacular successes and the Ottoman Empire was on the verge of collapse. At sea, the Battle of Jutland was not a decisive victory for the Royal Navy. It had taken the edge off the German Navy, which had received a minor trouncing, but it was still a formidable force, but as matters stood, the war could have continued interminably. In the spring of 1918 the Germans mounted several fairly successful attacks on the Western Front but the arrival of fresh American troops pushed the Germans back and, in November, the Germans sued for peace. This was the first time that an army had surrendered while its forces were intact and sitting in enemy territory. This unusual contretemps was commented on by a British General, who sought an explanation from General von Ludendorff, who in turn had no answer. The British General then suggested that Germany's defeat must have been caused by 'a stab in the back'. Ludendorff immediately picked up this refrain 'Yes, of course. It was a stab in the back.' This unfortunate conversation was overheard by a slightly wounded corporal lying in hospital. The corporal was none other than Adolf Hitler, who had been mulling over Germany's ignominious surrender and at last had found an answer. This was going to have dire consequences, as we will see. No German would stab his country in the back. It had to be the work of an alien. The only so-called 'aliens' were the Jews. That will have to suffice for the moment.

9

The Spoils of War

The Treaty of Versailles was signed in Paris in 1919, which formally ended WW I. There were several controversial clauses in the treaty. The first was Article 231, which assigned total blame and responsibility for the war on Germany and her allies, and demanded reparations for the damage caused. The reparations demanded by the Allies were ruthless and rapacious, and would cripple the German economy to such an extent that repayment of any reparation became an impossibility. The Allies demanded their 'pound of flesh' and dismantled German industries, which were shipped off to the Allies, which explains the origin of companies like Merck, Schering, GAF (General Aniline und Sodafabrik) and countless others, in the USA, Britain and France. Germany was stripped of her miniscule colonial possessions in Africa and Asia, and in 1924, Poland was given a large slice of Upper Silesia. Probably the worst indignity was the demilitarization of the Rhineland and its occupation by the Allies. Germany was a cripple, with raging inflation and unemployment. The Allies had unwittingly, and stupidly, paved the way for the arrival of Hitler and the Nazis.

The Ottoman Empire had collapsed and its possessions in the Middle East would be parcelled off between Britain, which got the lion's share, covering Mesopotamia and Palestine, and the French mandate, which covered Syria and the Lebanon. Britain now controlled all the oil rich territories, which it proceeded to sub-divide into manageable kingdoms like Trans-Jordan, Iraq, Kuwait and Saudi-Arabia. Egypt was ruled by the

Turkish Khadive but was a British protectorate. Palestine continued to be under direct British rule. A trickle of Jews had migrated into 'the promised land of Zion' and there were between 80,000 and 100,000 settlers. Arabs accounted for fewer than 250,000, who led a precarious existence as nomadic herdsmen. Britain prevaricated implementing the Balfour Declaration for fear of offending the Arabs, plus there was a strong anti-Semitic bias. The Arabs had the oil spigot in their hand and Britain needed oil. Even though Israel had not been formally created, the handful of Jewish Zionist migrants had made it mandatory to adopt the principle of ALIYAH, under which any Jew born of a Jewish mother had the inalienable right to migrate and settle in Palestine. Between 1919 and 1923, 35,000 Jews migrated and this figure increased to 80,000 between 1924 and 1928. Finally the rise of the Nazis between 1929 and 1939 opened the floodgates and 250,000 Jews arrived in Palestine. This ignited riots and massacres by the Arabs, fed by vitriolic preaching in mosques and rumors that the Jews were planning to destroy the al-Aqsa mosque in Jerusalem. The British made half-hearted efforts to bring the situation under control and convened the PEEL COMMISSION on 7 July 1937 that virtually abrogated the Balfour Declaration and confined the Jews to a tiny strip of land along the Mediterranean Sea and the Sea of Galilee. The Arabs were not going to have a bar of this and, led by Haj Amin Husseni, the Grand Mufti of Jerusalem, a violent revolt erupted The revolt was finally suppressed by Stanley Baldwin, the Prime Minister, in 1939. The Mufti fled to Beirut and then to Europe, where he espoused the Nazi cause. To cut a long story short, the State of Israel was finally created by a UN resolution on 14 May 1948, which would precipitate a series of Arab-Israeli wars. It is time to leave Palestine and return to India.

India in the Inter-Regnum between WWI and WWII

The clamour for Independence had been laid to rest as a wartime concession to a Britain that was immersed in a battle for survival in WWI. Several hundred thousand Indians fought and died for Britain in this gory and meaningless conflagration, which had no political significance whatsoever for the Indian, but to oppose an embattled Britain was like kicking *'Hamara Sahib'* when he was down, an action which would have violated a deep code of Honour and Chivalry in the psyche of the Indian soldier. Other than India Gate, in New Delhi, there are next to no monuments to commemorate the sacrifices made by the Indian fighting man for a foreign ruler. This is 'Izzat-o-Iqbal' ('Izzat above all else'). But now that this bloody interlude has blown over, it is time to pick up the threads and start squabbling again.

The British had an instinctive distrust of the Indian. As Robert Clive said, 'In India everything is for sale. You buy the Hindu with money and the Muslim with women.'

An extravagant exaggeration, of course, but we must bear in mind that, over centuries, Hindu culture and civilization had degenerated to such an extent that guile and cunning had replaced honest decency and values. Beset with pillage, rape and massacre by marauding conquerors, the Hindu was in 'survival' mode. The Muslim, on the other hand, had become decadent and morally corrupt, consumed by lewd lasciviousness. What a choice to pick from! Till the time that the British finally left India, they felt that the Indian did not have the inherent qualities of leadership that were necessary to administer and run a country independently. The Indian could be trained to work as a most proficient subordinate under British tutelage but, left to himself, he would quickly deteriorate to a corrupt self-serving official and revert to the age-old practice of cronyism, which had survived for centuries under the euphemism of *Dastoor* or *Sifarish*—'it is the custom'—which was supposed to explain and justify everything.

Winston Churchill had spent four years in India with a crack British Cavalry Regiment, the 4th Hussars, but that did not alter his contemptuous attitude towards India and Indians. He epitomized the obstinacy and pugnacity of John Bull on the one hand, and the courage and muted ferocity of The British Lion on the other. He was, after all, the grandson of the Duke of Marlborough, and was born in the ancestral home of Blenheim Palace. Pride of race and the proverbial British arrogance flowed freely through his veins since his birth. If you were not 'British' you were a 'bloody foreigner' irrespective of your own so-called 'nobility'. One year a very heavy fog descended on the English Channel. The London Times printed the headline, 'Heavy fog in the Channel! Continent isolated!'

That says it all. Even the fact that thousands of Indians had fought and died for England changed nothing in Churchill's eyes. That is after all what England expects of its subjugated Colonials! What really got up Churchill's nose was that the Indians quite honestly believed that they would be better off without the British. What absolute 'balder-dash!'. The stupid Indians did not know when they were well off. This is what Churchill had to say about Indian Independence: 'When independence comes to India, power will go into the hands of rascals, rogues, free-booters and men of straw.'

Post WWI, Britain was licking its wounds! It had won the war but had been bled white. The swaggering 'bully boy' had got a bloody nose and a chastened Britain picked up the reins of government in India. Princely India and the Indian Army had given total and absolute support to Britain in its hour of need, but it highlighted the inescapable truth that Britain could only rule India with the tacit consent of the Indian. The bulk of the Muslim population was a pampered minority, which was quite content to thrive under British tutelage. The Sikhs were only a small minority and had been given pride of place in the army. Massive irrigation projects in the Punjab had give prosperity to the landed peasantry of the Sikhs and the Punjabi Mussalman. That left the cavilling Hindus to agitate for 'Swaraj', (freedom) led by Gandhi and a cabal of Brahmin lawyers who were champing at the bit. The British were not going to hand over their 'Crown Jewel' to the thieving Nationalists without a fight and they kept up a pretence of gradually inducting Indians into the process of governance by appointing Provincial Ministers to run portfolios like Education and Local Government, whilst keeping the key areas, like Finance, Defence and Law and Order, in their firm grip. The 1857 Mutiny had shaken their confidence and the drubbing in WWI had well and truly disturbed their aplomb. This increasing sense of insecurity led the government to promulgate the iniquitous Rowlatt Act in 1919, which gave it draconian powers to suppress any move towards insurrection or sedition. The whole concept of Habeas corpus was abolished and imprisonment and internment without trial became the order of the day. Fear is a dreadful tutor and makes individuals react irrationally, particularly when privilege and pre-eminence are threatened. At Amritsar on 13 April 1919, a peaceful crowd of men, women and children had gathered to hold a meeting in an enclosed enclave called Jallianwalla Bagh. There was no hostile intent or rowdiness' but the meeting was held in defiance of an order banning all public meetings and a gathering of more than four persons under the Rowlatt Act. Brigadier General Reginald Dyer ordered his Gorkhas to open fire on the crowd, killing 379 persons and wounding over 1200. There was only one entrance to the enclave, which was guarded by Dyer's Gorkhas so there was no way that the crowd could have dispersed. To add insult to injury, Dyer demanded that all individuals had to crawl on their hands and knees before him. As he said afterwards, he was 'going to teach the Indians a lesson that they would never forget.'

All Indians had to *salaam* every European, and young Indians were mercilessly flogged without any trial.

He certainly succeeded and India never forgave the British for this inhuman and heinous act. Dyer was recalled to England, where he was assassinated by an Indian patriot. The sad sequel to this horrific act was that many Britishers approved of what he had done. The fate of the British in India was now sealed. Without the Indian, the government would grind to a halt. But, typically, the timid Hindus, led by Gandhi and his cohorts, did not rise in open revolt and crush the handful of Britishers who lived in India, but started a surreptitious campaign of 'civil disobedience' against the regime. The intention was to court arrest and fill the prisons to bursting point. As usual the Muslim was nowhere in sight, and, with only a few exceptions, contributed 'zilch' to the movement. As I have said many times, the Muslim was only too happy to live as a pampered minority under the British umbrella. Anything was better than having to become a second rate citizen under the despised, idolatrous

Hindu that the Muslim had ruled over for nearly 800 years. Many pathetic excuses were put forward but the all-time classic was the overthrow of the Ottoman Empire by the British and the demise of the Turkish Khalif in 1922. This led to the Khillafat Movement in Kerala by the Muslim Moplahs, who wanted the reinstatement of the Khalif. This was an absurd and strange logic, as post war Turkey had been totally revitalized by Mustaffa Kamal Ataturk and the new regime had no intention of reinstating the deposed Khalif. Yet here were Indian Muslim Moplahs going on a rampage, demanding his return. What is even more absurd is that a totally confused and muddle- headed Gandhi sided with their cause. The frustrated Moplahs then vented their spleen on their innocent Hindu neighbours, which led to massacres and demands that they must convert to Islam. Hindu women were raped and Hindu property was looted and destroyed.

Gandhi arrived back in India from South Africa in 1914. The Indian National Congress, which was going to spearhead the Independence movement, was founded by an Englishman, Allan Octavian Hume, the Secretary for Agriculture in the government of Earl Robert Bulwer Lytton (1876–80). Lytton was a sick man, suffering from a severe affliction of piles that made him an opium addict. During his reign India went through a dreadful famine that killed over seven million persons. Many Indians could have been saved by importing rice from Burma, but he refused permission because he was a follower of Trevelyan's ridiculous dictum that famine was God's 'Providential Event', which was beyond the power of any government to avert. To compound matters, he prohibited farmers in Orissa from making salt, which would have augmented their meagre income and enabled them to buy food. All this sickened Hume, especially the callous indifference of the government to the suffering of the Indian people. Like in Ireland, the Liberal Government in London seemed to be incapable of developing a plan for self-government for the two countries. Hume was only one of a galaxy of English persons to espouse the cause for Indian Independence. Annie Besant started off as a Theosophist under the spell of Madame

Blavatsky but rapidly moved into political life and, with Pandit Madan Mohan Malaviya, they laid the foundation of The Benares Hindu University. In 1917 she started the 'Home Rule for India League' and in 1918 she became the President of The Indian National Congress. Gandhi arrived in India in 1914 when the Independence Movement was already a well-established entity. Gandhi was a strange, mixed up and confused man, suffused with Hinduism's unrealistic, ascetic beliefs, that the world of the senses was a trap for the unwary. In India, all religions permeate through the entire fabric of the nation, particularly Hinduism, with its amorphous philosophy of total tolerance of everything. Gandhi was quick to grasp the nettle and he shed his European garb and donned a hand-spun 'dhoti', the simple garb of Hinduism's mendicants and holy men. So far so good and now he could preach to the Brahmins, demanding Independence with the authority of a 'saint,' who had renounced the carnal pleasures of sex and soft living. The rejection of Bradford's woollens and Manchester's cottons would hurt Britain where it was most vulnerable- its hip pocket. A very clever ploy, but Gandhi was also about to damage India's Industrial base as he rejected Capitalism per se, as a corrupting influence of the West, based on the profit motif. In its place he wanted to introduce the concept of 'swadeshi' or self-reliance based on the totally unrealistic ideal of handspun and hand-woven cloth, called *'khadi'*. The *khadi* concept became the uniform of the Indian National Congress and its Brahmin coterie, including Motilal Nehru and his son, Jawaharlal, who got rid of their expensive suits and donned the new uniform. In all fairness it must be said that rural India got a boost from the *khadi* innovation, but the villages could not possibly clothe India's millions. Gandhi's denunciation of Capitalism did not fall on deaf ears. This absurd credo was now picked up by his heir apparent, Jawaharlal Nehru, a crypto-Communist, who was enamoured by socialism. Under Nehru, India was going to be denuded of its miniscule industrial base and, in its place, Nehru was going to introduce a Russian-styled planned economy, with the nationalization of all banks, insurance companies and coal mines. But worse was to come with the creation of the so-called

'Public Sector Units' (PSU), or government-owned companies run by incompetent and untrained Indian Administrative Service (IAS) Officials. A 'Monopolies Commission' (MC) was created to ensure that the existing business houses did not use their financial muscle to intrude into new ventures, which were arbitrarily going to be the preserve of small entrepreneurs. Private enterprise was well and truly smothered, and all new ventures or the expansion of existing facilities needed the imprimatur of officialdom. All these rules and regulations made the public servant the linchpin in all matters of running the country. Single-handed, Nehru had created the infamous 'Permit Licence Raj' (PLR), which was rated as one of the most corrupt and venal systems in the world. 'Babudom', or the vicious rule of the totally corrupt civilian underdog, had India by the throat. India's GDP was one of the lowest in the developing world and there were shortages of everything and endless waiting lists for every commodity.This dreadful policy destroyed every shred of competitiveness in Indian industry, which survived under a blanket of exorbitant import tariffs. Nehru's vindictiveness towards business and the wealthier segments of society, knew no bounds and taxation reached absurd and extortionate levels. Every source of income was taxed, and even expenditure was taxed. India was crippled by Nehru for generations. This was the miserable legacy created by this dogma-ridden couple. Gandhi, a quasi-religious freak, and a crypto-Communist, Nehru. Smuggling, boot legging, bribery, corruption and black marketeering became not only survival mechanisms but necessities. Rapacious and unscrupulous politicians and a thieving bureaucracy thrived under Nehru's PLR, and India groaned under all this iniquity. But Nehru's legacy to India was still incomplete. He was destined to take India to the very edge of annihilation, as we will see

But now it is time to get back to the archaic world of Earl Lytton's Delhi. His daughter, Emily, married an up and coming architect, Edwin Lutyens, who was destined to become the creator of the magnificent city of New Delhi on Raisina Hill in 1912–18. His marriage to Emily Lytton was a disaster as the young lady had become a Theosophist, and eschewed sex and any form of intimacy. During Lytton's Vice-Regal tenure, in (1877–8), millions of tons of grain were shipped to Britain to stabilize prices, while India reeled with shortages and soaring prices. At the same time he promulgated 'The Anti- Charitable Contributions Act,' that prevented aid to flow from Britain to India and from Indian cities to the countryside. It was as though he had assumed the role of persecutor of India's rural poor. For example, Sir Richard Temple bought Burmese rice in 1873–4 and distributed it free to the neediest in India. This action was strongly opposed by Trevelyan and Lytton. To compound the misery of India's suffering poor, Lytton cut back on water storage facilities on the grounds that these were part of the game plan of so-called 'irrigation fanatics'. Admittedly Lytton was a sick man, but he proved to be a total disaster for India.

It is time to pause for a moment and do a cursory stock-take of the state of affairs on the sub-continent after WW I. On the one hand we have a rather subdued British Government that had lost some of its pristine, flamboyant hauteur and was chary to 'cuff and kick' the native after the unmitigated disaster of Jallianwalla Bagh. An iron fist in the velvet glove was the order of the day in order to play along with Gandhi and his Brahmin cohorts, baying for 'Swaraj'. The British had the Indian Princes well and truly heeled with titles and decorations and the paraphernalia of pseudo-royalty and protocol imitative of the British Royals. The Muslim population was meek and subdued and was thriving as a privileged minority under British tutelage that had craftily bestowed a disproportionate number of job vacancies in all the services, particularly in the army, under the misguided views of General Roberts, the C-in-C, who created the absurd myths of the 'martial classes' and the 'Punjab as the Sword Arm' of the Indian Army. The Muslims constituted barely 9 per cent of the population but were given over 30 per cent of seats in the Viceroy's Legislative Council. This was all a part of the British Realpolitik of 'Divide and Rule'. In one deft stroke the British emasculated the Hindu majority and created a solid pillar of support for the Empire with the Muslims in tow. Administration was in the capable hands of a brilliant

Indian Civil Service (ICS) with the unquestioning support of the Anglo-Indian community filling the lower echelons of the railways and postal services. Business was thriving in Calcutta and Bombay and the Koi Hais (KH) were having a field day, particularly in Calcutta, with their 'managing agencies' controlling the tea, jute and coal trades. These were the halcyon days of the Raj, and 'Pax Britannica' reigned supreme. The only discordant note was the incessant chatter for 'Home Rule' being spewed by Gandhi and his cohorts. Indianization of the army was put on hold. This suited the British who continued in the belief that the Indian did not have the pre-requisite qualities to command. The Nationalist leaders were suffused with Gandhi's Hindu-inspired beliefs of 'ahimsa' or non-violence and were fundamentally opposed to the military mindset. To them the army was a waste of money. This purblind attitude was destined to have disastrous consequences in years to come. Britain's 'Divide and Rule' Policy reaped a rich harvest, quite beyond their own expectations. Invaders from Central Asia and refugees escaping religious persecution found a haven in India and over the years they were assimilated and became Indians. They lived in isolated ghettos and rarely socialized, but language and culture produced a tenuous bonding. The true aliens were the British, who had no intention to assimilate. Pride of race created aloofness and the British, with some rare exceptions, lived in an ivory tower of their own making. India was the classic 'milch cow' that the British were going to unashamedly exploit and use to make enough money to retire to a small farm 'back home'.

Unwittingly the British were paving the way for the dismemberment of India by pandering to the Muslim minority and feeding them with the political garbage that they were a separate nation. A divided Nation with squabbling factions made for easy pickings and control. A United India was a nightmare for the Raj, which had no intention of relinquishing its Empire. To this end the British artificially fostered communal riots between Hindus and Muslims. The concept of two separate nations fell on fertile ground. Among the Muslims, Sir Syed Ahmad Khan founded the Aligarh Muslim University (AMU) to provide modern tertiary education, through the English language, to up-and-coming Muslims who, otherwise, would have to compete against their Hindu counterparts. The AMU strongly fostered the two-nation theory. Even among the Hindus there was growing distrust of the pampered Muslims, who were thriving on British patronage. Unfortunately Gandhi had introduced a distinct Hindu flavour to the Independence Movement, which made the Muslims uncomfortable and they opted for the creation of the Muslim League (ML,) to fight for their cause. The creation of separate Muslim electorates by the British furthered this dichotomy.

Compared to the vigorous Brahmin legal coterie of the Congress, the Muslims were like 'Babes in the Wood'. They were basically ingenuous farmers or *zamindar*s (landowners) or skilled artisans. The professions were dominated by the Hindus. When it came to the wily game of politics, the Muslim floundered and the community languished for want of leadership.The fear of becoming second-class citizens in a Hindu-dominated government, led by the Congress, was a very real cause for concern. Muhammad Ali Jinnah was the 'deus-ex-machina' that the Muslim community needed to bond it into a political entity. He was a prominent barrister in Bombay, who joined the Congress in 1906, but left after disagreements on leadership and joined the ML in 1913. He was by no means a rabid Muslim. As a matter of fact he was a Muslim by birth and little else. He was married to a Parsi lady. He dressed in expensive, beautifully tailored suits and loved his Scotch. He was one of the few Muslims who had political acumen and quickly realized that in a secular society the Muslim could never compete with the Hindu and, inevitably, would fall further and further behind. The only solution out of this conundrum was the partition of India, and the creation of a Muslim Majority country, called Pakistan, which would also be the home of minority Hindu and Sikh communities. The white band on the Pakistani flag was supposed to represent this minority. He quite genuinely believed in this political solution, but being a 'fringe Muslim', he had a poor understanding of the underlying bellicose fundamentalism of his co-religionists. Once partition took place, all hell broke loose. This hecatomb claimed over a million lives and displaced millions. The stupidity of creating Pakistan rests squarely on the shoulders of that dreadful duo: Gandhi and Nehru, who were so hungry for power that they could not wait and sacrificed the integrity of Mother India. The Muslims declared 'Direct Action Day', when they were going to unleash a bloody mayhem on the placid Hindus if they were not going to be bullied into giving them what they wanted. On 16 August 1946, Jinnah said, 'We shall have India divided or we shall have India destroyed!'. Here were a miniscule nine per cent of the population threatening 91 per cent of the population with extinction. Sounds like a pantomime or a comedy-turn, straight out of 'Music Hall' or Vaudeville!! Just imagine the shock if the Hindus had decided to embrace the 'Night of the Long Knives', took on the Muslims on their own terms and gave them a taste of their own bloody game plan. At long last we have the scenario of 'The Mouse that Roared'. Or alternatively, let the British sort out this imbroglio that was created by them by their Divide and Rule Policy. Nevertheless, all this is wishful thinking when you have to deal with an emasculated Hindu leadership that has never confronted a National Problem with decisive and resolute action and, instead, has always retreated back into the odious Hindu philosophical garbage of *'ahimsa'* and *'satyagraha'* ('and truth will prevail'). Don't take my word for it but look at what this idiocy of Partition has achieved. Pakistan was created by the Islamic intelligentsia of the United Provinces, Bihar, East Bengal and the fanatical seminaries like Dar-ul-Uloom in the town of Deoband and its sister school, Mazahir-ul-Uloom in Saharanpur. Having done their mischief, these organizations are still alive and thriving and the citizens of these states have not migrated to Pakistan in any appreciable numbers Those who have are labelled with the derogatory label of *'Mohajirs'* or refugees. But I will deal separately with the parlous state of these unfortunate individuals when I shift the focus to Pakistan. So what has been achieved by Partition other than a dreadful genocide of Hindus and Sikhs in Pakistan? The bulk of the Muslim population in the three states mentioned above has not moved, in fact the population has mushroomed right across what was undivided India. Here are some facts and figures to consider:

1. The total Muslim Population in undivided India in 1947 was 9 per cent. The population in present day India is 147 million or 13.4 per cent in 2006. The population in Pakistan is 161 million and in Bangladesh it is 122 million
2. The population of Pakistan was about 40 million in 1950. It is 161 million today.
3. There is no way that Pakistan can feed this burgeoning population or provide employment. To the West is the arid wasteland Afghanistan. The only conduit is India and infiltration has already reached alarming levels. India should be sealing her borders, but instead the borders are becoming more porous by increasing rail and road transport between the two countries.
4. It is estimated that there are over 1 million illegal immigrants from Bangldesh living in India and nearly 9,000 illegal immigrants enter India every day. The main targets are Assam and West Bengal because the border is hopelessly porous and the 'Muslim vote bank' of the totally corrupt state and national governments are not deporting the illegal migrants, even when they are identified, but issue them with ration-cards and other papers, which blends them with Indian citizenry. If India does not wake up and act decisively, another Partition is in the making in Eastern India.
5. Muslim fecundity is going to turn India into an Islamic country by stealth. This is all a part and parcel of the long-term plan of Pakistan's Inter Services Intelligence (ISI). This subject is vast and intricate and will be covered in depth when we deal with Pakistan.

Partition would have made some sense had it resulted in an exchange of populations and an expulsion of the majority of Muslims into Pakistan. Jinnah quite genuinely believed that Pakistan, in his ideology, would be some sort of secular state with a Muslim majority to counter balance India with a secular Hindu majority. Jinnah, the ideologue, had not envisioned that Islam is basically a vicious, bigoted creed, that has no tolerance for other faiths and secularism is anathema to Islamic thinking.

Jinnah said and I quote: 'You are free, free to go to your temples, free to go to your mosques or any other places of worship in this State of Pakistan. You may belong to any religion or caste or creed that has nothing to do with the business of State'.

Wishful thinking by the founder of Pakistan. Other than Religion there is no common bond to unite the very disparate people who live in the territories that constitute the State of Pakistan. The country is dominated by the Punjabis, who make up over 40 per cent of the population and over 80 per cent of the military that virtually runs the country. The Punjabis are the peasant yeomen farmers and soldiers who thrived on the largesse provided by the British with the massive irrigation schemes that converted the semi-arid and desert countryside into the food bowl of pre-partition India. In every sense, Pakistan is the aborted offspring of Britain's 'divide and rule' agenda that firstly planted the seed of the 'two nation theory', and then created the myth of the 'Punjab being the Sword Arm' of the Indian Army and amply rewarded the soldiery with large tracts of fertile irrigated land.

Pakistan was created under the myth of Islamic solidarity. The *ummah* or Muslim brotherhood transgresses all territorial boundaries and owes loyalty only to Allah and not to any one nation. In fact Islam over the years grew into a mish-mash of contentious sects that were forever at each other's throats. Each sect claimed authenticity and dubbed the others as charlatans and apostates. About 80 per cent of the population is Sunni Muslim and 20 per cent is Shia and a lively hatred has continued over the centuries, with regular bombings and killings punctuating life in this Islamic paradise and elsewhere. The minority problem has been permanently solved by the genocide of Hindus and Sikhs. Rightly or wrongly Pakistan, 'the land of the pure', has cleansed' itself, unlike the bumbling Hindus in India, who have a growing Muslim fifth- column in their midst, thanks to the muddle-headed and utterly confused leadership of Gandhi. India is going to pay dearly for this arrant stupidity. I am not suggesting that Indian Muslims should be forcefully evicted from their homeland. This would be tantamount to a Nazi-style racial purging but state and the national governments continue to pander to the Muslim voter by granting special concessions and privileges. The classic example of this stupidity is the granting of the 'Haj Subsidy' to pilgrims. No Muslim country in the world, including Pakistan, pays money to the Haj pilgrim to subsidize his expenses. As a matter of fact, this act is considered to be 'Haram' or forbidden, under Muslim law. Yet a purblind Indian Government persists in this folly. But this is only the tip of the iceberg. 'Affirmative Action' gives huge concessions to Muslims in entrance to elite Tertiary Institutions like the Indian Institutes of Technology (IIT) and the Indian Institute of Management (IIM), let alone Medical and Engineering Colleges. Leaving aside Islamic countries, Common Law is the prevailing Law that applies to all citizens. Muslims living in the EU, USA, Australia and every other country have to conform to the country's Common Law, which prohibits bigamy. Once again a pusillanimous Indian Government has not enforced its Common Law on the Muslim and bigamy is rife in this community. If the majority Hindus and every other race and creed are covered by Common Law, why are the Muslims outside the purview of the law? Those Muslims who persist in demanding the infamous rights of bigamy are most welcome to pack their bags and migrate to the Islamic 'hellholes' of Pakistan or Bangladesh. In one fell swoop this would put a brake on the Malthusian abyss of fecundity that is engulfing the Muslim population. It would engender a new respect to the female gender and give women equal rights, denied under the Shariat Law. Above all else it would clip the wings of fanatical religious seminaries like the Dar-ul-Uloom in Deoband, which regard themselves as the arbiters on all Islamic issues. It would bring the Muslim into the mainstream of India, but first of all the obsequious Hindu will have to grow up and become a 'Man'.That is a tall order.

I have repeatedly stressed that Islam cannot coexist with other religions as it regards all non-Muslims as Infidels. It is the bounden duty of every Muslim to convert the Infidel to Islam or to behead those who refuse. This is a injunction straight out of the Quran. Furthermore Muslims are prohibited to associate or have any contact with the infidel as this creates 'Najas' or pollution of the Momin or true believer. How on earth can any religion coexist with such blind bigotry?

The Students' Islamic Movement of India (SIMI) is a fanatical *jihadi* organization, a protégé of the Jamaat-e-Islami Hind (JEIH) founded in Aligarh on 25 April 1977, by Dr Shahid Badar Falahi, Professor of Journalism at Western Illinois University. SIMI was banned as a terrorist organization in July 2005, under the Unlawful Activities (Prevention) Act 1967. The basic tenets are

1. The establishment of a world Islamic Caliphate
2. The rejection of the Indian Constitution and the establishment of an Islamic government in Delhi
3. Rejection of Secularism and the establishment of Shariat Law.

This is total sedition. The avowed intention is to woo young Muslim students and professionals to al Quaida and Islamic fundamentalism. In spite of being banned, SIMI seems to be growing and has been involved in numerous bombings incidents in India. Obviously the current laws are inadequate to put a lid on these traitors. I would like to say unequivocally that SIMI and other traitorous organizations of this ilk must be hounded out and its members exterminated ruthlessly. This would also send a salutary message to the ISI in Pakistan and Bangladesh that their days are numbered and that they, and their sister terrorist organizations, are also on India's 'hit list.' As though in anticipation of this turn of events, the ISI has changed its tactics and is switching its focus from infiltration into Kashmir to targeting a wide range of bomb attacks throughout India and Nepal. Crucial to this strategy is the recruitment of operatives from organizations like SIMI, who are being trained in Pakistan and Bangladesh. Initially the Indian recruits are smuggled into Iran via the Zahedan border town and then back into Quetta for training with the Taliban. The trained operative now enters back into India, often with a Bangladesh passport.

The ISI has a very clear agenda, the destruction of India as a secular Nation and the establishment of an Islamic 'Belt', stretching from the Caspian Sea to the border of Myanmar, with the Caliphate located in Pakistan, the only Islamic nuclear power. That would finally close the chapter on the two-Nation theory, with the destruction of the Dar-ul-Harb in India and the installation of Dar-ul-Islam. This is all a part of Islam's 'Divine Destiny', awash with Allah's cornucopia of oil and gas. Democracy is a colonial conspiracy to subjugate the Muslim. The Islamic Caliphate would flourish under the shade of the Islamic Sanjir or sword. Within seven months of Jinnah's death, the Constituent Assembly of Pakistan passed the Objectives Resolution in March. 1948, that ISLAM would be the basis of the future Constitution. Pakistan had finally thrown off the pretence of being a democratic nation and emerged as an Islamic Republic.

The ISI functions like a state within a state. It professes to be the Intelligence wing of the Pakistan Army, and is manned by officers from the service, but the Heads of the Army only have a tenuous hold on its activities and leadership. One would imagine that since the Army controls the purse strings, that the old adage 'he who pays the piper calls the tune' would take the mickey out of the ISI. Likewise, since the civilian government of Pakistan theoretically funds the Army, it controls the Service. Both assumptions are incorrect. The ISI functions as a semi-autonomous unit, with funds coming from the Arab Gulf States and a steady flow of 'narco-dollars' from the cultivation of opium along the Pakistan-Afganistan border by the Taliban. The civilian government of Pakistan is the official recipient of American aid, but the government is run by an Army dictatorship that siphons off nearly a third of the budget for defence. The bogeyman is India, and the clandestine war in Kashmir, which silences any criticism. For the Services, and particularly the Army, the stakes are high to ensure perpetual military control of the country's economy. The Pakistan Army is the biggest stakeholder in all spheres of agriculture and industry. It owns and runs some of the most lucrative businesses in the country and is not about to forego its privileged 'pot of gold', which enables its flabby retirees to live in the lap of luxury. To hell with all the 'clap trap' about democracy! That is meant for consumption by the foreign media and the Americans, who were being mercilessly milked by that master of deception, President Pervez Musharraf, who took with both hands and gave nothing. The Americans have been taken for a ride with empty promises by Musharraf. If Osama bin Laden and his sidekick, Aiman al Zawahiri, were hiding in Afghanistan, they were protected by the ancient 'Puchtunwali' doctrine of 'refuge' which prohibited any harm to be inflicted on them while they were in Pushtun custody. The leadership and the Afghan President, Hamid Karzai, knew that the pair were 'untouchable' but the charade continued. The Americans were still good for many more billions of dollars in aid.

Pakistan's Punjabi army has wreaked havoc in Balochistan, which has never taken kindly to its involuntary inclusion in the country. It is by far the largest state in the country with 135,000 square miles and a miniscule population of barely 6 million inhabitants. It is rich in minerals, like copper and gold, and its SUI gas-fields supply 40 per cent of Pakistan's energy, but Balochistan gets a meagre 12.4 per cent in royalties. This blatant exploitation has never been addressed, resulting in the periodic blowing up of the gas lines to Karachi and the Punjab. Balochistan is a feudal country, ruled by the Bugti, Marri and Mengal tribes. The leader was Nawab Akbar Khan Bugti, a 78-year-old Sardar, who was killed on 26th August 2006 in a bombing by the Pakistan Air Force. This was a tactical blunder by Musharraf, who seems to have had a penchant for lashing out without considering the consequences. His earlier escapade was the fracas in Kargil in Kashmir, where the Pakistan Army got its fourth hiding from the Indian Army. The Pakistanis were in headlong retreat and were saved from total annihilation by the intervention of the Americans, who prevailed upon India not to cross over the LoC (Line of Control) and escalate the conflict. Stupidly, India acquiesced.

When Pakistan was created it consisted of a part of the Punjab, the NWFP, Balochistan and Sind, plus East Pakistan, hived off from West Bengal. A 1,000-mile corridor separated the two wings of the country. East Pakistan was racially different and the language was Bengali. In West Pakistan the national language was Urdu, which had been artificially superimposed on the people who spoke their own regional languages. Urdu is a hybrid language of the Muslims in North-Western India, who, by and large, have not migrated to Pakistan. East Pakistan had a larger population than West Pakistan and generated bigger export earnings for the country, but the Pakistan Army was predominantly Punjabi and ran the country. The Pakistani Punjabis had an arrogant racial dislike for their eastern countrymen and mercilessly exploited them and discouraged them from moving to West Pakistan for work. Clearly this state of affairs was not going to continue and when the East Pakistanis began to claim their rights, the Pakistan Army moved in to forcibly stop all dissent. What followed was another holocaust with rape, pillaging and slaughter.The first victims were the Hindus, who fled across the border into India, followed by the Muslim Intelligentsia. The Pakistani army was on a bloody rampage. India was inundated with 10 million desperate refugees and there was no staunching this flood. In 1971 the Indian Army entered East Pakistan at the request of the President of the Awami League, Mujibur Rahman. The Pakistan Army was routed and 90,000 prisoners of war were captured and taken to India. East Pakistan declared its independence and emerged as a new nation called Bangladesh. Over 340,000 Pakistani civilians of Indian origin, mostly from Bihar, were left stranded, as the West Pakistan Government would not allow them to return.

It is now time to return to Pakistan and the fate of the Indian émigrés who moved to Pakistan in 1947. The majority of Urdu-speaking Indians settled in the port city of Karachi, where they rapidly became the predominant business community and filled the bureaucracy. They constitute nearly 50 per cent of the population of Karachi and are resented by the less affluent Pathans, Sindhis and Balochis, who refer to them as 'Mohajirs', a derogatory term for a refugee. The Mohajirs felt defenceless against the belligerence of the other communities who resented the success of these 'aliens in their land'. The Mohajirs retaliated by forming their own political party, 'The Mohajir Qaumi Movement' (MQM), led by a charismatic leader, Altaf Hussain, who spends most of his time in London and periodically comes to Karachi. The relatively docile Mohajirs now went on the offensive and the streets of Karachi became a battleground. Karachi was like a city straight out of the American Wild West. The city was under siege, with the wealthy hiding behind high walls and protected by armed guards. Karachi was becoming ungovernable. The financial hub of Pakistan was in chaos and the country survived on American largesse. But there were other serious problems facing the country. The fanatical Taliban came into being, as an offshoot of the ISI, when the Soviets invaded Afghanistan in 1979 to buoy up their Communist puppet, Muhammad Najibullah, in Kabul. For the Americans this was a God-sent opportunity to give the Soviets a bloody nose without involving their own troops. All the fighting was going to be done by the Mujahidin, the Afghan Islamic warriors, trained by the ISI, funded and equipped by large shipments of arms provided by the Americans. This Machiavellian plan worked and the Taliban occupied Kabul and established a dreadful, barbaric Islamic regime. The Soviets retreated in 1989 and the Americans, having achieved their nefarious objective, left a war-torn and shattered country to the Taliban and the ISI. Little did the Americans realize that they were going to be 'hoist by their own petard,' and that they would be involved in a long and bloody war in Afghanistan, trying to establish a democratic government in a country that had never heard of this strange phenomenon. The horrific regime of the Taliban was ended with massive bombing by the Americans, who were hoping to kill the al Qaida leaders. This plan failed miserably and the warriors were allowed to escape across the border into Pakistan, with the help and complicity of the ISI and the Pakistan Army. As in Iraq, the Americans and their NATO allies, are bogged down in an un-winnable war. With the covert connivance of Pakistan, the Taliban has risen from its ashes like the proverbial Phoenix, and, from its bases in Pakistan, it is fearlessly attacking the Afghan Government establishments, the Americans and the NATO forces, who are fighting with their hands tied behind their backs, for they cannot pursue the Taliban across the border into Pakistan. In the meantime, Musharraf signed the Waziristan

Accord, which handed over control of this vital border to the Taliban, and released 2,500 foreign Mujahidin prisoners to join the Taliban. In addition, the Pakistan Army has been pulled back into their barracks. The Afghan tragedy rapidly deteriorated into a terrible farce, with an incompetent American leadership floundering helplessly like a rudderless ship. The Taliban and the ISI thrive in this imbroglio. Fighting and sniping is the National pastime of the Pathans, and the only way of handling this fratricidal community is to destroy them in their hideouts in the Tora Bora Mountains. But this can only be done once the Americans and their NATO allies bite the bullet and cross over into Pakistan. The Taliban is biding its time. It knows that the foreign forces in Afghanistan are getting weary and disheartened by their lack of success in establishing a workable democratic government in Kabul and building a reliable infrastructure, and sooner or later they will be going home. It is extremely unlikely that Hamid Karzari will survive on his own and the government in Kabul will collapse. This is when the Taliban, supported by the ISI and the Pakistan Army, will once again occupy Kabul. For Pakistan, its Afghan neighbour must be subservient and in its sphere of influence.

Musharraf and the Pakistan Army loved to play 'footsy' with the Americans as their very survival depends on them, but there is no love lost when its comes down to the man in the street who, regards America and Israel as the 'SHAITAN', or the Devil Incarnate. Unlike India, where the Americans are admired and respected, the situation in Pakistan is just the opposite. Since the 9/11 fracas, the USA has paid Pakistan $600 million in cash and $350 million in military aid; $ 3.6 billion in USA and IMF credits; postponed repayment of $ 13.5 billion debt to a US-led Consortium, and a $1 billion debt relief. In exchange for this massive bail out, the USA was allowed to use some airfields for fighting the Taliban. The sheer size and nature of the military aid given to Pakistan was obviously intended for use against India and has de-stabilized the entire sub-continent. The bumbling Americans have not learnt the harsh reality that you cannot buy love and respect, and they continued to be lead by the nose by that master of deceit, Pervez Musharraf.

But this game of political roulette has a very dangerous down side. Musharraf has lost his hold on the top brass of the army, which is getting indoctrinated into Islamic fundamentalism ever since General Zia-ul-Haq took the reins of Office. In order to consolidate his dual role of Chief of General Staff (CGS) of the Army and President of Pakistan, he has had to divest power to the Muttahida Majlis-e-Amal (MMA), a group of six religious parties who now govern two states, Balochistan and the NWFP, and have introduced strict Sharia laws. The MMA include the terrorist groups that Musharraf is supposed to eliminate. This is done in name only. The organizations are supposedly banned and then re-emerge under a different name. This is a game of charades and achieves absolutely nothing. But what is even more stupid and dangerous is that Pakistan has now emerged as a nuclear power with rockets bought from North Korea and China, and all with the full knowledge of the Americans. This lack a daisical attitude of the USA towards Pakistan and its protégé, A.Q. Khan, whose skullduggery stole the technology of manufacturing the atom bomb, has prompted Iran to play 'copy cat'. If Pakistan can get away with it and 'thumb its nose' at the Americans, then so can Iran' The Americans will rue the day that they were so naïve as to allow Pakistan to go Nuclear.

In the meantime events were moving fast as Musharraf was losing popularity and support. He stepped down from being the CGS of the Army and handed over to General Ashfaq Pervez Kiyani, who was commanding the ISI. In Islamabad, a fanatical Islamic Sect called Salafists, occupied the Lal Masjid, or Red Mosque, and had to be forcibly evicted by the army with considerable loss of life. This increased his unpopularity. The Americans, meanwhile, were still singing their paean for democracy and an embattled Musharraf was unwillingly compelled to remove the sanctions of exile imposed on Benazir Bhutto, the leader of the Pakistan Peoples Party (PPP). She returned to Pakistan to contest an election, but was assassinated on the 27 December, 2007. The leadership of the PPP passed to her husband, Asif Zardari, who was released from prison, being charged for corruption. Erstwhile Prime Minister, Nawaz Sharif, who had been deposed by Musharraf, also returned from exile in Saudi Arabia. Zardari and Nawaz Sharif formed a coalition of sorts and hoped to oust a shaky Musharraf, who was hanging on precariously. The net result was, and still is, a restive, unstable country, with a massive population that cannot be fed and employed. As the economy weakens there will be an increase in religious fervour, spurred on by organizations like the Tablighi Jama', which foster Islamic regeneration. India's burgeoning economy is like a red rag to a bull, and there will be an escalation of infiltration and terrorist attacks by the ISI on every centre that thrives on tourism, like the recent unprovoked attacks in Jaipur, airports, and Bombay. The biggest threat is posed by possible offshore attacks on oil and gas drilling rigs in the Gulf of Cambay and the Arabian Sea. It is vital that the Indian Navy and the Coast Guard are equipped to safeguard these installations. However it must be remembered that Islam only respects the sword. It is basically a cowardly regime and has the mentality of a bully. If India presents its usual Hindu soft belly, it will once again face Islamic intimidation and persecution. The best medicine to treat the ISI menace from Pakistan and Bangladesh is with the ferocious 'quid pro quo' mentality of 'I am bigger and stronger, so watch your p's and q's little man'. But the very first step is to seal the frontiers and stop infiltration. The second step is to re-introduce the POTA (Prevention of Terrorism Act) and forcefully expel the 1 million illegal Bangladeshis who are living in India. The third step is to complete the fence around Bangladesh and ensure that the Bangladesh Rifles get the message that they will be smashed by the Border Security Forces (BSF) and the Indian Army, if they try to, or remove, the Border Post. Fourth, is to infiltrate into Bangladesh and smash the insurgent forces like ULFA in their home bases and cease the political 'blarney' of trying to negotiate with seditious groups. Fifth step is to populate the frontier along the Rajasthan Canal with ex-army personnel. Give them irrigated farmland and small arms to protect themselves and their property. Sixth step is to strengthen the Indo-Tibet border, particularly in Arunachal Pradesh, as the Chinese are likely to take advantage of the uncertainties created by India's more bellicose stance vis-à-vis Pakistan and Bangladesh. The incredible Quinghai-Tibet Railway to Lhasa, built at a cost of $ 4.2 billion, has radically changed the military and socio-economic climate along the entire border, as China can move troops and armaments rapidly right to the Indian border. China is greedily eyeing Arunachal Pradesh, as the territory is very rich in timber and has abundant rainfall, which the Chinese desperately want to tap for the relatively arid alto-plane of Tibet. Strategically, they would be sitting on the high ground, overlooking the entire Assam Valley and Bhutan and the massive river systems flowing south into India. Annexation of Arunachal Pradesh will be the precursor to moving into the Assam Valley eventually, and linking up with their Naval Bases in Chittagong and the Greater Cocos Island in Myanmar. The eventual intention is to build a massive hydroelectric facility in the world's deepest gorge, where the Tsangpo drops from 12,000 feet to about 2,000 feet, and enters India as the Dihang. This giant hydroelectric plant will be the biggest in the world, generating over 40,000 MW's of electricity. Once Assam is annexed, China will link up with the Communist government in West Bengal and the Maoist-Naxalites in Nepal and Eastern India. This dismal scenario can be averted, provided India wakes up and mobilizes itself. Once again the threat to Arunachal Pradesh must be realized as a very real danger and the realization must dawn that Indian Territory is not negotiable and must be defended. India must call China's bluff and prepare itself for a drawn out military conflict. If China tries to occupy India's redoubt in Tawang, India must retaliate by attacking Chinese posts in Tibet by air. There is a Chinese saying, that China has five fingers on India's throat. The palm of the hand is Tibet and the five fingers are, the Karakorum Highway into Pakistan and the Bara Hoti out-posts in Garhwal, Nepal, Sikkim and Arunachal Pradesh. China has scant respect for India as a political force, and regards its leadership as a pack of 'paper tigers'. However, only time will tell. Nehru's disgraceful 'Hindi Chini Bhai Bhai' (India and China are brothers) mantra, and the absurd Pancha Shila political garbage, have not only put egg on India's face, but has caused the disgraceful defeat of the Indian Army in 1972 at the hands of the Chinese Peoples Liberation Army (PLA).

The disastrous earthquake in Sichuan Province on 12 May 2008, temporarily diverted China's attention from Arunachal Pradesh, but they are back in force now the Beijing Olympics are over. Unlike India, China is a determined adversary with a clear-cut plan for the future. The only impediment to achieving its' objectives is a determined riposte from India. Is this likely to materialize? Can a corrupt, puerile society throw off its' ancient antecedents overnight and meet the challenges of the future head on? I have my doubts, but such is the fate of wishes that 'even beggars could be kings.'

10

The 'Quit India' Movement

It is now time to return to Delhi and the burgeoning 'Quit India' Movement (QIM), which was gaining momentum every day, with strikes, street protests and '*hartals*' (shut downs) paralysing the country. Because of Gandhi's philosophy' of 'ahimsa' (non-violence) there was very little physical confrontation with the British, who, nevertheless, reacted by arresting the Congress leaders and incarcerating them. The Muslim leadership was conspicuous by its absence, but this was only to be expected for the Muslims prospered under British preferential tutelage. The Grand Durbar of 1911 was an outstanding success and put the stamp of British Sovereignty over India.

Lord Curzon had moved the capital from Calcutta to Delhi, but the administration was cramped for space in the walled 'Old City' of Delhi. It was decided to move out southwards and to build a brand new Capital on Delhi's Raisina Hill. The work was entrusted to an up-and-coming architect, Edwin Lutyens, who had married Emily Lytton, the daughter of the Viceroy, Lord Lytton. Lutyens did a spectacular job and created a magnificent city called New Delhi, with its spectacular Vice-Regal Lodge and gracious North and South Blocks for government offices and a circular Parliament House. In addition, he laid out an entire city, with palatial houses and gardens for the civilian administrators, with radial streets, lined with lovely trees. In one fell swoop the British left an indelible stamp of Imperial Britain on a squabbling Nation and bolstered its' diminishing image.

It is time to recount the developments taking place in the Indian Army during the 'inter-regnum', between WW I and WW II. I have covered this period fairly thoroughly with the Indianization of the Indian Army, and the building of the Indian Military Academy (IMA) in Dehra Dun. This entire process was shunned and ignored by Gandhi and his cohorts in the Indian National Congress, as this went counter to Gandhi's Hindu-based philosophy of 'ahimsa' (non- violence). The army, according to these misguided Nationalists, was a total waste of money. The only dissenter was Subhas Chander Bose (Netaji), who took voluntary exile in Germany and finished up in Japan at the start of WW II. Netaji, or revered leader, was destined to create the Indian National Army, which fought with the Japanese against the British and their former compatriots in the Indian Army, in Burma. I will cover this segment in more detail when I cover the disastrous debacle of the collapse of Singapore.

The leadership of the Indian National Congress (INC) was a strange triumvirate of three totally disparate individuals. The only common bonding of this group was the vision of Indian Independence from Britain. There were several subsidiary players but the stage was dominated by this triumvirate of Gandhi, Nehru and Vallabhbhai Patel. These three individuals are going to have such an enormous influence on the fate and future of India that it is imperative that we have a character profile on each:

Without any doubt, the leader of the pack is Gandhi, so he must have pride of place. As said before, he was a strange mixture of a quasi-Hindu ascetic and a confused, muddle-headed politician, who could never draw a line between the harsh cruel world of politics, religion and self-abnegation. He adorned himself with the pseudo-honorific of 'Mahatma' (great soul), obsequiously bestowed upon him by that most highly respected Nobel Laureate, Rabindra Nath Tagore. Such is the spiritual ego of the man that he never once questioned his right to wear this most venerated title, which had not even been used by the true giants of the Hindu faith, like Swami Vivekananda. It speaks volumes about the man who professed the creed of 'ahimsa', or non-violence in public, but was a tyrant to his children at home. One son, in open rebellion, became a Muslim. The tragedy of the man was that he held strange beliefs, which often defied rational reasoning. A classical example of this irrational behaviour was his espousing the Khillafat Movement by the Moplah community in Kerala, who wanted Turkey to reinstate the deposed Caliph. Patent nonsense of course, but this resulted in the massacre of hundreds of innocent Hindus. However, Gandhi had this terrible penchant to interfere in areas where he was a total ignoramus. He was totally opposed to industrialization and held the absurd, half-baked, view that India could achieve self-sufficiency and total employment by hand-spun and hand-woven cloth, made in villages, called Khadi. I have written on this subject earlier and the disastrous effect this was going to have on Indian industry. However, credit must be given to Gandhi for his famous 'Salt March', to wreck the iniquitous 'Salt Tax', imposed by the government. Thousands walked down to the sea to make salt. This defiance, once and for all, established the power of 'civil disobedience' as a weapon against the government's draconian diktats. The second accolade is for his valiant effort to eradicate the scourge of 'untouchability'. As he said, and I quote: 'I regard 'untouchability' as the greatest blot on Hinduism.'

He elevated the status of the persecuted by calling them 'Harijans', 'the beloved of God.' Unfortunately ingrained prejudice and blatant bigotry defies logic and reason and no amount of legal Statutes will get rid of this centuries-old scourge. The Hindus of India are still plagued with this despicable blemish to their image. The only difference is that today the so-called underprivileged are enjoying a boom as 'Dalits' and are cashing in on 'affirmative action' which a guilt-ridden government has bestowed on them It is a strange travesty of circumstances that have doomed the Hindus to continue in this '*danse macabre*' with the absurd caste system of antiquity.

It is now time to get back to Gandhi and his weird views on politics. The man had a fixation on his sexuality, which he kept on testing in absurd ways. His second obsession was the ridiculous Hindu belief of 'ahimsa' that had opened the door to Islamic domination and persecution of Hindus for 800 years.

We are about to witness how an obsession can blind rationality and reason. Gandhi's solution to Partition was that the Hindus and Sikhs who had survived the charnel house of Pakistan, should go back for another dose of this holocaust, and the Indian Muslims who had fled across the border should return to their homes. This inanity is not an isolated example of a demented mind. His views on the European Holocaust were, and I quote: 'Hitler killed five million Jews. It is the greatest crime of our time. But the Jews should have offered themselves to the butcher's knife. They should have thrown themselves into the sea from cliffs.'

These are the grotesque pronouncements of a totally irrational mind. These are the so-called 'words of wisdom' from 'the Father of the Nation'. The tragedy was that Gandhi was a very poor judge of people, as evidenced by choosing Nehru as his heir. The only person who understood Gandhi was Dr. B.R.Ambedkar who had this to say and I quote: 'Gandhi was a man with no vision, no knowledge, no judgement. A worse man could not have been chosen to lead India's destiny.'

Ambedkar came from the untouchable cast of Mahars and had the distinction of writing India's Constitution. But the harm had been done and Nehru donned the mantle of leadership of an emerging Nation. The man was totally ill-equipped for the task. Gandhi was a pseudo-Hindu and Nehru was like a peanut, brown on the outside but a white, pseudo-Englishman inside. A dreadful duo, cast in the roles of leadership of a Nation, which had forgotten the meaning of the word over centuries of subjugation and servitude. What India needed was a strong and motivated leadership and, instead, it got a serve of moral platitudes from Gandhi and a fistful of pallid, Fabian Socialism from a crypto-Communist, Nehru. I have already written at length on Nehru's dreadful imprint on India's Industry and Economy. The country was salvaged from total ruin by the intrinsic resilience of its business community and a people who, over centuries, had learned to bounce back like a rubber ball when squashed by ruthless overlords. India owed nothing to Gandhi and even less to Nehru, who ruined the country for the better part of two decades. Nehru was an arrogant, narcissistic popinjay, who covered a deep-seated inferiority complex with irrational outbursts of anger and tantrums.

He had a mortal fear of the popularity of General K.M. Cariappa, India's highly popular C-in-C ('Kipper' to his men) and he distrusted the Army. He was forever opposing his own GOC, Lt. General Sir Robert Lockhart, whose staff had prepared an intricate Strategic Defence Plan, which needed the imprimatur of the Cabinet for implementation. When Lockhart presented the plan to Nehru, the PM, true-to-form, hit the roof and began to rant and rave, and this is what he had to say to the poor, dumbfounded GOC: 'Rubbish! Total Rubbish! We don't need a defence plan. Our policy is *ahimsa*. We foresee no military threat. Scrap the army! The police are good enough to meet our security needs.'

Here is *ahimsa* in action! What saved the Indian Army from this rank stupidity was, ironically, the invasion of Kashmir by Pakistan in October 1947. The Maharaja of Kashmir, Hari Singh, kept dithering as to which country to choose to join, until the Pakistanis took Baramulla on 24 October 1947. In the meantime the Kashmir State Forces, under the command of Brigadier Rajinder Singh, fought to the last man and last bullet, at Uri, and stopped the enemy for two crucial days, as Kashmir acceded to India. Nehru became totally catatonic, until a furious Sardar Patel shouted at Nehru and said—'Jawaharlal, are you going to save Kashmir and order the troops?'

Lt Col Ranjit Rai and Major Som Nath Sharma flew into an embattled Kashmir with their valiant troops and perished to a man. Kashmir had been saved by the valour of the men of the Indian Army, who routed the Pakistanis. Generals Cariappa, Thimayya and Kulwant Singh requested permission from Nehru to throw the Pakistanis out of Kashmir. Permission was refused and no reason given. This utter stupidity of a moronic PM has caused four wars with Pakistan and the loss of thousands of lives. The tragedy is that Nehru is dead and gone, as is Gandhi, but their dreadful legacy is alive and well. The long reach of Nehru from beyond the grave still plagues the country. Egged on by Count Louis Mountbatten, the first Governor-General of independent India, Nehru ignored the advice of his Generals to eliminate the Pakistani presence in Kashmir, and foolishly, took an entirely domestic issue to the United Nations for arbitration. The UN recommended a referendum to ascertain the wishes of the people, totally vitiating the agreed principle of accession of Indian Princes to India or Pakistan in 1947. The highly suspect relationship of Nehru and the Mounbattens will be covered in more detail later. Let it suffice to say that, with one stroke of the pen, Nehru jeopardized the fate of Kashmir and India and destabilized the entire region. This stupidity is going to have far-reaching consequences when China forcibly occupies Tibet and sits looming over India.

Nehru's pernicious influence is going to pervade the entire defence establishment with the appointment of Krishna Menon as the Minister for Defence. Krishna Menon was a dyed-in-the-wool Communist; with an ego that even overshadowed that of Nehru. Both Nehru and Menon pranced across the International Stage like two puppets-on-a-string, puffed-up with their misplaced sense of importance. True to form, the Services were starved for funds. 'Ahimsa' was going to save India like it had done for 800 years of tyrannical Muslim rule; only the stakes were much bigger this time. Krishna Menon was an ignorant fool, who persisted in interfering in military matters that he did not understand. India was in desperate need of a first rate Main Battle Tank (MBT) to replace the ageing 'Centurions' and 'Shermans' that had provided such salutary service against Pakistan's American 'Patton' and 'Chaffe' tanks, in three earlier wars, but time was running out. The Germans had offered to supply, and later manufacture, locally, the magnificient 'Leopard' MBT. This Offer was turned down. Menon over-rode the Army and demanded that India should manufacture the British 'Conqueror', an untested tank that was named the 'Vijyanta'. The venture was a total failure and India was left without an MBT. This blunder was going to be covered up by the purchase of Russian tanks. What follows is an even greater fiasco, but, in all fairness, we have to let the deadly duo off the hook. The Indian Army decided to build its own MBT called the 'Arjun', named after the famous warrior in the epic battle of the Mahabharata. Bad planning and constant vacillations in function and design, created a lumbering Behemoth that was too heavy for combat. Talk about a 'camel being a horse, designed by a committee', the Arjun came straight out of the Mad Hatter's Tea Party. An absurd sequel, as India had fought three major tank-wars with Pakistan and won them.The Indian Armoured Corps is a highly experienced body of battle-hardened veterans, who could have drafted a Qualitative Requirement (QR), outling the function and equipment of the MBT needed by the Army, with their eyes closed. The cardinal rule is that the planners must NEVER change horses in midstream, as the turn around time is too long. And this is precisely what the Army did. The General Staff had originally written a QR for a 40-ton tank, armed with a 105mm gun. The Arjun that finally emerged from the Heavy Vehicles Factory at Chennai was a gas-guzzling behemoth of nearly 80 tons, powered by a huge BMW diesel engine of 1,500hp and sporting a huge 120mm gun. The MBT had 'grown like Topsy'. The Arjun cannot be used on the battlefield and will be used for training purposes only. So it is back to the drawing board and a fresh QR!!

It is time to get back to Nehru and the Congress Party that donned the mantle of government after Independence. True to form, the absurdity of Gandhi's ahimsa still cast its ominous shadow over the Army, which was starved for funds and equipment, but what was worse, was the constant political and bureaucratic interference at all levels, which degraded the Service. Promotions and postings, used as weapons to succour political favours and corruption scams in the purchase of armaments, dominated the defence establishment. Jockeying for political mileage destroyed the élan of the Officer Corp and spelt the 'coup de grace' of the Army families, who had supplied the PWRIMC and the IMA with the superb manpower that had been the backbone of the Service. The Army became just another tawdry employer of second-rate officer material. The '*Hamara Sahib*' had been finally buried by a venal, self-serving, political class.

We are not through with that 'Scaramouche', Nehru, but time and space demands that we switch our attention to Sardar

Vallabhbhai Patel, literally the giant in the triumvirate. Patel was the Prime Minister that India needed, and did not get, because of that bumbling 'Mahatma', who was such a poor judge of character that he succumbed to the pestering barrage from Motilal Nehru, who pushed his son's case unashamedly. Sardar Patel finished up as the Deputy Prime Minister and Minister for Home Affairs, a portfolio that involved integrating the 560 Princely States into the Indian Union. The sagacity and clever diplomacy exercised by Patel won over the arrogant Princes. The Indian Government offered the princes a privy purse in exchange for their ancestral property. The privy purse would be defined on a sliding scale, getting progressively reduced with succeeding generations. This munificence would give the Princes the breathing-time necessary to adapt to their new, reduced circumstances. Little did the Princes foresee the duplicity and crass dishonesty of Indira Gandhi, who, as PM, abrogated the clause from the Constitution to punish the Princes, who were repeatedly elected by their former subjects against Congress candidates. The Congress Party has shown scant regard for the country's Constitution, which has been ruthlessly torn to shreds, time and again, to achieve political advantages. Tragically Sardar Patel passed away soon after India achieved Independence. India lost its one true leader, leaving the field open to an irresponsible popinjay, who is going to play havoc with the country. One of Nehru's first blunders was the signing of The Indus Water Treaty in 1960, which partitioned the riparian rights of the whole Indus and the five Punjab river systems. Without any sensible logic, based on land use or population demands, India got the tiny Beas and Sutlej rivers and Pakistan got the Indus, Jhelum, Ravi and Chenab—a totally disproportionate distribution, heavily skewed in favour of Pakistan. The absurdity of this arrangement becomes evident in the case of the Indus, which is handed over to Pakistan, lock, stock and barrel, thereby depriving the whole of the Ladakh and Dras Valleys of water

For the sake of continuity I have had to over-run the historical chain of events leading to India's Independence. Intervening was the commencement of WW II, which was going to drag India, willly-nilly, into this morass, although the country was not directly involved in the politics leading up to war. Such is the fate of subjugated nations. Since Britain was at war, so was India. WW II was the result of expansionism,' Lebensraum', by the two European powers, Germany and Italy, who were 'late arrivals' and had missed out on the enormous 'land-grab' by Britain, following the advent of the Industrial Revolution. They were about to make up for lost time under the dictatorships of Hitler and Mussolini. On the other side of the massive Asian land mass was another island nation, Japan, that had recently emerged out of its centuries-old isolation with the arrival of the American, Commodore Matthew Perry, in Tokyo Bay in 1853, demanding that Japan must open its doors to American trade. This incident brought about an end to the Tokugawa Shogunate, the military dictatorship rule of the Samurai, and the restoration of the Imperial Japanese Meiji Dynasty in 1868. With this came the harsh realization that the Samurai sword alone would not be able to preserve Japanese Sovereignty against the industrialized might of the Europeans and Americans. Japan had to industrialize fast, and catch up with the rest of the world. We are now going to witness the incredible gestation of the Zaibatsu, the handful of powerful commercial enterprises, which were going to pioneer Japan's leap forward into industrial and military might. Unlike Britain, Japan was an impoverished landmass, with hardly any natural resources. This paucity led to the Sino-Japanese War of 1895, which gave Japan control of Taiwan and Korea and brought Japan face-to-face with Russia, who had occupied Manchuria in1900.

Japan desperately needed the mineral wealth of Manchuria for its factories, but it first had to neutralize the Russian 'Far-Eastern Fleet', with its headquarters in Port Arthur, which was heavily defended by General Anatoli Stossel, commanding 41,000 men and 500 guns.The Russo-Japanese War began on 8 February 1904, by a surprise torpedo-boat attack on the Russian fleet, at anchor in Port Arthur, by Admiral Hethachiro Togo. This was followed by a land attack on 25 May. Port Arthur was a city under siege, with massive, determined attacks by the Japanese Army, suffering heavy casualties. The Russians surrendered on 2 January 1905, with 10,000 starving defenders. The siege cost Japan 59,000 casualties, plus another 3,400 succumbing to disease. The Russians lost 41,000—killed or lost to disease. But there is another sequel to this war, which was the final blow to 'white supremacy'. A small Asian country had smashed a huge European Power with relative ease. But there was still some fight left in a battered Imperial Russia, which was determined to redeem its honour, and relieve its Far-Eastern Fleet, bottled up in Port Arthur by the Japanese. The Russians dispatched their Baltic Fleet from its base in Kronstadt, near St. Petersberg, under the command of Admiral Rozhdestvenski. Ahead lay a huge 18,000-mile voyage around the Cape of Good Hope to Port Arthur.

I can't intend to give a 'blow-by-blow' version of the battle, but suffice it to say of Tsushima in 1905, which was going to go down as one of the most decisive naval battles in history. It was a battle between a much larger Russian fleet against a smaller, but faster and more determined, Japanese fleet, under the command of the redoubtable Admiral Togo. The Russian fleet was well and truly routed and surrendered. Japan, which had earned its laurels as a land army, now emerged as a major naval power. Japan had also realized that its dependence on Asian raw materials for its factories necessitated a powerful Navy to protect its sea-lanes.

Enough of Japan and its genesis into the twentieth century. It's back to India and the 'Quit India' mantra:

As I mentioned earlier, India was going to be sucked into the vortex of European politics without being involved in the process. The ruthless war machine of the German Wehrmacht brought about the rapid capitulation of Austria, Belgium, Holland, Denmark and Norway, followed by the attack on Poland, which brought France and Britain into the war. The Fuhrer was now the Master of Western Europe and would unleash the fury of the *'blitzkreig'* by an armoured thrust through Sedan in Belgium. It was a replay of the old Schlieffen Plan of WW I. WW II had begun in earnest. It is not the intention to write a military or political history of this conflagration but to introduce a preamble to India's induction into the war.

At the commencement of hostilities, the Indian Army had shrivelled down to a peacekeeping force, a buttress against the periodic intrusions by truculent tribesmen on the North-Western Frontier. It was literally living off scraps of the British Army. This miserly treatment was going to have dire consequences in the debacle of Singapore, which will be covered more comprehensively later on.

The intentions of the Italians were unclear. They had occupied Libya in 1911, after defeating the Turks, but consolidated their presence under Mussolini. As a part of Italy's expansionist design, Ethiopia was invaded in1935 by forces sent from their colony of Eritrea. Indianization of the Indian Army was deliberately slowed down by the British, who felt that, since there was no military threat in the pre-war years, the Indian Army was unlikely to be used overseas. History is going to prove how wrong this policy was going to be.

The IMA was well and truly established by General Sir Philip Chetwood in 1932 in Dehra Dun. On the walls were inscribed the following words, which he addressed to the first cadets and I quote: 'The safety, honour and welfare of your country come first, always and every time. The honour, welfare and comfort of the men you command come next. Your own ease, comfort and safety come last, always and every time.'

What glorious words of inspiration by a true leader of men. While Britain could produce such incredible men, her future as the Empire's leader is assured. But for how long can a small nation keep gestating such a brood of prestigious leaders? Sooner or later mediocrity, that great leveller of people, must come into its' own and the 'Common Man' will have ascendancy, with all its disastrous consequences.

The German Blitzkreig, led by General Guderian's 'Panzers', flustered the Allies, who had overwhelming numerical superiority, but true, to WW I tactics' they were 'dug in'. The Germans out flanked the 'dug in' Allies and arrived behind their enemy's unprotected rear. The Allies had never experienced this new, fast-moving kind of modernized and motorized warfare, and were routed into headlong retreat. The front-line was ragged and the situation was critical for the British

Expeditionary Force and the French First Army, which could have been annihilated by the German Army Groups A and B. Then, out of the blue, came a reprieve. Hitler over-rode his Commanders and stopped the Panzers in their tracks. In the Fuhrer's feverish imagination, the capture of Paris would redeem German honour and the defeat of Germany in WW I. Thank God for little corporals! The British were pinned down, with their backs to the sea at Dunkirk. True to form the British Nation rallied and sent every seaworthy vessel, and just about anything else that would float, across the channel, to evacuate 338,226 troops, including 120,000 French troops, from the beaches. The RAF did a sterling job protecting the stranded soldiers from being staffed by the Luftwaffe. The RAF destroyed 179 enemy aircraft for a loss of 29 of their own. The RAF was getting a fore taste of 'The Battle of Britain'. In France the fate of the remnants of its First Army was sealed, as was the rest of France's forces. Britain had gained a reprieve with the evacuation of the BEF, but a shaken nation sat licking its wounds behind the security of the English Channel, the only thing to arrest the murderous onslaught of the Wehrmacht. Britain needed time to rebuild its shattered army. The RAF was desperately short of aircraft and pilots and time was running out. Britain suddenly realized that it did not have the manpower to confront the Germans and Italians and the call went out to mobilize the Indian Army in a hurry. The response was dramatic and the army expanded to almost twelve times its peacetime strength. But there were serious bottlenecks that slowed down mobilization. First and foremost was the fragile political situation, with the Congress and the Muslim League facing each other in a hostile environment? Although the Muslim League claimed to represent the Muslim community, it floundered in the main recruiting areas of the Punjab and the NWFP. The dominant Congress Party was not convinced of a British victory in the war and the 'Quit India' movement deliberately disrupted supplies and communications, leading to the arrest and imprisonment of its leaders. The other serious bottleneck was the mechanization of the cavalry. The trusted and beloved horse was going to be replaced by a lumbering vehicle and the simple, rustic peasant-recruit was going to be inducted to the subtlety of the petrol engine. The IMA was working flat out but there was no way that it could provide the officers needed to command an army of 2.5 million men, the biggest volunteer army in the history of the world. This huge hiatus would have to be filled by the recruitment of Emergency Commissioned Officers, (ECOs) who would receive a crash-course in military training. Compared to the pre-war ICO coming out of the IMA, the ECO fared badly. The majority of the ECOs were neither militarily motivated, nor came from an army background. They had entered the service for totally selfish reasons of hoping to get permanent commissions and promotions. They were a 'stop gap' measure and nothing else.

The Indian Army was going to be 'blooded' in North Africa, against the Italians, who had enormous superiority in numbers and equipment. The Indian Army is going to be heavily involved in the North African Desert, first against the Italians and then against the formidable Afrika Korps, commanded by the redoubtable, General Erwin Rommel. This narrative cannot faithfully cover the trials and tribulations of this Desert War involving the British and Commonwealth 8th Army and the Axis forces, so we have to be content to briefly refer to the sterling service performed by the 4th, 8th and 10th 'Tiger Divisions' of the Indian Army and the heroic defence of Tobruk by the 9th Australian Division. With the defeat of the Afrika Korps, Rommel was left with the distressing responsibility of extricating the tattered remnants of his Army and evacuating them back to Europe. He achieved this most successfully, leaving an exhausted and demoralized Italian army caught between the victorious British Eight Army under Field Marshall Montgomery and the fresh American force, under General Patton, advancing from the west. The Afrika Korps lost 59,000 men killed or captured, 500 tanks and 400 guns. The war in the desert was over.The victory at El Alamein saved Egypt and the Suez Canal. In the meantime Germany had declared war on Russia in June 1941, and launched Operation Barbarossa, driving the Russians back to within 50 kilometers of Moscow. The victorious Allied armies were now waiting to be deployed against the Germans in Europe. They were faced with three choices. The first was an invasion into Southern France but this would involve considerable delays in mustering naval and amphibious landing craft to transport sufficient troops against a well-entrenched and strongly fortified enemy.Winston Churchill was in favour of an attack in the Balkans, but the Germans had already occupied Yugoslavia and Greece, to help an embattled Italian ally who had tried to subjugate the area and earned a bloody nose. The foray into the Balkans delayed the launching of Operation Barbarossa by a few months and would have a crucial effect, as the invasion was now going into the Russian winter with ill-equipped troops. The Allies were now left with the worst possible option and that was the invasion of Sicily, followed by a slow slog up the Italian Peninsula, in rough, mountainous terrain, to the heavily fortified German 'Gustav Line', south of Rome. The 4th, 8th and 10th Indian Divisions were heavily involved against crack German Panzer and Parachute Regiments, fighting under Field Marshal Albert Kesselring. Some of the bloodiest fighting took place at the crossing of the Sangro and Senio Rivers and the attack on the Citadel of Monte Cassino. This redoubt eventually fell to the Poles on 18 May 1944. It is time to return to India where new developments were going to bring the war closer to home.

After the defeat of the Russians in 1905, an overconfident Japan was going to turn its eyes on its old prey, China, brimming with the mineral wealth that Japan needed for its bustling industries. China had already lost Taiwan and Korea to Japan in 1895. Manchuria had been annexed by Russia in 1900, and was occupied by Japan after the Russo-Japanese War of 1905. Japan continued its aggression against China, which was convulsed with Civil War between the Communists, led by Mao Zedong, and Chiang Kai Shek. The Americans had been supporting the Nationalists in their fight against the Communists. The Secretary of State, Cordell Hull, issued an ultimatum to Japan to get out of China or face sanctions on supplies of oil, iron ore and other commodities. A military power like Japan was not going to submit meekly to this type of hectoring. The Americans were pushing Japan into a corner and were literally spoiling for a fight. The riposte was the attack on Pearl Harbour on 7 December 1941, by the Japanese Navy under Vice-Admiral Chuichi Nagomo. In Japan there were divided opinions on the right course of action. The Army, under General Hideki Tojo, was spoiling for a fight, whereas the Navy, under Admiral Isoroku Yamamoto, was more circumspect. Yamamoto had first hand experience and knowledge of America's industrial might and was aware that Japan could not survive in a prolonged war of attrition against this enemy. If war was inevitable, Japan's only hope was a surprise, debilitating attack against the American Pacific Fleet in Pearl Harbour. Once Japan had supremacy in the Pacific Ocean, it could threaten the American mainland and the Americans would be forced to sue for peace. The plan nearly succeeded. Three out of the eight American battleships in the harbour were sunk, one capsized and the remainder were severely damaged. Three light cruisers and three destroyers were also sunk. Out of 231 US Army planes, 65 were destroyed outright and many were seriously damaged. Out of 250 planes belonging to the Marine Corps, 196 were destroyed. The Japanese lost 29 aircraft. The Americans lost 3,226 killed and 1,272 wounded. A dreadful carnage, but, fortuitously, 3 aircraft carriers, which were Nagumo's prized target, were not in the harbour and thus escaped. These three carriers would play a pivotal role in the Battle of The Coral Sea, which arrested the advance of the Japanese towards Australia. The attack on Pearl Harbour brought America into the war.

After Pearl Harbour the gloves were off and the Japanese went on the offensive in the Pacific and the Philippines. They were unstoppable. By 7 January 1941, the Japanese had the upper hand in the Philippines and General Douglas MacArthur was forced to retire into the Bataan Peninsula, pursued by the Japanese. The Americans surrendered on 9 April and MacArthur escaped by the skin of his teeth, to continue the fight from Australia.

Japan now switched its attention to Southern Asia, where the British presence in Malaysia and Singapore was a thorn in their side. The Japanese 25th Army, under General Tomoyuki

Yamashita, landed on the southern peninsula of Thailand and Malaysia, on 8 December 1941, a day after the attack on Pearl Harbour. Obviously a part of a very carefully planned attack on the Americans and British in the Pacific. At the same time the Japanese 11th Fleet bombed Singapore. This offensive caught the British totally unprepared and they were going to experience their most humiliating defeat in history at the hands of an Asian power that was destined to finish 'European Supremacy' in Asia forever. Singapore was supposed to be impregnable and was the lynchpin of Britain's Sovereignty in South Asia. Over confidence and insouciance was their undoing. The British never dreamed that an attack on Singapore could come through the impenetrable jungles of Malaysia to the north. All the gun emplacements faced out to sea, plus the harbour was protected by the battleship 'The Prince of Wales', and the battle cruiser, 'The Repulse'. They and 4 destroyers sailed out as Force Z on 8 December, under Admiral Tom Phillips, to attack the invading fleet. The flotilla was destroyed by bombers and sunk. This encounter made Naval history, as this was the first time that capital ships had been destroyed by aircraft. The Japanese had complete supremacy in the air and at sea, but Yamashita's army was out numbered on the ground. He crossed the Straits of Johore on 8 February 1942, and attacked the Australian forces. Lt. General Arthur Percival was GOC in Malaysia, with 90,000 troops, made up of the 9th and 11th Indian Divisions, the 8th Australian Division and the recently arrived British 18th Division. Numerically the Allies had roughly a 2:1 advantage over Yamashita, but the Indian troops were under-trained and poorly equipped, and about 3,000 Australians of the 8th Australian Division had never fired a rifle. The Japanese, on the other hand, had very high morale. The troops were battle-hardened veterans, equipped with excellent weaponry and had excellent air and naval support. General Sir Archibald Wavell was the Supreme Commander of the recently formed ABDA (American, British, Dutch, Australian) Force, and when he visited Singapore he was taken aback at the relatively low élan among the senior officers, who had nicknamed their commander, General Percival 'the Rabbit', unlike the Japanese who had nicknamed Yamashita 'the Tiger'. Unfortunately, Percival was a poor commander, who did not listen to advice from his senior officers. In spite of being told that the Japanese were advancing in strength down the west coast he was convinced that the invasion of Singapore would come from the east and mustered his forces on the wrong coast. Yamashita's rapid advance was creating supply problems and his extended lines of supply would slow him down. As it happened, Kuala Lumpur fell on 11 January. The railway-yard was full of wagons filled with essential supplies that solved the problem. No one had bothered to destroy or move the wagons.

Unfortunately the troops under Percival were unaccustomed to jungle warfare. The rare exceptions were the Argyll and Sutherland Highlanders. Percival did not have a clear plan for the defence of the Malayan Peninsula and, in spite of having numerical superiority; he lost to Yamashita in tactics and élan. The Allies had 110 antiquated American-built Brewster Buffalo fighters out of which 60 were shot down. The rest flew south. The Japanese had 617 planes and total air supremacy.

Percival had no choice but to vacate the Malayan Peninsula and put up a futile defence of Singapore, which was being pounded by air-attacks. Yamashita sent two demands for surrender to Percival, which were ignored. Singapore had its back to the wall. On 14 February, the last British ship left port, and on 15 February, Percival surrendered, unconditionally, to Yamashita Left behind were 30,000 British, 15,000 Australian and 5,000 Indians as POW's, who were going to be brutalized in terrible camps. The Japanese followed their warrior code of Bushido, which demanded death rather than surrender. In their eyes, POWs were cowards and worthy of only contempt and humiliation. The code of Bushido did not apply to non-Japanese, who were covered by The Geneva Convention, which demanded respect and the humane treatment of POWs. The Japanese ignored all these rules. But brutality seemed to be ingrained in the Japanese Nation, as evidenced by the disgraceful massacre of innocent women and children in Nanking, and the harsh, inhuman treatment meted out to the civilians in all the Countries they conquered. The Japanese were feared and despised.

In the aforesaid, I have mentioned that 5,000 Indians were POWs. These were the handful that refused to break their oath of allegiance to the Sovereign, and were treated disgracefully. A friend of my family from Mussoorie, Hari Badhwar, was a young Captain in a Cavalry Regiment, a big, strapping man, who was strung up in a tiny cage for months on end. He came out a pathetic shadow of his former self. Others were shot or beheaded. Singapore and Malaysia finally laid to rest the last vestige of '*HamaraSahib*', for it seemed to the Indian contingent, that their British C.O. had let them down, with little or no regard for them, the 'Brits' or 'Aussies', all of whom had been pushed into battle with no adequate training or equipment, and delivered into a dreadful fate. So much for oaths of allegiance!! About 40,000 men joined the Indian National Army (INA) and fought alongside the Japanese against their former compatriots in the Indian Army. The INA was the brainchild of the Indian patriot, Subhash Chandra Bose, who had gone into voluntary exile in Japan. The raison d'être of the INA was the liberation of India from British rule. There was even a regiment of Indian women in the INA called 'The Rani of Jhansi' Regiment, named after the famous Warrior Princess of the Indian Mutiny of 1857. The regiment was commanded by a Capt. Lakshmi. Three senior officers of the INA were imprisoned and tried as traitors by the British after the war. Their trial will be treated separately.

11

Burma

The Japanese juggernaut was unstoppable. After the relatively easy conquest of Malaysia and the rout of the Allies in the supposedly impregnable fortress of Singapore, it proved to the Japanese that the so-called supremacy of the Colonial European Powers of Britain, France and Holland, was just sham and bluff. For the loss of just over 9,000 Japanese soldiers killed in these campaigns, Japan had destroyed European Colonial rule in South Asia forever. Burma was just a hop skip and a jump from Malaysia and promised to be an easy plum ready for picking. The country was rich in minerals and forests, but ahead lay the real prize—India.

Once again, Britain was caught 'napping' in Burma. The British had two weak Divisions defending a huge land mass, surrounded by impregnable mountains, swathed in dense forests to the west, north and east of the Irrawaddy River, which ran down the middle of the country. The only real access to the country was from the delta of the river. No one had ever threatened the country, so the British were securely ensconced in the capital, Rangoon, with a thriving business community plying their trade up and down the river in steamboats. Other than the river, there was a railway-line that ran north, past the major city of Mandalay, to the important trading-outpost of Myitkyina. Oddly enough, there were very poor connections by road to its giant neighbour, India, and no railway line. The two countries were separated by the Arakan Mountains in Burma and the fairly formidable Naga Hills in India. Before the start of WW II, a road had been built from the border town of

Lashio, to the Chinese city of Chungking. This was the famous 'Burma Road' and was a vital supply-line to the embattled Chinese Army, fighting the Japanese.

Rangoon was abandoned on 7 March 1941, and the victorious Japanese made a beeline for the Burma Road, which had to be cut. This was imperative to give relief to their men fighting against the Chinese Army of Chiang Kai Shek. The British and Indians were in headlong retreat. They were even less prepared than in Malaysia. To compound their misery, the monsoon had broken, drenching everything. The roads turned into quagmires and rivers became torrents. To make matters worse, the roads were crammed with fleeing Indian civilians trying to get to India. The scene was like a mad house. Burma was lost, and the axis of the war was going to shift to India.

The Japanese opened the account by sailing into The Bay of Bengal in April 1942, sinking a lot of Merchant Shipping. They attacked the ports of Trincomalee and Colombo in Ceylon, and destroyed the RAF bases there. India's Army had grown from 189,000 in 1939 to 2,500,000, but most of the troops were trained to fight in arid terrains and not in the moist, dense jungles of Burma. A huge retraining programme in jungle warfare was initiated under General Auchinleck. But there was also another problem emerging, and that was the increasing integration with the Americans, who were going to be heavily involved in supplying the Chinese Armies, under Chiang Kai Shek, now that the Japanese had cut the Burma Road. The only alternative was supplies by air, over the Himalayas, from bases in India. This was the famous 'flying the hump': a highly hazardous flight in Douglas DC3 'Dakotas', whose flight ceiling was not sufficient to fly over the peaks. The Dakotas had to weave between the peaks and in and out of clouds.

The Command Structure in India was complex. The retraining of the Indians in jungle warfare; fresh recruitment of troops and familiarization with new weapons was the responsibility of General Auchinleck. The Overall Command of all three services, rested with Lord Wavell. And, lastly, there were the Americans, who were fighting an intense island war in the Pacific, and leap-frogging over the 'hump', to supply the

Chinese and also sustaining General Claire Lee Chennault's 'Flying Tigers' of the 14th(Volunteer) Army Air Force, which had destroyed 300 Japanese aircraft. In order to coordinate this fragmented Command Structure, the British appointed Admiral Lord Louis Mountbatten as the Supreme Allied Commander of SEAC, South East Asia Command.

Wavell was champing-at-the-bit as he felt that the Japanese had over- extended their resources and lines of supply, and should be hit before they could re-organize. Even more pressing was a morale issue. After the debacles in Malaysia, Singapore, and now in Burma, a defeatist element had crept into the British ethos, that the Japanese were unbeatable in jungle war-fare. It was vital to recover this self-confidence. All very commendable, but there is no substitute for careful planning and assessment of the enemy's capability.

Wavell launched the poorly prepared 'First Arakan Campaign' with the Indian 14th Division, moving down the Mayu Peninsula from Chittagong, towards Akyab, on the Burmese coast. A frontal attack against a well-entrenched enemy was a recipe for disaster. The Japanese counter-attacked and the operation ended as a failure, with heavy losses in men and equipment.

Space and time do not permit this narrative to cover the details of this critical conflict in Burma. On the other hand this battle-ground is going to be the turning-point in reversing the fortunes of the Japanese, and the cardinal elements must be highlighted. I have had to pick the eyes of the battles and discard the matrix.

This brings us to the crucial Second Arakan Campaign, designed and executed by General William Slim, commanding the British-Indian XIV Army. The troops under his command had been initiated into jungle warfare by General Auchinleck, and could be trusted to give a good account of themselves against the Japanese. The main objective was to take the initiative and go on the offensive and hurt the enemy on their own turf. The biggest problem for the Japanese was their extended lines-of-supply through dense forests, raging rivers and dreadful roads, where they existed. Supply and communications were the soft under-belly of the enemy and the logical targets. A frontal attack had been tried in the First Arakan Campaign with disastrous results and the rout of the Indian 14th Division. The air was still dominated by the enemy. This left only one alternative and that was a clandestine guerrilla war behind enemy lines. Enter a strange, enigmatic officer, Orde Charles Wingate, a maverick Commander, who had won his stripes under Wavell in Abyssinia. His 'Gideon' guerrilla force had proved its' worth, and Wavell was anxious to use Wingate's unusual talents in Burma. Wingate created a deep-penetration Force which he named the 'Chindits', supposedly named after a mythical Burmese lion called '*chinthe*' or possibly named after the Chindwin River in the Arakans. The Chindits were specially selected Commandos, who could be airlifted and dropped behind enemy lines to cut railway lines, attack depots and small troop formations. The Chindits were specialists in jungle warfare and carried all their supplies and weaponry on their backs. They had a one-way ticket, as there was no way that they could be relieved or extricated. Once their job was done, the Chindits had to claw their way back to India as best as they could. The Chindits were a mixed bag of Indian and British soldiers. Casualties were high, but, besides military successes, the morale soared as the Chindits proved that the Japanese soldier could be defeated, and was by no means invincible. At this point I have to digress and mention that the legacy of the Chindits lives on in the Indian Army, and, in the IMA, every cadet has to successfully complete his 'Chindits' exercise before he can graduate. We are not through with Wingate, who moved to Israel after the War, and helped train the Haganah, the incipient Israeli army. His memory is greatly revered in that country—a most unusual man, very much in the mould of Lawrence of Arabia.

Now it is time to go back to the redoubtable General Slim, commanding the British-Indian XIV Army. General Slim was an Australian who had transferred to the Indian Army, and served with the 6th Gorkha Rifles and had fought with the regiment at Gallipoli. He made a name for himself by extricating the embattled 1st Corp in Rangoon in 1941, followed by a dogged slog of 900 miles to Imphal, in appalling conditions. He was raring to go as he realized that there was an essential morale problem with his British troops, who badly needed a victory to vindicate their honour. Unfortunately his First Arakan Campaign had fared badly. His Second Arakan Campaign had already started, with Wingate's Chindits cutting the railway line at Myitkyina. All this was a prelude to his reclaiming Burma. He had the troops and airpower, but he had to lure the Japanese into a battle where he could decisively beat them, leaving the road open to invade Burma. He did not have to wait long as the Japanese launched their offensive on India on 15 March 1944. The Japanese 15th Army, under Lieutenant General Renya Mutaguchi, laid siege on Imphal and Kohima. The battles surged relentlessly for nearly six months, on both fronts, in heavily forested country. It turned into a war of attrition.

The Japanese had hoped to capture the railway town of Dimapur and secure badly needed supplies. This was denied to them by the arrival of fresh British and Indian divisions and a heavy pounding from the air by British and American planes. Japanese fighting strength was seriously depleted by starvation and disease and the relentless pursuit by General Geoffrey Scoone's IVth Corps, General Montagu Stropford's XXXIII Corps and of course, Slim's 14th Army. Mutaguchi's 15th Army fell back to the Chindwin River, having lost 65,000 dead, 250 guns and most of its tanks and transport. British and Indian losses were 13,000. The Japanese had fought with their usual tenacious ferocity throughout the entire Imphal-Kohima Campaign but, by June, the tide had turned against them. This campaign ended in September 1944, after a full six months of some of the most gruelling and bloody battles of WW II. But the war in Burma was not over. Ahead lay some intense fighting. In February 1945, the 20th Indian Division crossed the Irrawaddy and established a bridgehead which was attacked in strength by the enemy. The bloody battle of Meiktila had begun and was won. The Japanese surrendered Rangoon on 1 May 1945. Slim had the rare distinction of conclusively defeating a Japanese Land Army for the first time in its history.

Burma will go down in India's Military Annals as an

incredible victory against insuperable odds. Twenty-seven V.C.s were awarded, out of which twenty went to the Indian Army. One single battalion, the 2nd/5th Gorkha Rifles, earned three. Their Regimental HQ is in Dehra Dun. The Burma war brought out the best in the great Martial Triad of the British, Indian and the Gorkha soldiers who fought and died in the gory battlefields of that distant land. It also, sadly, laid to rest that incredible bond of '*Hamara Sahib*' and the Indian soldier, who, without question, followed him into the jaws of death. It was also the harbinger of the end of 'Pax Britannica'. Once Great Britain lost its 'Jewel in the Crown', it seemed to crumble into mediocrity and quiet indifference. It was the end of an era.

The war in Burma was over but there was still plenty of fight left in the Japanese and heavy fighting against the Americans continued in the Pacific. This narrative covers the trials and tribulations of the Indian Army and not the Pacific. The dreadful carnage of Imphal and Kohima had saved India from conquest by the Japanese. India would have been savagely brutalized despite all the protestation by Bose, who was living in the dream world of the Greater Asia Co-prosperity Sphere, in the event of a Japanese victory. He had already formed The Provisional Government of Free India with himself as the head of state. Such is the chimera that dreams are made of. All the aspirations of an intense patriot were going to be cut short by his demise in an air-crash over Formosa. Left behind were the tattered remains of his progeny, the I.N.A. By late summer of 1945, the eventual capitulation of the Japanese was a fore- gone conclusion. Remnants of a dispirited and half starved I.N.A. began to trickle back into India. There was no tumultuous reception awaiting a hero's return. They were going to be mercilessly politicized by the Congress, once their Leaders were imprisoned by the British and tried for sedition.To the men and Officers of the Indian Army, the I.N.A. was an object of contempt for fighting against them. But much worse was their terrible performance on the battlefield. The 1st I.N.A. Division of 6,000 men went into the Battle of Imphal—715 deserted, 8oo surrendered, 400 were killed in action, 1,500 died of disease and starvation and 2,600 retreated. Although the I.N.A. was fighting alongside the Japanese, they cracked much more readily. They were badly armed and poorly officered by relatively junior cadres who had been jumped up to fill senior vacancies. The 1st I.N.A. Division once again crossed swords with the Indian Army at the great battle of Meiktila. It surrendered en masse, including its commander, 150 officers and 3,000 men. They did not have the stomach for a fight.

After the war ended, the British were faced with a nightmarish dilemma. Here were thousands of dispirited men whose futures had to be determined. They could not be lined up and shot as traitors, although, technically this should have been their fate. But the British were not Nazis. With very few exceptions, they could not be taken back into the army, as this would have sent the wrong message, that loyalty was tradable. On the other hand, examples had to be made. The Commander-in-Chief, Auchinleck, chose three prominent Commanders, Saigal, Dhillon and Shah Nawaz, and put them on trial for sedition. Unfortunately they were imprisoned and tried in Delhi's Red Fort, the epicentre of the Mutiny and the symbol of the Independence Movement. This was a tactical mistake. The country erupted in National hysteria. Overnight the I.N.A. became a National Army fighting for the Independence of Mother India and the accused were patriotic heroes.

If the truth be known, Britain had had a gut full. It had been bled white in two sanguinary wars; it was broke, owing war debts to the USA, India and others; it had broken its back saving its Empire; its cities hadbeen mercilessly bombed and had to be rebuilt; its enormous Industrial Might had been ruthlessly whittled down by labour unrest; ridiculous extortionist-taxation laws had drained all entrepreneurial initiative; and here was its 'Jewel in the Crown' slavering for Independence. There seemed to be no end to this tale of woe. To make matters worse, the very bastion on which the Empire rested—the integrity and loyalty of the Indian Army and Navy—was now questionable, with mutinies and disloyalties tearing at the very fabric of the Imperial Edifice. Britain was getting ready to quit. To hell with the I.N.A. trials! It was an Indian problem. Let the Indians sort it out.

12

Partition

Britain was going to be 'hoist by its own petard'. It had perfected its policy of '*Divide et Impera* ', literally 'divide and rule'. Soon after the arrival of the East India Company, it saw a country at loggerheads with petty and not-so-petty Princes at each other's throats, and quickly grasped the nettle. The arrival of the British was like a life raft for the Muslims who were rapidly losing their ascendancy over the vastly bigger Hindu population. This scenario has already been covered in depth and does not merit repetition other than to remind the reader that the British craftily decided to introduce 'affirmative action' in favour of the Muslims. As a part of this agenda was the mischievous myth that Hindus and Muslims were separate nations and could not live together. The seeds of partition had been sown. On the other hand, the same British rulers were responsible for welding an incredible bond of camaraderie and brotherhood of all races in the Indian Army, because it suited them. Talk about running with the hares and hunting with the hounds, the British were past masters at this game.

Idealistically, a pluralistic society is feasible where people of different faiths and beliefs can live peacefully together as a Nation. But there are certain criteria that must be met before this can become a reality, and the fundamental, cardinal plinth is a separation of the 'Church' and the 'State.'The two are totally incompatible. Religion is a personal matter of faith and belief and must not intrude into the Civic realm of Law and Order and the secular functioning of society. The problem is that overlapping is inevitable especially in matters relating to morality and inter-personal relationships like marriage, family responsibilities, education and births and death. Religions over the years have been the custodians of social mores and morality and are chary to hand this function over to Civil Law. This dichotomy becomes impossible in Islam, where there is no differentiation between the dictates of religion, the Shariat or Divine Law, with all 'temporal' power being vested in a 'Caliph', nominated by the *'ulemah'* or Clergy .The trouble is that Islam is not just a religion. It is a social order, a total way of life. It is not surprising that Islam cannot live side by side with other religions. It is supposedly the religion of 'peace' as the name implies, but strictly on its terms and conditions. The whole world should embrace the Faith, as dictated by Allah, the 'all merciful'. If you refuse, then be it on your head, which you will literally lose! It is all very simple!!

The mischief is done, and cannot be undone. The virus of 'Partition' had been released by conniving politicians and fanned on by a Muslim *'ulemah'* that could see its power growing. The architect of Pakistan, Mohammed Ali Jinnah, in his Islamic naïveté, honestly believed that once Pakistan was a reality, nothing would change other than the government. As a successful barrister in Bombay he had led a life of ease and luxury and had been totally insulated from the grime, ignorance and bigotry, which cloaked the underdog in a fog of hatred and resentment. This 'cauldron of hate' bubbled over on 15 August 1947. The frontier between India and Pakistan was still on the drawing-board, but this did not deter roaming bands of vicious looters and rapists from inflicting mayhem on innocent peasants and their families, who had no idea of what was happening and why. They were trapped and fled for their lives, leaving their ancestral homes and lands behind. Overnight, their neighbours had become their enemy, hell-bent on killing them, and plundering anything that they could lay their hands on. The world had gone mad. Nothing made sense anymore. Hatred fed revenge and more hatred. Civil authority had collapsed and a rudimentary semblance of law and order was maintained by the army, spread paper-thin over a huge area. The world was witnessing the greatest 'migration' in history and certainly one of the worst massacres of innocent people, whose only crime was that they followed a certain faith. There is no proper tally of the death toll but it is believed that over 1,000,000 perished. The agony of Partition was going to run its course. Hatred is blind and has neither 'rhyme nor reason'. Eventually the fuel of hate is consumed and sanity returns.

But life will never be the same again. Wounds will heal but the scars will remain. Families have been wrenched apart, one section staying in India and another moving to Pakistan. I personally know of one case where two brothers, both Generals in the army, one opted for Pakistan and the other served in the Indian Army. Ridiculous, but true!!

The British Army fought side by side with the Indian Army. They tasted the heady wine of victory together and perished together. Over generations British and Indian officers and men had forged a bond of *'espirit de corps'*, unparalleled anywhere in the world. And, overnight, this intimate fabric was going to be unravelled by a political will, which decreed that loyalty and allegiance had outlived their usefulness and were now defunct. Regiments in the erstwhile Indian Army were going to be splintered, and would finish up fighting each other on the ramparts of the 'Line of Control' on the frontier.

We are now approaching the end of British Rule in India, but the concluding chapter cannot be written until the war in Europe and the Pacific comes to an end.

The Russians launched a ferocious assault on Berlin. On 30 April 1945, Hitler committed suicide and the once-unstoppable 'Wehrmacht' surrendered to Russia's Marshall Zhukov. The insane dreams of a glorious 'Third Reich' had finished as a 'Gotterdammerung' of the German people. The Pacific War was also in its death throes. The Americans were relentlessly pushing north towards Japan. On 6th August 1945, the city of Hiroshima was devastated by the explosion of an atom bomb, dropped from a B29 Superfortress nicknamed the 'Enola Gay', which had flown from its base in Tinian in the Mariana Islands. In less than a second, 78,000 Japanese were killed by the blast and heat, and thousands received a lethal dose of radiation that would finish the victims in an agonizing, protracted death in the months to come. The Americans coded the device as 'Little Boy', which was powered by Uranium 235. Three days later the Americans bombed the city of Nagasaki using a Plutonium 239 bomb, which was coded 'Fat Boy'. The Americans had not even waited to get a response from Tokyo offering to surrender, but there were cold-blooded reasons for this. The first was that the Americans wanted to see whether there were any major differences between the two devices. The Japanese were merely the 'guinea pigs'; the second reason was a 'pay back' for 'Pearl Harbour', and all the suffering that Japan had inflicted on the Americans during the war; the third reason was political. After the defeat of Germany, the Russians had emerged as the most powerful military machine in Europe, and, under the ruthless dictatorship of Stalin, had subjugated the whole of Eastern Europe. The 'Cold War' had commenced. The USA, Britain and France could not contain the Soviets on the ground. The USA had to demonstrate its possession of nuclear warheads to the Russians, who were desperately trying to catch up, but still lacked a Nuclear Capability. Russia exploded its first atom bomb in1949. Now the two countries were running neck-and-neck, amassing arsenals that could annihilate the entire world. This was 'jingoism' gone berserk. But, once the 'hounds of war' have been unleashed', madness clouds judgement. The tiny little kiloton atom bomb was now going to be superseded by monstrous, megaton Hydrogen Bombs. In 1963 the Soviets exploded a Hydrogen bomb with a yield of 58 megatons of TNT. Britain, France and China have also now entered the Big League. In the meantime the Big Powers were also developing missile delivery systems and anti-missile defence shields. This is a race with no end in sight.

Now it's back to India:

> Partition had truncated India. Pakistan was a reality, but nothing had been achieved, other than an abortion that was held together by the myth of a Muslim *ummah*, the factitious 'Islamic Brotherhood', which existed only on paper, and in the imagination of the *ulemah*, the fanatical clergy. The reality was very different with Shias and Sunnis at each others throats and both ex-communicating all other sub-sects like the Sufis, Ahmediayas,

Kadianis and many others, as apostates. The country teetered on the verge of collapse, barely surviving on American largesse. Democracy and military dictatorship alternated in the dreadful game of a political carousel. Pakistan was Britain's legacy to India, but it could never have become a reality had there been a true sense of patriotism and nationhood in the Indian ethos. Instead, India was a gaggle of self-interested religious and princely groups, held together by the iron will of a ruler sitting in Delhi, or the EIC in Calcutta. India had no sense of nationhood, as understood by Countries in Europe or Japan.

13

Independence at Last

As I have said earlier, Britain had had a gutful, and was ready to quit India.

A glorious chapter in British history was coming to an end. It is a strange travesty of fate that threw these two totally dissimilar nations together. The British had not come to India as conquerors or even colonialists. They came as merchant traders, like the Portuguese, Dutch and the French before them, lured by the fabled riches of the Orient and the demand for spices by the gourmet cuisines of the City States of Europe. Asia literally fell into the lap of these opportunistic traders, always beady-eyed for easy profit. What started off as a straightforward mercantile venture, gradually became acquisitive of land and territory. The asian countries were not countries in the European sense, with a common sense of history, lineage and nationhood, but were petty Principalities, which were forever warring against each other for paltry gains. The European traders came, armed with guards to protect their trading posts, and naval vessels to safeguard their ports and harbours. Compared with the rag-tag militias of the local Chieftains, the Europeans had regular, well-trained troops, which could be hired out to the local Chiefs for a handsome consideration, by way of money or land. The petty-trader was on his way to becoming a colonialist, with settlers and farmers trickling in from the congestion of the Homeland. The two main contenders in India were the French and the British. The Portuguese were militarily too weak and retreated into the safety of their enclaves along the west coast of India. The Dutch were more interested in Ceylon and

Indonesia. After the Napoleonic Wars in Europe, French power began to slip behind Britain and this was reflected in India. The coast was now wide open for a single European trader to exploit the wealth and riches of India. The Mughal power in Delhi was rapidly declining, eaten from within by decadence and lasciviousness. India was open slather for exploitation by the British who were quick to grasp the nettle and fill their coffers with their ill gotten gains. Huge fortunes were made by the Directors of the EIC. The disease even percolated down to the lower echelons of the EIC. India was the proverbial treasure-trove, where the British were going to amass huge fortunes and retire back to 'Good old Blighty', the envy of those had not taken the plunge. These were the 'Nabobs' like Robert Clive, who was probably the richest man in England. In the famous words of Lord Acton,

> 'Power corrupts and absolute power corrupts absolutely.'

Once the British had tasted the heady wine of power and wealth, they had stepped onto an unstoppable whirligig. India was destined to power the Industrial Revolution in England, which, in turn, was going to become the workshop and factory of the world. Britain climbed to its Empyrean Heights on the shoulders of India. It is not surprising that it earned the accolade of 'The Jewel in the Crown of the British Empire.' We are now witnessing the return of the 'Crown Jewels' to their rightful owners, the People of India, and the inevitable sinking of Britain into Its dismal slot of mediocrity. But this narrative is beginning to look lop-sided, with a heavy bias against Britain, which is emerging as a ravenous ogre, with an insatiable appetite for power and wealth. The facts belie this absurd sentiment. If the truth be known, Britain and India had a strange tryst with Destiny. I have already covered India's ruthless exploitation. It is time to turn over the page and look at the enormous legacy that the British have left behind from their sojourn in India. Before we embark on this eulogy it is vital to lay to rest the bitter and resentful Indian Nationalists, who have pen and paper poised and are ever ready to blame the British for all the failings and pitfalls of a country in decadence.

The list of achievements are legion, so where does one begin and how does one apportion a 'Value judgement? Every unbiased Indian will have his own opinion on what constitutes Britain's greatest bequest to India. It would be senseless to get involved in this dissection of minutiae. We all have a right to our opinion, so let's leave it at that.

As the writer of this expose I reserve the right to kick off. One way or another I have had a lot to do with the British. They are a strange race, to say the least. When they are good, they are incomparable, with an abiding sense of justice and fair play rarely seen in any other nation. It must have something to do with playing that incomprehensible game called Cricket!! They give with both hands and take the same way. Their most outstanding quality, and they have so many, is their sense of duty and responsibility, like my headmaster, Mr Foot, insisting that on Saturday night all boys must wear their National dress and Mrs Foot wearing a sari on formal occasions, (to the horror of the '*burra memsahibs*' in the Dehra Dun Club) which the HM refused to join because Indians were not allowed to become members. I could write volumes in this vein but that is sidetracking the main issue. In my carefully considered opinion, the greatest gift was Macaulay, bestowing the English Language to India. English is such a rich, eclectic language containing shamelessly borrowed words from every-where, that it has become the 'lingua franca' of the world! English is no longer a foreign language in India, which has developed its own quaint spoken variant called 'Indish'. India is the second-biggest English-speaking country in the world, after America. It is incredibly prolific in its output of books and literature in the English language.

India has 22 major languages and hundreds of dialects. The great and only uniting force is the English language, which makes communication possible in this 'Tower of Babel'. This must sound like heresy to the protagonists of Hindi and Sanskrit. Both these languages, and the other vernacular languages, have a very important role to play in conserving provincial and national history and culture. Their study is intrinsic to the education system, but for sheer practical reasons, English must have the Centre Stage. Proficiency in English has given India the edge over China in the burgeoning IT industry, and in Silicon Valley, not to mention work for thousands in Telephone 'Call Centres'! So much for the blessings of English. It's time to move on.

True to form, the imprint of Britain runs through the entire fabric of India. I cannot think of any aspect of Indian life that has not been touched by the British presence. It was the British who wiped out the disgraceful custom of '*sati*', the immolation of widows on the funeral pyres of their husbands. Thanks to the British, the scourge of 'Thugee' was ruthlessly eliminated, as were the roving bands of 'Pindaris' and other 'dacoits' who roamed the countryside. The British brought Law and Order into Civil Life and promulgated a Civil and Criminal Code, which became the Judicial System that survives to this day. The rapacious *Zamindari* and *Talukdari* system which bled the peasant farmer for centuries, was replaced by the Indian Civil Service (ICS) Revenue 'Collectors'. The ICS became the 'crème de la crème' of Civil Services throughout the world. The 'Sword arm' of the ICS was the Indian Police Service.' Another British innovation was the Indian Irrigation Service that finally wiped out the endemic scourge of famine in India. Modern education at all levels is another bequest to India. The British Public School education was emulated by India and has been covered in considerable depth earlier in this expose. India has the second-longest Railway System in the world with, 39,000 miles of track. The USA has 96,000 miles. The intricate relationship of the British and the Indian Armies has been extensively covered and does not need any further commentary. The beautiful City of New Delhi, with its superb governmental buildings, is an inheritance to treasure, along with other great architectural landmarks; irrigation; forestry-management; and the list of indelible contributions to India is endless. It is futile to visualize an India minus the British presence. It is all-pervading in every aspect of life in the country. In concluding this eulogy it is imperative to interject that Britain could never have achieved what it did without the solid help and support of the Indian. The two made an excellent team when they were yoked together.

India helped Britain climb to its apogee of greatness and contributed enormously to the success of the Industrial Revolution. It provided the manpower for its civil and military machine. Britain revolutionized a decadent and senile society and brought it, kicking and screaming, into the nineteenth century. The two countries were destined by divine providence to travel together in tandem.

The terrible carnage of WW II is over and a pallid Britain is pausing to get its breath. With typical racist prescience, Winston Churchill said:

> 'When Independence comes to India, power will go into the hands of rascals, rogues, free-booters and men of straw.'

On the sub-continent, India had been mindlessly truncated and the triad of Gandhi, Nehru and Sardar Patel were going to take the reigns of power from the British. True to form, Gandhi resigned from the contest and it must be said to his credit that the 'Father of the Nation' could have asked for anything and a grateful country would have bent over backwards to fulfil his wishes.

He asked for nothing other than to pursue his evangelist 'uplift of the Harijans' from the disgusting pit of untouchability. Unfortunately, as a poor judge of human character, he chose Nehru as his successor instead of the solid and brilliant Patel. This was a tragic blunder that would cost India dearly in the years to come. Nehru was a 'flibbertygibbet', puffed up with his own importance, burdened with a huge inferiority complex, which he covered up with tantrums and outbursts of irrational anger. His blunders and faux pas were so numerous that they have to be addressed separately. Patel on the other hand was a man of enormous prescience, who had clarity of vision and persistent fortitude, coupled with sagacity and tact.

Patel warned Nehru that China had designs on India in his letter of 11 November 1950, and that Nehru's mantra of '*Hindi Chini Bhai Bhai*' (India and China are brothers'), was a lot of 'codswallop', and a sensible strategy had better be evolved. Needless to say, Nehru totally ignored this warning as it went counter to his absurd Socialistic bias. Tragically, Patel died in

December 1950, leaving the field wide open for the shenanigans of Nehru, but more of that anon.

Britain is now packing its 'kit-bag', preparatory to leaving India, and appoints Admiral Lord Louis Mountbatten as the last Viceroy. Mountbatten was not an outstanding success as a Naval Commander but he was greatly admired and respected as the Supreme Commander of SEAC, South-East Asia Command. He had charm, good looks and an enormous stature. He was an instant success with Nehru and had him eating out of his hand. Nehru appointed him as India's first Governor-General, after Independence. In hindsight this was a strategic blunder. Nehru was a weak, indecisive man and was like putty in the hands of a person like Mountbatten, whose first loyalty was to Britain. In October 1947, Pakistan invaded Kashmir. I have covered this event thoroughly and the tragic aftermath that followed. Kashmir had acceded to India and this made it an internal affair, but at the instigation of Mountbatten.

Nehru referred the matter to the United Nations for arbitration, against the advice of Patel. Three Generals, Cariappa, Thimayya and Kulwant Singh, asked Nehru for permission to totally eject the Pakistanis from the whole of Kashmir. The Pakistanis had been thoroughly trounced and were in headlong retreat. Permission was refused and no reason given. The present-day imbroglio is the direct result of this stupidity. Thousands of valiant Indian soldiers have perished in three wars with Pakistan and nothing has been resolved, thanks to the blundering idiocy of Nehru! The man was an unmitigated disaster. The United Nations offered India a permanent seat in the Security Council. Nehru turned this down and wanted China to get the seat instead, which it gleefully grasped with both hands. India is clamouring for this seat today, which is opposed by, guess who? China!! Such is the gratitude of rascals. The mischief of this rapscallion is endless! Without proper consultation, he signed the 1950 Indus Valley Treaty with Pakistan, which gave India the riparian rights over the tiny Beas River and the sizeable Sutlej. The Indus and the remaining three Punjab rivers went to Pakistan. This absurd partition had no logic, rhyme or reason. India is now stuck with this absurdity.

With great magnanimity, Nehru bequeathed The Greater Cocos Island to Myanmar, which sits over the head of India's Naval Base in the Andaman Islands. Sure enough, China has set up an Observation Station, which in years to come will become a Naval Base in the Bay of Bengal. But, much worse is to follow, with the rape of Tibet by China in 1950. Tibet has been a sovereign independent country for hundreds of years. China had a loose suzerainty till 1912, but has never had sovereignty over the country. No Chinese citizen has lived in Tibet since 1912. China, under Mao Zedong, was an expansionist, rapacious and revanchist country. His armies had defeated Chiang Kai Shek and pushed the Japanese out of China. Next came the Korean War (1950–3) when the combined North Korean and Chinese armies fought the UN Forces to a stale mate. When China invaded Tibet on 7 October 1950, it was still licking its wounds from Korea. It took a calculated risk in venturing on this highly questionable foray. To the south of Tibet was India, which had at its helm a pedantic buffoon with his ridiculous chant of 'Hindi Chini Bhai Bhai', and the absurd political garbage of 'Pancha Shila'. There was no danger or opposition likely from this quarter. The USA and the USSR were still playing the 'Roulette of the Cold War' and had enough on their plate. Tibet was 'somewhere out there', a Buddhist Monastic State of 3 million souls and no oil or gas to whet the appetite of the oil-oligarchs. So, who was interested, other than China? Its amazing how ignorant the political Czars are of the world of 'Realpolitik,' even when it is staring them in the face. China is probably the solitary exception. Tibet is a semi arid 'altoplano', sitting at an average elevation of about 12,000 feet, wind swept and freezing cold, with no known mineral wealth. The Tibetans are ethnically totally different from the Han Chinese, with a different language and a culture more akin to India than China. So what was the attraction to occupy this wind-swept deep freeze? There were many and these need to be enumerated:

First: There is the fact that Tibet sits on the source of most of Asia's giant rivers, like the Indus, Sutlej and Brahmaputra, which flow into India. The Yangtse, Kiang and Hwang Ho, flow into China, and the Salween, Mekong and Irrawaddy are the life-blood of South-East Asia. Whoever sits across the headwaters of these rivers has a distinct riparian advantage over the Countries down-stream. Theoretically this aquatic Bonanza could irrigate the parched lands of China and generate huge amounts of hydroelectricity.

Second: China and India did not share a common frontier. By occupying Tibet, the two Countries now sit cheek by jowl, with China glowering down on India. China realized that sooner or later the two Countries were going to be locked in a tussle for dominance in Asia. I remind you of the Chinese saying that:

> Tibet is the palm and the five fingers on India's throat are the Karakorum Highway into Pakistan, the Bara Hoti salient near the Niti Pass in Garhwal, Nepal, Sikkim and Arunachal Pradesh in Assam.

The Chinese want to eventually dominate India and have instigated a Maoist Insurgency in Nepal and the Maoist/ Naxalite Insurgency in Eastern India.

Third: The Chinese needed an easy access-route to their western-most province of Xinjiang through the Aksai Chin plateau, which they have already annexed from India. They have already built an all-weather Military road.

Fourth: The Chinese have completed the Quinghai/Lhasa Railway, which will eventually wind across the plateau to Xinjiang. The steel necklace around India will be complete. The railway will give China a huge tactical advantage as men and weapons can be brought to India's very doorstep in Arunachal Pradesh. China is just biding its time to move into this area. It remains to be seen whether an effete and flaccid country will have the gumption to take on the Chinese Dragon!

China's brazen occupation of a peaceful nation like Tibet is a part of a huge Strategic Operation. The key player should have been India, which missed its cue and 'moment of truth'. It did nothing and left its friend and neighbour to be savaged by a ruthless bully. Sadly this opprobrium of 'Mea Culpa' adorns the entire Western World, which sat on its hands and did not even bother to chastise China in the Security Council or the United Nations. Nehru even went to the extent of actively opposing taking the Tibet issue to the UN. Tibet asked India for help, which was refused. Nehru's stupid advice was that the Tibetans should negotiate a peaceful settlement on their own. It is like asking a rabbit to negotiate with a fox and somehow persuade the fox not to eat it!

India was a nation that was fast asleep, lulled in the ambrosia of '*ahimsa*' or non-violence. It had shamelessly neglected its Armed Forces who had extricated the Congress leadership out of a 'pickle' on three occasions, at a great cost to the lives of its valiant soldiers. Its comeuppance was going to be delivered by China, who had surreptitiously annexed 38,000 sq km of land in Aksai Chin, and Pakistan had illegally ceded them 5,180 sq km of land. When Nehru was made aware of this transgression he did not make this known to his Cabinet or the Public for several months. When this information eventually leaked out he said that the 'Aksai Chin' was only an inhospitable wasteland that could sustain no grass and no population.' Excuses do not solve problems; they only create new ones. China had always suspected that the Indian leaders were men of straw and had no stomach for a fight. Its troops kept probing into Border areas, and in September 1959, China laid a formal claim to 50,000 sq miles of Indian Territory in Ladakh and NEFA, in Assam. Nehru and his sidekick, Krishna Menon, monopolized Foreign Affairs, and did not even allow any interjection or discussion, even within the Ministry. The Chinese kept over-running far-flung Indian Outposts. In 1959, the Chinese ruthlessly suppressed a Tibetan uprising in Lhasa, forcing the Dalai Lama and thousands of his followers, to flee to India. He and his followers were given asylum on the condition that they did not pursue a political agenda. His Holiness and his followers were accommodated in my family's estate, the Happy Valley Club, and its vast environs, in Mussoorie. This instigated a vicious tirade from China, who accused India of being a lackey of British Imperialists. Problems were also brewing in the Ministry of Defence between the Minister, Krishna Menon, and the Army Chief, the redoubtable General Thimayya. The Chief could see storm-clouds gathering on the border but could not convince Nehru and Menon that China was building up a heavy concentration of troops. There are 'none so blind as those who will not see' and fools who will not listen to their appointed specialists because it does not suit them. The General's worries were ignored and Thimayya, in sheer desperation, submitted his resignation. He was persuaded by Nehru to withdraw his resignation, which he did, but the whole episode soured him.

Nehru loved to prance around the international stage, playing the part of an elder statesman, and being the 'big man', which he certainly was not. He hated being pushed into a corner and forced to be decisive.The whole confrontation with China unnerved him. This was not the way 'the game' was supposed to be played! Here was a crypto-Communist being upstaged by a dyed-in-the-wool Communist. It did not make any sense!

The year 1959 found India flapping around helplessly with its defences in tatters and its soldiers armed with old, discarded WW II Lee Enfield rifles. India did not even have a Defence Plan or Policy. Its only strategy, if one can call it that, was endless chatter and the desperate hope that it would be able to bring the Chinese to the negotiating table. China on the other hand is a hard-nosed, dogged, pragmatic country that knows what it wants, and will get its way. It did not accept the McMahon Line (MML) as the border between India and Tibet, as it had not signed the Simla Convention of 1913–14, yet it accepted the extension of the MML into Burma as the frontier.

China had other plans for India. Burma was just a pliant neighbour. Chinese intrusions into India continued in NEFA and elsewhere. Belatedly, India decided, feebly, to assert itself and embarked on an ill-conceived 'Forward Policy,' entailing the setting-up forward posts on the frontier with no regard to their ability to defend and sustain themselves. This was taken as an aggressive stance by China. To compound the Army's enormous problems, Nehru and Menon promoted Major-General B.M. Kaul to Lt. General and brought him to Delhi in July 1959 as the Quarter Master General, against the advice of the Army Chief, General Thimayya. This was typical of that fool, Krishna Menon, who meddled in promotions to suit his political agenda. Thimayya was against the silly Forward Policy that made military nonsense, but worse was Nehru's futile attempt to cover up India's lack of readiness with bluff and bravado. Nehru and Menon needed the imprimatur of a Senior General to gain credence for this policy. Kaul was their man. Kaul had no experience in commanding troops in the battlefield but he took on the responsibility of pursuing Nehru's stupid Forward Policy. He was a political appointment and loyally obeyed his political master, come what may. Reliable and capable Generals, who understood the realities of the field situation and expressed their reservations, were over-ridden and pushed aside. A game of Army 'musical chairs' was being played, with resignations and a shuffling of Senior Generals to suit the political 'pied piper'. Kaul was related to Nehru and was politically trust worthy. A deadly combination that was guaranteed to brush aside any professional inadequacies. Kaul superseded at least six Generals to become the Chief-of-General-Staff (CGS). Nehru was embarking on a very dangerous and slippery road. Bluff and bravado can be useful tools but they must be used judiciously. India was militarily totally unprepared to take on a determined and belligerent China. It did not have a clear Defence Strategy other than the ill-conceived 'Forward Policy,' but it foolishly announced, in October 1962, that Kaul was going to evict the Chinese from NEFA. In August 1959, Cabinet decided to hand over control of the NEFA border to the Army instead of the Assam Regiment, which was under the Ministry of External Affairs. In 1960, the Border Roads Organization (BRO) was created as an independent body. It lacked the heavy road building equipment which had to be imported. There were next to no roads to move supplies and the troops had to be sent supplies by irregular and uncertain airdrops. The Chinese on the other hand had busily constructed military roads right to the border. India was living in a twilight world of unreality and the ridiculous belief that China would never attack India. The Chinese were totally prepared for war and would pick the time and place to teach the Indians a lesson that they would never forget.

It is not my intention to write a detailed expose on the Sino-Indian war, which was bubbling away in the crucible. At the same time, it would be inexcusable to ignore the momentous events that were developing. Once again, I reserve the right to glean the kernel from the chaff and present this to the reader in a logical and comprehensible form.

Unlike a bumbling India, the Chinese preparations were immaculate, politically and militarily. The Chinese were fully aware that the Indian Army was hamstrung, and that its Generals could not act independently without political consent. The appropriate time to create an incident would be when the top political brass was away from Delhi. Nehru was attending the Commonwealth Prime Ministers' Conference in London. Menon was pre-occupied with his forthcoming visit to the UN, to address the General Assembly Meeting in September. The Finance Minister, Morarji Desai, was accompanying Nehru. So much for the three-man, Defence Committee of the Cabinet. To cap it all, the CGS, General Kaul, was holidaying in Kashmir. The stage was set. The Chinese crossed over the MML on 8 September 1962 into NEFA and assaulted the undermanned Indian Outpost on the Thagla Ridge. Clashes had already taken place in Ladakh, which should have heralded the aggressive intention of the Chinese. The Chinese laid siege to the tiny Indian outpost in the Galwan Valley in Ladakh, manned by 40 Gorkhas. The post was overrun in October 1962. Kaul is now entrusted with the dubious task of 'evicting the Chinese from Thagla, 'Irrespective of the loss of lives.' A deadline was set for October 10th to evict the Chinese.

14

The Fiasco

Sham and bluster cannot cover up a lack of preparation and ineptitude. Sooner or later, accountability will prevail. Unfortunately India had over-played its hand of 'Blind man's buff', and had been caught napping. The cardinal rule in the world of Realpolitik is to 'know ones enemy', and his intentions. The second indispensable rule is that in 'Realpolitik' there are no friends, only cultivated alliances of convenience. In the Sino-Indian debacle of 1962, India ignored both injunctions. Nehru was an idealistic, naive and basically weak man, who was full of his own importance. Unlike Sardar Patel, who was a hard-nosed realist, with enormous prescience. Menon, on the other hand, had risen from poverty in England, into a position of eminence on the shoulders of Nehru. He had no political following. He was an absolute opportunist, with an ego rivalling Nehru. Plus he was more than a Fabian Socialist like Nehru. He was a dyed-in-the-wool Communist. Nehru and Menon made a deadly duo who could not ascribe any capitalistic aggrandizement to a Communist China. It was inevitable that they wore blinkers when China arrived on India's doorstep. India had an army of over 400,000 men, but a mere 600 soldiers of the 7th Infantry Brigade were going to meet a ferocious assault by two Divisions of well-equipped and acclimatized Chinese troops. The terrible carnage on Thagla Ridge, Dhola and Namka Chu, will go down in Indian Army history as a Memorial to the valour and fortitude of the 2nd Rajputs, 1/9th Gorkhas, 9th Punjab, 1st Sikh and many others. This was a ridiculous David and Goliath struggle. The full strength of the Indian Army was never brought to bear on the victorious Chinese, who now raced down to the Brahmaputra Valley and reached it on 20 November. In this entire debacle the Indian Air force was never used to strafe the entrenched Chinese, who were a stones throw away from Indian airfields. The Indian politicians were a timorous, emasculated bunch of weaklings who were petrified of escalating the conflict with the Chinese.

15

A Post Mortem – The Blame Game

The Sino-Indian conflict extended over a period of barely a month, with roughly ten days of actual fighting. Militarily it was a miniscule affair. The aftermath was horrendous and the consequences completely outstripped the size of the actual event. To start with, India finished with egg on its face. In one-fell-swoop the Chinese trashed India's image as a nation of some consequence. It was rather like the Japanese in WW II, who, for the loss of barely 9,000 lives, annihilated European Colonialism in South Asia forever!

China not only defeated India militarily, by throwing two Divisions against a paltry handful of determined Indian soldiers, but showed the Indian Leadership to be men of s^traw, as predicted by Winston Churchill The Indian Politician had no Patriotism or Pride. All he could do was to whimper and snivel and talk about being 'stabbed in the back by China'. The consequences of this debacle were going to be monumental. The ignominious defeat of the Indian Army in 1962 provoked the Pakistanis to attack India. The audacious plan was to sever the supply-lines to the Indian troops in Kashmir and make an armoured thrust and capture Delhi. Once again the Indian Army blunted the move towards Delhi and reversed the tables and thrashed the much vaunted Pakistan 1st Armoured Division, freshly supplied with the latest Patton tanks by the Americans. The Indian Army redeemed its honour at the Battle of Asal Uttar and turned it into a graveyard for the Patton tank. So is there any point in playing this game of Mea Culpa? Yes there is. It is vital that we exonerate those who have been falsely accused by the Press, Political Propaganda and Public Opinion, of 'Dereliction of Duty' and bring the guilty to bear the responsibility for the disgraceful debacle they visited on India.

This Post Mortem falls into two distinct sections, although overlapping is inevitable:

The first tier of responsibility is political and administrative. The second is military organization of the defence establishment. So let's start with the first.

I have written at length on the muddled thinking of Gandhi in particular, who was a quasi-Hindu ascetic imbued with the unfortunate Hindu philosophy of 'ahimsa' or non-violence. Because of this patent absurdity, Gandhi and his acolyte, Nehru, abjured even the need for an army. I have already covered this dismal and pathetic stance in depth. The neglect and deprivation of India's defence establishment sits squarely on the shoulders of Gandhi, but principally on Nehru, as he ran the country. India's rueful and pathetic lack of military preparation is entirely the fault of a sycophantic, Communist fellow traveller, Nehru, and his rabid Defence Minister, Krishna Menon. To throw ill-equipped, badly-armed, and un-acclimatized troops into battle is criminal negligence, and is totally reprehensible. The outcome is a foregone conclusion. But let's continue in this silly game of trying to dupe a determined China into accepting a political settlement that is at total variance with its aims and objects. India betrayed Tibet in its hour of need and now it is doing the same thing apropos Nepal.

India is stuck with a belligerent neighbour that is going to nibble away at Indian Territory, in cahoots with Pakistan and Bangladesh. It has already helped Pakistan become a Nuclear Power and has given it missiles–the Shaheen I and II–that can hit every city in India. Its Naval Base at Gwadar on the Makran coast gives it a powerful Naval facility in the Arabian Sea. The armed forces of Bangladesh are equipped with Chinese weaponry and Chittagong is being upgraded to become a Chinese Naval Base in The Bay of Bengal. Politically, India has badly blotted its copybook vis-a-vis China.

Today, India is governed by coalition parties, a hotchpotch mixture of totally opportunistic political groups with huge variances in their aims and ideologies. The only uniting cement is a selfish grab for political power. Coalition governments are a poor substitute for a one party rule, with clearly defined aims and objectives.Unfortunately, the Indian voter has learnt a bitter lesson of political 'mis'-governance and corruption under decades of Congress rule, and has become totally suspicious of politicians and their avowed intentions.

Now let's turn our attention to the military. This is another story of prevarication and ineptitude. Constant interference by politicians and the bureaucrats has progressively destroyed the élan of the Services, particularly the Army. There are about 12,000 unfilled vacancies in the officer corps. The army loses about 1,000 officers every year by premature retirement, attrition and obsolescence. The concept of the 'Army family' is dead and gone. This was the bedrock, which ensured a supply of excellent Officer material to the services, and in particular to the Army. Poor service conditions, loss of respect and prestige, political promotions and patronage, have killed the glamour of being a service officer. There are very few senior service officers whose sons are opting for a commission. Nearly 50 per cent of the applicants for the IMA are sons of JCOs (non-commissioned officers). Nothing wrong with that. They make excellent field officers who can climb to the rank of majors and colonels. What is missing are the Staff Officers, who can head for Staff College in Wellington. They are the 'bright boys' who formulate the strategic plans for the Services, prepare defence budgets and ensure that the Services are equipped and supplied with the latest military hard ware. I have covered the fiasco of the Arjun (MBT), an inexcusable waste of time and resources, which should never have happened. Mistakes are bound to happen, but what is crucial is the ability to Learn from these errors. Unfortunately India seems to be caught in a warp and web of history and make-believe, which prevents it from getting a clear over-view of the political scenario. It exploded its first nuclear device in 1974, and then sat on its hands until 1999, because it could not make up its mind to become a nuclear power. Now it's the turn for its missile programme to be put on hold.

Its AGNI 3 Intermediate Range Ballistic Missile (IRBM) is

an excellent and reliable vehicle, which could easily become the precursor for a fully-fledged ICBM, but pressure from the USA has halted the programme. In the meantime Pakistan has emerged as a nuclear power, bristling with missiles, acquired from China and North Korea. While an irresolute and complacent India continues to slumber, its enemies are busy squirreling away reserves and resources. And this neglect and complacency continues apace. Tragically this dereliction of duty and responsibility continues without any let up. The Indian Air Force (IAF) is reputed to be the fourth largest in the world, but this is in name only. The JRD Tata Committee recommended that the IAF should field 65 squadrons. The backbone of the IAF is the outdated MiG 21, which is 40 years old and way beyond its prime. The intention is to replace the MiG 21 with India's own Light Combat Aircraft (LCA), the TEJAS. The project has been totally mismanaged and is years behind schedule, partly due to the embargo placed by the USA on the power plant, the General Electric GE 404. It was then decided by the Defence Ministry to replace the GE 404 by the Indian designed and built Kaveri engine from The Gas Turbine Research Establishment (GTRE). Very laudable, but jet engines are complicated pieces of machinery and very soon the Kaveri project ran into technical problems. Instead of trying to re-invent the wheel on its own, the GTRE should have sought collaboration with an experienced manufacturer like the French Dassault Company, whose Mirage 2000 is already in service with the IAF. The Tejas is years behind schedule. In February 2005, the IAF placed an order for 20 Tejas which will take at least five years for delivery, by which time the Tejas will be an obsolete aircraft. This is what India is desperately short of - Strategic Planners!

Before we leave the IAF in its dreadful predicament, we have another problem to resolve and that is the IAF's front-line fighter, the brilliant Russian Sukhoi SU 30 MKI. According to plan, 140 of the planes are going to be built by Hindustan Aeronautics Ltd (HAL), but this will take at least a dozen years. In the meantime the IAF is desperately short of aircraft and can barely field 35 Squadrons, as against a projected requirement of 65 Squadrons. The IAF had requisitioned for 200 medium-range multi-role fighters as far back as 2002. This order has been trimmed down to 126. India has still not decided on the aircraft that it wants let alone placing an order. The main contenders are the Mirage 2000-5 and the MiG 29M/M2. The Americans are pushing the F 16 Fighting Falcon, which is in service with the Pakistan Air Force. It looks as though India is, once again, going to be muzzled by an inept Defence Ministry and its lack of strategic planners.

Now it's time to switch the searchlight onto the Indian Navy, whose Achille's heel is its dismal shipbuilding record for both merchant and naval vessels. China, on the other hand, has pursued a determined programme to build a huge flotilla of gas and oil tankers, to transport these vital energy supplies from around the world to China, protected by a powerful blue water Navy. The world's biggest shipbuilding yard is nearing completion in Shanghai. India must take its cue from China and start a vigorous campaign to build its own flotilla of Merchant ships, flying the Indian Ensign, instead of relying on hired vessels, which could be de-commissioned by the foreign owners in the event of conflicts in the Persian Gulf. India has a small shipbuilding facility in the port of Vishakhapatnam, and Hyundai should be encouraged to build oil tankers and LPG carriers at this venue. Hyundai already has a substantial investment in building cars and trucks in nearby Chennai.

The biggest problems facing the Indian Navy are threefold:

First and foremost is patrolling its huge coastline, protecting its shore establishments and prevention of smuggling and illegal immigration. Add to this the safety of its off shore oil and gas platforms which could easily become the target for terrorist attacks. This needs a vast Coast Guard service of fast vessels with a low draft and sufficient firepower to ward off any intruders, protecting Indian fishing boats and maintaining maritime sovereignty of its continental shelf right upto its international waters.

The second major role is safeguarding India's shipping lanes in the Arabian Sea, the Indian Ocean, Bay of Bengal and into Indonesian and Australian waters. The main danger is from pirates operating from the Horn of Africa and the Straits of Malacca. This is a huge undertaking and beyond the capability of a single nation. It needs collective action like The Proliferation Security Initiative (PSI) involving the USA, UK, France, Germany, Spain, Portugal, Italy, Australia, Japan, Poland, Netherland and India, under whose aegis these Countries can stop and search air, land and sea cargo for Weapons of Mass Destruction. The Indian Navy needs to collaborate with the Americans, Australians, Japan and Singapore to safeguard the dangerous Straits of Malacca and develop its Naval facilities in the Andamans.

Thirdly, the Navy needs to expand its hitting-power against potentially aggressive enemies like China and Pakistan. Oddly enough the Navy has opted for a flotilla of three Aircraft Carriers, a disproportionate number compared to the defensive shield of destroyers and frigates that would be needed to protect these 'Capital ships' from attack by submarines, air and other surface vessels. Furthermore an aircraft carrier is essentially an offensive weapon that takes strike aircraft to the enemy. The Pakistani ports of Karachi, Gwadar and Pasni are all within range of India's land based aircraft, so what is the need for three aircraft carriers? So far China's blue water Navy does not pose a threat. This looks like a case of 'overkill'. But there are many other problems associated with aircraft carriers that are highly sophisticated pieces of machinery involving multiple technologies. The purchase of the old, mothballed, Russian 'Admiral Gorshkov' looks like a colossal blunder. India has paid US$500 million upfront and now the Russians are demanding more money. The eventual cost could exceed US $1.6 billion and the delivery time is not fixed. But it does not stop here. Once the Gorshkov arrives in India, 16 MiG 29K will have to be purchased for use on this vessel. What aircraft are used on the Hermes? Eventually, which aircraft will be used on the 38,000-ton Air Defence Ship that is scheduled to be built in Kochi in collaboration with Italy's Fincantieri? A fundamental principle in military procurement is to minimize the inventory. A multiplicity of suppliers and stores is a nightmare for the Quarter Master. Once again it looks as though the Navy has not done its homework. India's defence establishment is in a mess, plagued with corruption and ineptitude. It has a huge budget for the purchase of military hardware from foreign suppliers because its own factories are unable to produce its needs. This is a planned strategy by corrupt and conniving politicians, who get enormous' kick backs' on defence contracts, like the infamous 'Bofors' deal, involving the Nehru/Gandhi dynasty. There is no money to be made on Indian production but foreign contracts are a bottomless 'El Dorado' for scams, craftily engineered by venal politicians. The latest example is the purchase of six Scorpene Submarines, supplied by the French company, Thales, through a middleman, Abhishek Verma, who purportedly stands to make a commission of 4 per cent on the contract price. Understandably corrupt politicians and bureaucrats in the Ministry of Defence love these huge defence tenders, which can set them and their families up for life, and with no accountability. In a 2006 report of the Swiss Banking Association, Indians are by far the biggest depositors of 'black money' in Swiss Banks, with deposits amounting to US $ 1456 billion, more than the rest of the world combined. Apparently, under Swiss law, details of these accounts can only be released if a formal request is lodged by the Government of India (GoI). It is highly unlikely that the GoI will put its own head in the noose The sufferers are the Services, Indian manufacturers like HAL, IRDO and scores of others, who get step-motherly treatment as there is very little money to be made on local manufacture.

India is the proverbial 'milch cow'. The hapless Indian public cannot bank on a non-existent shred of decency and honesty among its politicians. But there are more ways than one to 'Kill the Cat'. I shall give my views in another section involving a re-organization of India's defence establishment.

I think it is time to do a thorough stock-take of where the country stands and the huge political and military problems that it faces. Once again the subject is so vast and complicated that it has to be sectionalized and the problems tackled piece-meal. The logical dissection is political and military with the inevitable over laps.

16

The Political

'Know your enemy and you won't be defeated.' SUN TZU, Chinese sage. India's usual meaningless political waffle of 'Friendship towards everyone and malice to none' is just a lot of twaddle .The very first step in establishing a political road map is to identify the enemy, its aims and designs, its strengths and weaknesses and assign priorities to thwart any moves that threaten the safety and sovereignty of the country. India has three potential and real enemies, listed in order of priority:

CHINA
PAKISTAN
BANGLADESH

China

As far back as 100 years ago, Bipin Chandra Pal, a Hindu Nationalist, with great prescience, predicted that an Islamic and Chinese conspiracy will threaten Hindu India, which will side with a Judeo-Christian Alliance to survive. It looks as though Bipin Chandra Pal's prediction is becoming a reality. Unlike a soft, degenerate and pliable Hindu India, China is the world's most ruthless and pragmatic country. It has no idealistic illusions like India. Its objective is clear and that is to overtake the USA and to become the world's hegemone, economically and militarily. It is the only country that has successfully married two diametrically opposed systems like Communism and Capitalism, to produce a monolithic hybrid that looks as though it will dominate the economy of the world. With great dexterity it has melded the freewheeling, highly opportunistic world of

Capitalism under the firm hand of a Communistic Dictatorship. The USA, the EU and for that matter the rest of the Western World has lost its Work Ethic and is lying back on its oars, hoping that the Asians will fetch, carry, toil and loan them the money to keep their economies humming. An absurd fantasy. The world belongs to those who sweat and toil. History is replete with the rise and fall of great Dynasties and Empires. In all cases the precursor is indolence, the loss of moral probity, gluttony and eventual decadence. China and India are the main workshops of the world, with Brazil and Russia clambering close behind. These are the BRIC giants of Wall Street's Goldman Sachs blue eyed boys. China realizes that India is going to be its biggest competitor for dominance in Asia and possibly in the whole world and has surrounded this slumbering giant with a collar of steel. I have already covered this Chinese ploy but it needs further elaboration.

The 1962 Sino-Indian victory not only destroyed India's military image but it made it abundantly clear to India that the McMahon Line (MML) was just a scrap of paper and that China could ride roughshod over it at will, whenever it wanted. The enormous Quinghai/Lhasa Railway has radically changed the military balance, as China can now move men and weapons right to the border of Arunachal Pradesh. It is only a matter of time before it claims the entire area. Geography and topography favour China. The Tibetan plateau is on the leeward side of the monsoon winds coming from the south. It is very cold but gets little snow or rain. The ramparts of the mighty Himalayas were always regarded as an impenetrable barrier by India. In one fell swoop, the Chinese have changed all that and its divisions sit on India's doorstep at 12,000 feet, their forward base at Le is a hop skip and a jump from the Indian salient at Towang. Once again, the Indians have learnt nothing from the disastrous rout in 1962. Towang, Dhola, the Sela Pass and the Namka Chu are precariously supplied by an indifferent road from Misamari in the Assam Valley, crossing many ranges of heavily forested mountains in NEFA. During the Monsoon the road is often broken by landslides. I believe that it still takes about 6 days from Misamari to Towang, when the road is open. Logistics are against a road system. So is there an alternative? There is, and here we have to look at the incredible railway system that the Swiss have developed in the Alps. The 'Rack and Pinion' (R&P) system can virtually scale straight up the side of a mountain, eliminating the need for a tortuous road following the contours of the hillside. Furthermore the R&P can work in a loop with the ascending train being partly pulled up by the gravitational force of the descending train. These are details that can be worked out with a company like ABB Brown Boweri of Switzerland. Once India can master the R&P it could be used in the length and breadth of the Himalayas. The R&P needs a plentiful supply of electricity, which would be available in situ from hydroelectric plants harnessed from the myriad rivers debouching into the plains from the Himalayas. All this will take time, which is a scarce commodity. Time is running out and will India be able to thwart the Chinese when they decide to move into Arunachal Pradesh? There are two factors in India's favour. Firstly the Chinese have ambitious plans for Eastern Tibet. The Brahmaputra, that is, the Tsangpo, loops around the massif of Namche Barwa (7,755 metres) to the south and Gyali Peri (7,160 metres) to the North before looping south-ward to enter Arunachal Pradesh as the Dihang. The Tsangpo falls from 12,000 feet to 1,000 feet in the deepest and most awesome gorge in the world. This huge head of water is capable of generating 40,000 MWs of electricity, that is, more than twice the capacity of the 'Three Gorges' Dams on the Yangtse. The Chinese plan to divert the Brahmaputra and build the biggest hydroelectric plant in the world in Arunachal Pradesh. China needs this project to run the Quinghai Lhasa Railway and push it across the plateau to the Aksai Chin, and beyond to Xinjiang. In addition, giant pumps will draw the water over the Kun Lun Mountains to the arid country to the North and then water will be piped towards Shanghai and the nearly dry Hwang Ho River. If this project eventuates it will draw a huge amount of water from the Brahmaputra in Assam and Bangladesh. The latter country is so beholden to China that it will not utter a whimper. As for India, it is on the verge of losing the whole of Arunachal Pradesh. For China, India is only a nuisance and an impediment.

The ambitious water grid could cost China US $ 62 billion and this does not include the cost of the monstrous hydroelectric plant on the Brahmaputra. China is playing for big stakes. Its long-term survival hinges on balancing the abundant water available in the South and pumping it to the dry North. Arunachal Pradesh is pivotal in this scheme. It remains to be seen whether it will ride roughshod over India and walk into Arunachal Pradesh, or will it try and work out a quid pro quo. Either way, India had better wake up and start developing its long-neglected North-Eastern Areas with railways, roads and defence installations.

The second saving grace for India is purely fortuitous and that is the economic meltdown in the world economy. Like the rest of the world, China has been sucked into the vortex of lost markets and a sharp decline in growth and a sharp increase in unemployment. China's immediate concerns are parochial and India has been relegated to the back burner. India must realize that the problem has not gone away and that this is merely a respite in which to build its defences in Arunachal Pradesh. Be rest assured, China will be back in force once the economic turmoil has subsided.

But this is not the end of India's travail in this remote area. Illegal immigration from Bangladesh, aided and abetted by unscrupulous Indian politicians, has added more than one million Bangladeshis to the population. More than 1,000 illegal immigrants cross over the border every day and even when they are caught they are not deported. Today a lot of terrorism throughout India has a Bangladeshi imprint, in connivance with Pakistan's ISI, and homegrown Indian *jihadi*s. China has a ready-made fifth column in Assam all set to establish a 'Sonhar Bangla', an independent Islamic Republic. Another dismemberment of India could be in the offing. With Arunachal Pradesh in its pocket and a powerful Muslim Fifth Column in Assam, China could literally walk into the Brahmaputra Valley and link up with the Communist governments in West Bengal, the Maoists in Nepal and the Maoist/Naxalites in Eastern India. Menacing storm clouds are amassing around India. But more about this prognostication of doom in what follows.

Let it be clearly understood that India and China are pirouetting in an endless Danse Macabre. On the one hand we have a fragile democracy governed by venal, self-serving politicians and their bureaucratic helpmates, and on the other we have a sinister Communist Dictatorship, which brooks no contest or any opposition, 'nolo contendere'. China is the past master in the ruthless game of Realpolitik. It thoroughly exploited its Communist Mentor, the Soviet Union, while it suited its political agenda and then dumped it when the Soviets tried to control it at the end of WW II. It dominated the Korean and Indochina wars and was the armourer for the Viet Min and Viet Cong who gave the Americans a bloody nose. Then it gyrated in a merry Cotillion with President Nixon and Henri Kissinger. After the disastrous 'Great Leap Forward' of Mao Zedong, which killed 30 million Chinese, Deng Xiaoping opened the flood- gates for Capitalist Investment that has not abated. The USA is the cornucopia supplying China with its endless appetite for dollars and factories. But how long can any nation survive on myth and fantasy? For the USA the blissful 'dreamtime' is turning into a nightmare. It has lived way beyond its means for years, surviving on the largesse of Asian countries, which paid its bills. The day of reckoning has arrived and the country is struggling to keep its head above water. Laziness and greed for easy-profit are a dreadful combination and have finally brought the country to its knees. The once mighty 'Green Back' is losing its muscle and is gradually becoming a limp strip of paper that no one wants to overcome the credit crisis of some of the largest American and European banks there has been an infusion of money from 'Sovereign Wealth Funds' (SWF) as the Central Banks of emerging countries are flush with US dollars and bonds and are looking for new outlets for their cache. The US has tried to limit the lending to preference and convertible shares without voting rights, but the SWFs are not stupid and are looking at more profitable ventures like real estate, typified by the purchase of the Chrysler Building, UBS and Citigroup shares. This does not augur well for the world's largest and most powerful economy.

China is flush with US$ 1.9 trillion in hard currency reserves and has limited avenues for investment. America wants China to open its doors for American Banks to enter the market, but is averse to China operating on US soil. This deadlock cannot continue much longer. In the long run the Chinese will win as they have the money, the fortitude and the stamina. The USA is a tired, spent force that is hemorrhaging badly in its futile and ill-advised wars in Iraq and Afghanistan. Behind the scenes, China is waging a clandestine war against the USA with aid to Pakistan and, therefore indirectly, to the Taliban, which is growing in strength and popularity. It's a strange irony of fate that the Chinese are using the Taliban against the Americans, who had used it against the Russians. In the midst of all this squabbling, the Taliban is honing its skills to eventually topple the weak and corrupt government of Hamid Karzai in Kabul, when the dispirited foreign troops leave. Once Afghanistan is in the bag, Pakistan and the Taliban will transfer their attention to Kashmir and India. This fits in perfectly with China's plans for India. But more of that anon.

China has begun to intrude across the Amur River from its Northern-most province of Heilongjiang. Illegal Chinese immigrants walk across the frozen river to sell goods to passengers on the Trans-Siberian Railway and do not return. With the collapse of the Soviet Union, the impoverished country could not pay its border-guards who sat in their unheated barracks, stupefied with cheap vodka. They turned a blind eye to what the Chinese were doing. Hopefully with the turn around of the economy under President Vladimir Putin and now President Dmitri Medvedev, will continue to turn around this dismal scenario and Russia will tighten its border with China. Eastern Siberia is rich in oil, gas, minerals, furs and forests, and is a magnet for the enterprising Chinese who will continue to sneak across the porous border to find a new home and opportunity.

PAKISTAN

Enough said about China and India's 'Danse Macabre'. It is time to switch over to India's 'bete noire', Pakistan. There is a strange parody in Pakistan's virulent hatred for India. The two countries are virtually a mirror image of each other, which is understandable, because they both emerged from the same womb. So, what is the genesis of this festering hatred? A most intriguing study of human nature, which needs a thorough analysis.

My home state, the Punjab, was divided into two by the British 'Radcliffe Award,' an arbitrary line drawn across the map by Radcliffe, who had never been to India or studied its demography. Many tragic blunders were made because the British wanted to leave in a hurry and the deadline was drawing near. Overnight the population of Hindus, Muslims and Sikhs found themselves as aliens in a hostile land. This gave an excuse for marauding bands of ruthless renegades to rape, murder and pillage mercilessly.

The sheer horror of those dreadful days has seared the soul of all communities. Memories will only die when this generation passes away. One can neither forgive nor forget. The die is cast for a lingering hatred. Yet the strange thing is that when the three communities cross over the border they clasp each other in a close embrace like long-lost brothers, which is what they are. A strange love-hate relationship exists which boggles the intellect. Anyway, lets starts the ball rolling, but the convolutions are many and involved. It's time to try and unravel this mess and make some sense of this unbelievable tangle.

The overwhelming Muslim population of India and Pakistan were previously Hindus, who were forced to convert to Islam or be slain by the marauding Muslims from Afghanistan, Persia and Central Asia. The Muslims sent thousands of Hindu women and children across the Hindu Kush Mountains to be sold as slaves in the markets of Arabia and Central Asia, or were forced into harems as concubines. Tens of thousands of defeated Hindu warriors were mercilessly butchered and no quarter given. Those who survived had to pay the iniquitous *'jaziya'*, or poll tax, and were subjected to grievous inhuman indignities as 'Dhimmies'. Hindu India experienced the most ferocious and bloody genocide in the history of the world, which makes Hitler's 'final solution' of the Jews in Europe look like a picnic. A Nazi SS Gauleiter was asked how his Storm Troopers could kill innocent Jews without pity. His answer was 'because they did not resist.' The brutal sadist has total contempt for the submissive masochist. It is not surprising that barely 9 per cent of Muslims ruled over 90 per cent of Hindus for 800 years in India. The contempt of the Muslim for the timid Hindu was total and complete. It is not surprising that the Hindu convert wanted to forget and disown his origins, and tried desperately to assume the guise of the invading Muslim from Central Asia. Herein lies the genesis of the Muslims disclaiming their Hindu heritage and claiming to be a separate nation. This is also a part and parcel of the 'Stockholm Syndrome', where the oppressed, instead of hating the oppressor, actually begin to love him.

I have written at length on the Partition of India and I do not intend to dwell on this subject, other than to say that Pakistan became a nation 'piggy-backing' on India's Independence movement. Religion is a poor cement to bind disparate races and people. The Pakistani and Indian Punjabis are indistinguishable in looks, language and culture, but are very different from the Pashtun of the NWFP, or the Baluchis in Sind. India has the same and even greater diversity, but, unlike Pakistan, the cement is not religion but the more enduring and tenuous tentacles of democracy.

At this stage I have to apologize for some repetition, which is inevitable when one is covering several hundred years of history and a vast montage embracing so many facets of religion, races and their interaction. So please bear with me and let us continue on our journey of discovery. Islam professes to be the 'Religion of peace', as its name implies. Nothing could be further from the truth, 'Peace on Earth', but strictly on Islamic terms. The first absolute imperative is that the whole world must become Muslim; must accept Mohammad as the last and only true prophet of Allah, and the only universal law is the Sharia. It is all very simple and straightforward. Those who do not accept and obey are warmongers and have to be killed in a holy *jihad*. Islam is a very basic and simple religion. There are the true believers, the Momins. The rest are infidels or Kafirs who are doomed to burn in the fires of Hell and must be killed by the Faithful to save them from this terrible fate. But in the interregnum the world is split between the Land of Islam, the Dar-ul-Islam, and the Dar-ul-Harb, the Land of War, populated by the despicable idolators and other Kafirs. It is the duty of every Muslim to wage war, the Razzias, to convert these heathens or to kill them. But there is the added complication of Revanchism. Once a land has been under Muslim rule, it must revert back to the Muslim. It is because of this absurd belief that Islam is demanding that Andalusia in Spain and India must be under Islam. This is the law of Islam and is not negotiable. How can India hope to negotiate peace with a country that insists that it must re-conquer the country and establish Islamic rule once again? But this is only the tip of the iceberg. India is now lumped together with the USA and Israel as the conspirators of *'Shaitan'*, the Devil, whose sole aim is to destroy Islam worldwide and plunder the wealth of Muslim Countries. How can anyone cope with this absurd paranoia?

The mess gets messier because Islam is not just a religion, it is a total socio-economic creed that intrudes into every moment and thought of the Faithful from the time he wakes up to the time he falls asleep. It even dictates on ablutions, defecation and procreation. Nothing is left to chance. There is no choice. The Diktat is to Obey without question.

In Islam there are no nationalities or national boundaries.These were created by Western colonialists to control the population. In Islam there is only the universal Muslim Brotherhood, the *ummah*, guided and controlled by the learned clergy, the *ulemah*, who pontificates on the Divine Sharia and its intricate legal and social diktats. And, over-riding everyone is the Caliph, who masterminds all temporal and secular issues. Islam is at total variance with modern concepts of democracy. It is not surprising that democracy is strange and alien concept in the Muslim world. Which also explains why there is virtually no democratic Muslim country, with the possible exception of Turkey, which is now teetering on the brink. Mustafa Kamal Ataturk, the Father of modern-day Turkey, virtually abolished Islam after WW I, and the collapse of the dreadful Ottoman Sultanate.

There is another crucial issue that must be highlighted, and that is the imperative to internationalize the Arabic language and culture. The spread of Islam has spearheaded this movement. The Quran is recited, parrot fashion, in all Islamic seminaries called 'madrassas' even though the students cannot read or understand Arabic. The *'namaz'* or prayers recited five times a day are in Arabic, as is the *'azaan'*, the call to prayer by the *'muezzin'* from the 'masjid'. The virulent Wahabbi movement in Saudi Arabia was to purify Islam and also to purge the Turkish Ottoman pollution out of Arab lands. A much older civilization existed in Persia, which modified the Arabic script and created the Persian script, which was adopted by the hybrid language called Urdu in India.

Islam and Muslims cannot live in peace and coexist with other races and beliefs. When an admixture does occur as a result of history, the Muslim demands dominance, even when they are a minority. This results in incessant internecine friction and bloodshed. History abounds in such unfortunate juxtapositions, like Palestine, Kosovo in the Balkans, Chechnya in Russia, Lebanon, and of course India. So where is there a common meeting ground for a cordial rapprochement between India and Pakistan? There is none. The two Countries are destined to live in a constant state of conflict. India, as usual, has learned nothing from history and lives in the absurd Hindu euphoria that Peace can be bought and traded by abject pacifism. This is inevitably a philosophy for disaster.

Unfortunately Providence played a dirty trick on India and bestowed on it a worthless leadership, under a confused and muddle-headed Gandhi and a popinjay like Nehru. Pakistan, in typical Muslim fashion, which reduced the population from 25 per cent in 1947 to 17 per cent in 1948 and to its present 1.5 per cent level. Bangladesh followed suit with a Hindu population of 30 per cent in 1947 down to 25 per cent in 1948 and 7 per cent at present. The Hindus fared much better in Bangladesh under the benign leadership of Mujibur Rahman's Awami League, which tragically ended in his assassination in a Military Coup. In 1972 the Pakistan Army unleashed a virulent genocide against their compatriots in East Pakistan causing millions to flee to India for safety. The Hindus bore the brunt of the genocide, which forced India to invade the country and to put an end to this dreadful butchery. The Pakistan Army surrendered and India captured over 90,000 Pakistani POWs. Hindus in Bangladesh are still mercilessly harassed with forcible conversions, rape of their women and forced occupation of their homes and lands.

The Partition of India could have ended in a genuine exchange of populations in a peaceful and orderly manner. But, human nature,being what it is, turned it into a blood bath. I have already recounted that the Muslims of the U.P. and Bihar who spearheaded the creation of Pakistan, did not migrate in large numbers and still live in their traditional homes, courtesy of the secular Constitution of India. In fact the Muslims in India have thrived and the population has increased from 9 per cent in 1947 to 13 per cent at present.

The political situation in Pakistan has undergone a radical change in recent months. Musharraf has been deposed and forced into exile in Saudi Arabia. A short-lived coalition government was stitched together between Asif Ali Zardari, the widower of Benazir Bhutto, and who inherited the Pakistan Peoples Party (PPL) and Nawaz Sharif, the leader of the Pakistan Muslim League (N). The coalition fell apart as Nawaz Sharif wanted to reinstate the judiciary that had been dismissed by Musharraf, but Zardari was reluctant, as charges of corruption against him could have been revived. In the end Nawaz Sharif backed off and Zardari became the president, pro tempore. The Pakistan economy is a shambles with barely US$ 3 billion in reserves. This would barely last 2 months to pay for food and oil. China has declined to provide aid and Zardari has gone cap in hand to the IMF. Pakistan's traditional stand-by is the USA, but is itself in a parlous state and the Presidential election in November 2008 has projected Barak Obama as the President. Pakistan's long time patron, President Bush, is leaving Office with a dreadful legacy of a country in ruins. If Pakistan is unable to muster sufficient funds to keep running, the country could splinter apart, a highly dangerous situation for a nuclear power, whose arsenal could fall into the hands of extremists. The

Americans cannot risk this eventuality, plus the collapse of Pakistan would spell the end of the war in Afghanistan. In sheer desperation Zardari has gone, cap in hand,to the International Monetary Fund (IMF), for a bail out. The IMF will fund $4-5 billion immediately and a further $9.6 billion spread over 3 years. These loans come with stringent clauses, which are too extensive to be covered here but they will tether Pakistan to severe austerity.

To the north, China is girding its loins to advance into India's Arunachal Pradesh at a time of its choosing. To the west, Pakistan is literally falling apart. The frontier had better be slammed shut before a flood of refugees tries to force its way into India. Refugees have already started to stream into Afghanistan to escape the onslaught of the Taliban in the border areas.

In India's East, the Maoist/Naxalite insurgency continues to grow, due to ineptitude at the state and central government levels to take a determined stand. India is fast becoming a nation under siege. It is a nation that is running out of time. In the heartland of India, Muslim insurgency is growing apace and SIMI, and its offshoot the Indian Mujahidin (IM), are becoming more brazen as the Security apparatus is totally ineffective in catching and prosecuting the culprits. The Human Rights activists are forever on the side of the insurrectionists and against the poor victims, who are being blown apart by bombs. This puerile situation cannot continue and a revised, vigorous agenda has to be written and outdated shibboleths buried. What is being offered below are suggestions, *not diktats*, written in concrete. They can be transcribed, rewritten and modified as long as the gist remains at the core. I have tried to avoid prioritizing, as flexibility is cardinal to getting a proper format going.

17

National Security

India's Security System is seriously flawed. It consists of two wings. The Intelligence Bureau (IB) is entrusted with the responsibility of maintaining internal security within the country, rather on the lines of Britain's Scotland Yard, affectionately called the MI5. External security falls within the purview of the organization called the Research and Analysis Wing (RAW), whose British equivalent would be MI6. In recent times both organizations have become progressively emasculated and ineffective for the following reasons:

1. They are grossly understaffed. There are 126 police officers per 100,000 people in both services. The United Nations recommends 232 per 100,000. The IB has 3,500 field operatives. This handful of operatives is wasted, dealing with day-to-day crimes like drug running and smuggling instead of problems of terrorism.
2. Both the IB and RAW are manned by police officers seconded from the state cadres. They have no specialized training in espionage, spying or interrogation techniques. The second is not regarded as a stepping-stone to promotion or professional betterment, but as a handicap. The officers are moved around by the politicians and bureaucrats to serve their personal needs, or those of their family members. Both services are heavily politicized and sandwiched between the state governments and the central government, who are forever playing the 'blame game'. To crown the

misery of both the IB and RAW personnel is the strict political injunction that on no account should the minority community, that is, the Muslims, be offended.

3. Even when culprits are apprehended, the legalities are endless and the offender's sentence is either commuted or he is released, making a mockery of the judicial process.This is very disheartening for the security personnel. The classic case is the trial of Afzal Guru, the leader of the Pakistani-inspired attack on the Indian Parliament. He was sentenced to death-by-hanging by the Supreme Court but the UPA Government in Delhi has not carried out the execution for fear of a Muslim backlash. No Government worth its salt can rule under the blanket of fear.
4. National Security is way beyond the capability and financial resources of states. It must rest securely on the shoulders of the Government in Delhi. States should continue with the normal policing operations of maintaining law and order in their jurisdiction.
5. There is infiltration into both organizations. In 1980, Polish and French operatives raided the offices of the Prime Minister and RAW and removed files, documents and computers. The security of the coding system was breached. A Joint-Secretary in RAW, Ravindra Singh, illegally immigrated to the USA with his family without the knowledge of the government. He has never been extradited back to India.
6. There is a totally inadequate database, with very poor communication and sharing of strategic information between the police in the different states and Delhi. When investigation details are passed on, they are ignored and not acted on.
7. There is a total lack of planning, policy and direction, with contradictory instructions confusing the scenario. The classic example is the banning of SIMI in some states as a terrorist organization, and a lifting of the ban in others. This dreadful muddle is created by untrustworthy politicians who want the Muslim vote

at any cost. This shambles creates a field day for the terrorist and makes India a soft target for their vicious *jihadi*s.

To sum up, India has muddled through for the last 60 years but it is getting to a stage when only a radical shift in thinking is going to meet the demands of effective defence of the Land, which is threatened from all sides and even from within. There is no time left for prevarication. The first and vital step is for the timid politicians and bureaucrats to gird up their loins, banish fear and meet their destiny with a steady eye. The second crucial step is to disavow the contemptible attitude that every person and situation has a price and can be bought with filthy lucre. A disgraceful ignobility acquired by centuries of subservience and servitude. There is no substitute for raw courage and determination to confront any threat, external or internal.

The rot in the security system is so profound that patchwork remedies cannot plug up the leaks. The only remedy is to scrap the entire antiquated, degenerate structure and build a new edifice from scratch, inspired by the hoary wisdom of India's great sage, Chanakya. Protection and security of the country's territories and frontiers is the prime responsibility of any government in power. This is followed by peace, law and order, calm and prosperity for its citizens. With this in mind, I am suggesting the following modus operandi.

The security organization should be split into three totally independent organizations, with clearly defined areas of responsibility. For the sake of clarity, I have given them names to identify them. These names are purely for convenience and can be changed at will and as circumstances demand. These are as under:

(a) *Talwar,* the sword—In this thesis, National Security is paramount and is the first line of defence and attack against actual or potential enemies. The cardinal philosophy is that protection is proactive, not retroactive.

To be proactive, the fundamental rule is interdiction, which entails the destruction of a threat at source. The *Talwar* should be modelled on the Israeli 'Mossad', which identifies the henchmen who come onto the 'hit list' of *Talwar*. The key philosophy is to take the war to the enemy. It is the antithesis of 'ahimsa'.

(b) *Raksha*—this covers homeland security. The nefarious activities of SIMI, IM, Pakistan's ISI, and the Maoist/Naxalite threat fall within the remit of *Raksha*. This organization must develop teams of linguists in languages such as Arabic, Farsi, Russian, Mandarin, Burmese and many others, so that spies can penetrate these cells operating in and around India. *Raksha* must operate 'stings' to identify and destroy these cells. Like *Talwar*, *Rakhsha* is proactive, to find and identify the terrorist cells and then ruthlessly destroy them at source and no quarter given.

(c) *Baaz,* the Hawk—This is a surveillance organization to survey the Indian landscape for scams, and every type of corruption that is eating into the very heart of the Indian soul. The function of *Baaz* is firstly preventative. When corruption has taken place, the criminals must be taken to task and their ill-gotten gains must be repatriated and criminal charges laid against the offenders. Out of the three organizations, *Baaz* will meet the greatest opposition from venal politicians and bureaucrats as it eats into the very life-blood of their existence.

The survival and effectiveness of Talwar, Raksha and Baaz hinges on the following support mechanisms, which are the key vital ingredients. These are listed below:

(1) Total independence, and accountability to only one authority. It is imperative that the three organizations are shielded from politicians and bureaucrats. On the other hand the three organizations cannot be given unlimited reins to ride rough shod over National Governance, otherwise we are creating states within the State. Parliament must appoint three citizens of impeccable character to be the mentors for the three organizations. The mentors must be non-political, open-minded and their identity sanctified by secrecy, irrespective of the party in power. This Mafia-like *'Omerta'* or vow of silence is essential, as the politician and bureaucrat have proved to be totally unworthy vehicles of trust and confidence.

(2) The operatives must be nameless and faceless to prevent

reprisals and vendettas against families and associates.

(3) The operatives must have bogus second jobs to mask their clandestine activity.

(4) Legal processes must be short-circuited on the principle of '*interarma silent legis*'—'In times of conflict the Laws are silent'. We already have a precedence of this principle in the USA's National Security Agency (NSA) tapping private telephones under authority of the White House and in violation of the American Constitution. This is the Priority Act.

(5) It is inadvisable to take prisoners as they are often used to barter the freedom of incarcerated terrorists. Israel has had a major problem apropos Hamas and Hizballah, whose modus operandi is to capture Israeli soldiers and civilians and then barter them for prisoners. Select prisoners should be kept for interrogation before being eliminated.

All this sounds ruthless and it is. India is in a survival mode, threatened by vicious and ruthless enemies, both internal and external, who are determined to destroy the very fabric of the country, Balkanize the territory before eventually Islamizing the Dar-ul Harb and making it a part of Dar-ul-Islam. This is a part of the grand plan of Pakistan's ISI and Bangladesh's Directorate General of Forces Intelligence (DGFI), to create a vast Islamic State extending from the Caspian Sea to Indonesia with a Caliphate located in the nuclear-armed State of Pakistan. This is not Alice in Wonderland romanticizing, but a very real threat. Terror is the weapon of choice and I have covered this Islamic philosophy in depth. And we can see this happening all around the country while ineffective politicians keep carping about which government witnessed the greater number of bomb blasts in their regime. What utter rubbish!! The loss of a single life to terrorism is one life too many. It is a travesty of good governance and is unforgivable. The only language that terrorism understands is the language of ruthless reprisal and annihilation. The cadres of SIMI and IM must learn the harsh reality that they are going to be ruthlessly hounded and destroyed. The same deadly message must go out to the ISI and DGFI. India's citizens demand the right to live their lives in peace and tranquility.

As for the Maoist/Naxalite menace, this is becoming a growing threat due to the ineptitude of the Home Minister, Shivraj Patil, with the connivance of the Communists in the UPA Government, who are only too happy to see the Maoists succeeding in disrupting the eastern and southern part of the country. The Naxalites were totally routed by Indira Gandhi when she instructed the army to kill on sight. Admittedly the problem is much bigger now but so are the resources. The problem should be put under the command of the redoubtable police officer, I.P.S. Gill, who eliminated terrorism in the Punjab. Gill should be given a free hand and the resources to do the same with the Maoists/Naxalites. In addition, this insurrection is driven by despair and poverty. A concerted effort must be made to provide employment, education and health to a large segment of the population that has been by-passed in India's burgeoning economy. This neglect can only breed disaster and will not go away unless achieve steps are taken to ameliorate the parlous state of millions on the edge of poverty. Poverty breeds despair and despair breeds resentment and revolution.

India's spectacular rise to economic power is because of the business community, whose initiative and acumen are irrepressible. They have succeeded *in spite of the government.* An over-governed country like India has been a *total failure at all levels,* with the possible exception of the States of Gujarat and Uttarakhand. Politicians and their running mates, the bureaucrats, are an impediment not an asset. Tragically 800 years of subjugation and servitude have destroyed the moral fibre of the people and created an ethos of loot and plunder. Independence has meant *licence,* instead of *responsibility* and *duty*. The Government's over-riding polity is epitomized by the Indian vernacular word, *saudagiri,* meaning that you can buy or sell yourself out of every situation. Everyone and everything has a price and is available for purchase. There are instances galore, like the Haj subsidy paid to Muslim pilgrims from India—a totally unwarranted bequest, with no precedence even among Muslim countries. Then there is the absurd statement made by the PM that Muslims will have first claim on any aid given by the government and orders have been given to banks to give priority to Muslims in giving loans.This continuous 'sucking up' to the Muslim is a part and parcel of *'dhimmitude'*, forced on the subservient Hindus by the Muslim overlords through centuries. This inherent inferiority complex keeps bobbing up like a cork in the most unexpected places like the most recent announcement by Maharashtra's Chief Minister, Vilasrao Deshmukh that preference would be given to Muslims for recruitment into the police force. What on earth provoked this totally uncalled for 'sucking up' other than vote-bank politics? This sort of puerile mentality is positively dangerous in the current situation, when the country has to address the problem of Muslim insurgency stemming from SIMI, the IM and ISI. Muslims MUST be recruited to initiate 'stings', but it is absurd to make stupid statements about preferences. The politicians have proved their worthlessness, time and again. Since we cannot re-write the Constitution, and the country is pushed for time, the only solution is to marginalize the politicians and push them into a corner where they can continue to burble to their hearts content.

It is not the intention to write opprobrium on the inadequacies of the political system in India, but to systematize the huge amount of work that needs to be done. This subject is so vast and the dereliction so manifest that it has to be prioritized.

I have already covered the problem of Islamic terrorism in considerable depth but the rough edges need to be trimmed. But let us continue in this vein. First and foremost we have to get rid of hackneyed beliefs that Muslim terrorism is the result of poverty and discrimination. Nothing could be further from the truth. In fact the SIMI and IM activist is a well-educated, professional person like a doctor or engineer or a fairly prosperous businessman. This also fits in with the profile of the bombers in London, Glasgow, Australia and elsewhere. The activist is not driven by poverty but by a deviant, bigoted religious belief in the inevitability of Islam and the Shariat Law sweeping the world. The second myth is that terrorism is a justified reprisal against some International conspiracy against the Muslim World by international Jewry, the Americans and their ilk. The oft-quoted Palestinian question is merely a justification for violence. If the truth be known, the Muslim world could not care less for the so-called misery of Hamas, Iraq or Hizballah. The fact is that the Muslim world cringes at the impotence of a once-dominant power that had conquered a huge area of the civilized world and has now withered to an insignificant, poverty-ridden, in-the-main uneducated, mass of ignorant believers. A 'has been', in the true sense of the word. This sticks in the craw of the Muslim. The best that he can do is to revive the absurdity of reconquering India, but first he must terrorize the Indian into abject submission. The bombing of innocent Indians is not 'senseless', but a carefully planned strategy of unmitigated terror. As India has been ineffective in stopping this violence, this has only encouraged the perpetrators. There is no sense in trying to bring a bigot to the negotiating table. He takes this as a sign of weakness. The only language that a terrorist understands is relentless violence and reprisal. The treatment is to find them and destroy them. I am not even remotely suggesting a vendetta against innocent, law-abiding Muslims. Anything but! What I am advocating is a relentless war against the vicious *jihadis*. They must be eliminated by bearding them in their den, inside India, in Pakistan or Bangladesh. This is a war to the finish; a war to end all wars between the Muslim fanatic and a democratic, secular India, which should be a haven for all freedom-loving citizens of all faiths, races and creeds. We cannot quibble on minutiae. Allow me to quote from the wisdom of the incomparable politician, Sir Winston Churchill:

> If you will not fight for the right when you can easily win without bloodshed; if you will not fight when your victory will be sure and not too costly; you may come to the moment when you will have to fight with all the odds against you and only a small chance of survival. There may be a worse case; you may have to fight when there is no hope of victory. This is because it is better to perish than to live as slaves.

This, then, is the choice—freedom or slavery.

We have traversed through a vast spectrum of India's woes. It is not possible to prescribe a total compendium of remedies, limited as we are by space and time. A 'vade mecum' is the recommended alternative, but first and foremost a short stock-take is desirable to avoid repetition.

The problems, vis-à-vis China, Pakistan and Bangladesh, have been adequately covered, as have problems in defence spending and Procurement. What we still lack are suitable alternatives to corruption in the Ministry of Defence and its concomitant scams. The first step is to sideline the politicians and bureaucrats who deliberately engineer inadequacies in local defence production, as there is very little fat for kickbacks, and shift the bias to overseas contracts. The suggested modus operandi is as under.

The three Chiefs of Staff, for the Army, Navy and Air Force, and their key planning personnel, still have the responsibility for preparing the annual defence budget, which is presented to the Defence Ministry for approval and funding. The three services nominate their preferences for equipment, weaponry, and delivery schedules, which are passed onto the Purchasing and Requisitioning Committee (PRC), composed of the following personnel:

(a) The Minister and Secretary of Defence and a minimum number of staff

(b) The CEO or Chairman of the major Indian manufacturers of defence equipment in India, like DRDO (Defence Research & Development Organization); HAL (Hindustan Aircraft Ltd) and many others.

(c) A select group of seven Business Executives, including a chairman. This group will invite tenders from local and foreign manufacturers and place orders. Preference will be given to local suppliers, provided they are competitive in price, quality and delivery times. Middlemen and facilitators should be excluded in the tendering and purchasingprocess as they are the major culprits in initiating kickbacks.

The PRC will be responsible for following up on orders and their delivery on time. Any changes in the inventory by the Chiefs, subject to the approval by the Ministry, will also be implemented by the PRC.

We have now eradicated the pernicious influence of the

venal politician and the bureaucrat in the Defence Ministry. Hopefully the PRC will bring order and method into the ordering of defence equipment.

I am now getting to the end of this narrative. We have covered a huge mosaic of history and the intricate interplay between India and Britain over nearly two hundred years. Both countries are totally disparate in culture, ethos and history yet divine providence threw them together to fulfil a mysterious arcane destiny. Britain and India are travelling on totally different paths but each has left an indelible imprint on the other. In calm retrospect one can see sense in the intricate Cotillion that two such totally different cultures had to perform in history. India still carries the baggage of indigent poverty and misery, a legacy going back aeons. Inequality breeds resentment and despair and the two ferment violence and revolution in the crucible of social injustice. India's burgeoning economy could become the percussion cap to ignite a huge explosion of anger and resentment of the 'have nots'. The writing is on the wall and India had better take heed. Its biggest enemy is its own fecundity. The population bulge in the 15 to 30-year-old age group portends disaster of Malthusian proportions. China has contained its population growth by its Draconian 'one child' policy. India, Pakistan, Bangladesh, parts of South Asia, Africa and South America keep blundering into the future as if 'tomorrow will never come. 'They are all heading to disaster. But lets stick to India for the moment.

Until about two years ago, India was exporting cereals, pulses, vegetables and meat to adjoining Countries. All this changed dramatically when the current Congress Party came into power. India is still an agricultural country and nearly 70 per cent of the population is rural, yet only 5.2 per cent of the budget in the 10th five-year plan was allocated to agriculture. This is now a badly neglected area with deteriorating production and a once-flourishing agricultural economy is languishing. Wheat production in 2005–6 was 68.54 million tons, down from 76.37 million tons in 2001–2. Food production was down from 213.19 million tons in 2003–4 to 198.65 million tons in 2006–7 that is, down by nearly 15 million tons. India has imported 4 million tons of wheat from Australia in 2007. About 40 per cent of farmers feel that farming is unprofitable and are only too ready to leave the land and migrate into an already overburdened urban environment, looking for employment that is non-existent, and perishing in slums which breed corruption and crime. The commonsense solution is to revive agriculture, provide employment in rural India so that people do not have to move. The share of agriculture in the national GDP has fallen from 61 per cent to 24 per cent, whilst the rural population has risen from 299 million to 709 million in 2001. This is insane economics perpetuated by ineptitude and indifference by state and central governments who keep shifting blame. In the meantime nothing gets done. But in all fairness the problems are multifold. In India there is no primogeniture and all the male descendants are co-parceners in their inheritance. The result is an unmitigated disaster. The land gets divided and sub-divided into tiny un-farmable plots. This is a pernicious ongoing problem that can only get worse, aggravated by bad farming methods, a lack of irrigation, salination and deforestation. The key to revitalizing agriculture in India is to keep the rural population on the land and to stop this inexorable exodus to the cities that are choking with over-population and lacking in the necessary infrastructure. This agenda requires a departure from traditional methods and the very first step is to collectivize the patchwork quilt of miniscule land holdings and forge them into cooperatives. The cooperatives would be run on scientific methods and ensure proper storage of grain in silos safe from the ravages of rodents and insects. Perishables like fruit and vegetables would be refrigerated before transportation to the markets. The cooperatives would eliminate the endemic curse of the middleman who skims the cream by buying the farmer's produce cheap and selling it in the market at exorbitant rates. The farmer is no better than a serf of the middleman, who, incidentally, is also the local *'baniya'* or moneylender, who gives instant credit at usurious rates. The cooperative is an almost self-contained entity, providing essential amenities like schools, electricity from the power grid, clean portable water, and all the infrastructure of the community.